Starlight around New Zealand

The days with you were wonderful and look forward to meeting you again in your home country.

Love & Light
Linda Shoebridge

Published December 2005
by: October Enterprises Ltd t/a
River Press
P O Box 10, Picton
New Zealand
riverpress@xtra.co.nz

for: Mavis Millar
91 Kotuku Street
Elsdon, Porirua
New Zealand

PS This book was given to my by my mother as the author was my teacher at age 14/15.

Cover design: Liane McGee, Wellington
Printed by: Rainbow Print Group, Christchurch

ISBN 0-9582252-8-1

Front cover photograph: *Starlight* sailing across Cook Strait, 1 January 1981
Back cover: Mavis and Norm Millar on *Starlight,* courtesy *Kapi Mana News*
Other pics from top left: Laying the fibreglass mould for *Starlight;* Doubtful Sound, Fiordland; Bruce Bay Takeways; Mahitahi River, West Coast; Sam Medland
All photographs by Mavis and Norm Millar unless otherwise credited

.

* PPS. my trip sailing ... PTO ...
www.acapellalodge.co.nz mobile: 0275.933.758
info@acapellalodge.co.nz OR acapella@xtra.co.nz

To Linda
Best wishes from
Mavis Millar - April 2007

Starlight around New Zealand

a circumnavigation in a trailer yacht

Mavis Millar

24·4·13

Dear Judy

On this journey I 'knew' while on transit, travelling in my car, I would stay several days in Nelson.

Little did I know I would meet you ... a kindred spirit, and end in spending several days literally inside the CBD.

It's been a great few days, to the point, I am now querying if Switzerland should be my destination?

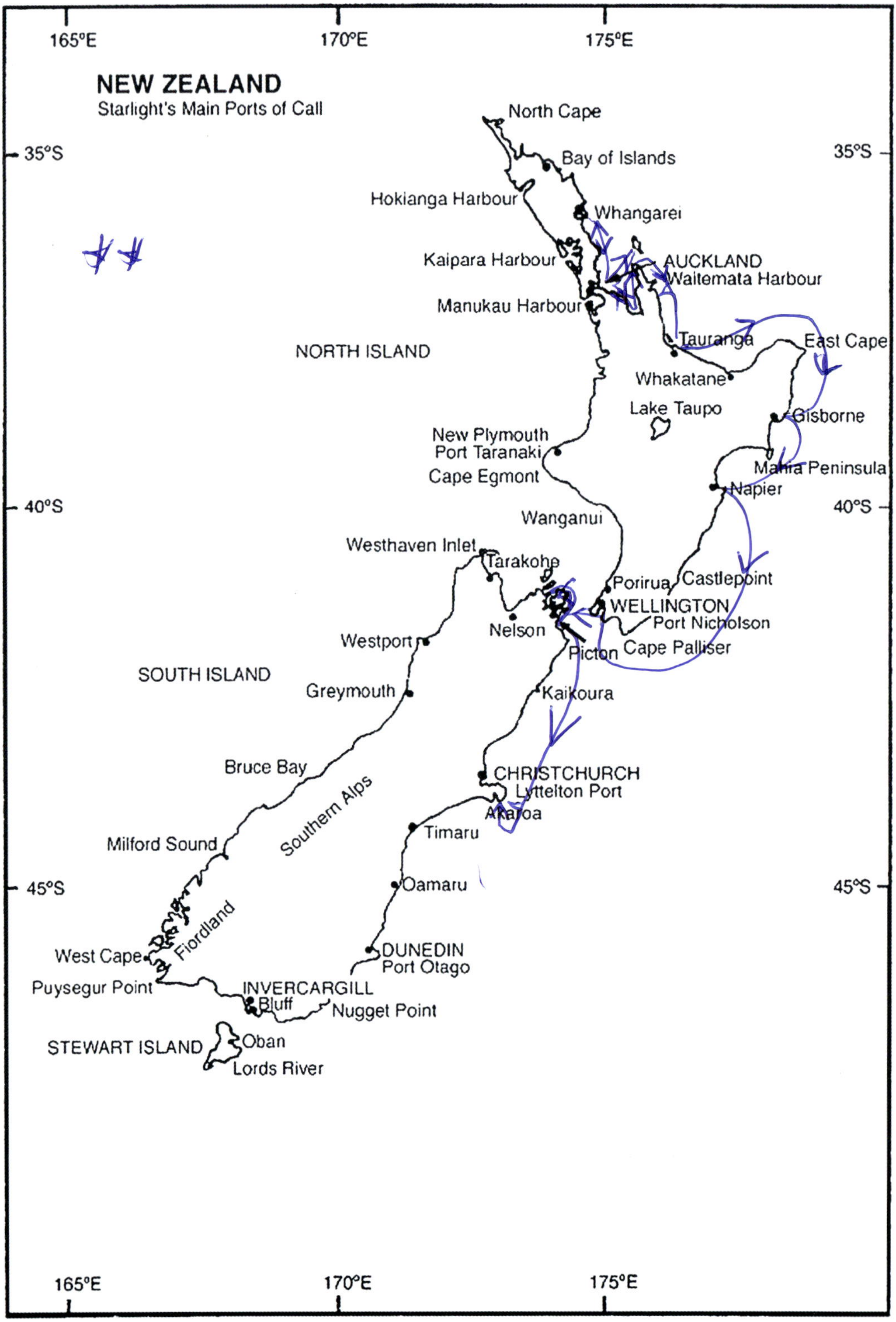
165°E
170°E
175°E
NEW ZEALAND
Starlight's Main Ports of Call
35°S
40°S
45°S
North Cape
Bay of Islands
Hokianga Harbour
Whangarei
Kaipara Harbour
AUCKLAND
Waitemata Harbour
Manukau Harbour
NORTH ISLAND
Tauranga
East Cape
Whakatane
Lake Taupo
Gisborne
New Plymouth
Port Taranaki
Cape Egmont
Mahia Peninsula
Napier
Wanganui
Westhaven Inlet
Tarakohe
Porirua
Castlepoint
WELLINGTON
Port Nicholson
Nelson
Picton
Cape Palliser
Westport
SOUTH ISLAND
Greymouth
Kaikoura
Bruce Bay
Southern Alps
CHRISTCHURCH
Lyttelton Port
Akaroa
Milford Sound
Timaru
Oamaru
Fiordland
West Cape
DUNEDIN
Port Otago
Puysegur Point
INVERCARGILL
Bluff
Nugget Point
STEWART ISLAND
Oban
Lords River

Preface

Where did you go? What happened? Did you have storms and big seas? What were the fiords like? How did you manage on such a small boat? These were some of the questions we were asked.

This book has been written not only to answer the many questions but also to share this adventure with others – especially trailer-yacht owners and boaties who dream of going around New Zealand or at least exploring part of it. It may stir up a dream or two for those not nautically minded.

It is not a 'how to do it' book but I expect readers will take note of some of the dos and don'ts. It is more a 'we did it' book. The fact that my husband Norm Millar and I, with the assistance of Sam Medland on sections of this adventure around both the North Island and South Island coasts, were retired meant that we could wait for suitable weather. However although we listened carefully to the weather forecasts and took note of local fishermen's advice, it was not all plain sailing. In fact we motored two thirds of the way around the North Island and hardly ever sailed in open seas around the South Island.

Even though *Starlight* could be put on a trailer and towed from one part of New Zealand to another, our dream was to circumnavigate – to go around the coastlines of both islands – in our trailer-yacht when we retired. It took four months to complete the North Island trip in 1997 and nearly six months to do the South Island circumnavigation in 2001.

The varied coastline with its many bays, headlands and capes made interesting viewing. We could take *Starlight,* with its retractable centre-plate, into shallow waters, up rivers and into tidal inlets. We could rest the yacht on beaches and go into harbours with big sand bars where the bigger keeler yachts could not enter. In this respect the journey was unique.

At each place we were greeted by overwhelming hospitality and spontaneously offered local knowledge, especially on how to negotiate the following leg of our journey at sea and how to enter the next port of call. To these kind, generous, friendly people we owe a debt of gratitude. Those whose names are known are mentioned in the text but there are many more, often unknown and unseen, who assisted us during our adventure. The VHF radio operators, the weather forecasters, the chart makers, the authors of books, the designer and maker of the stable and seaworthy Gazelle yacht, the sail-makers, rigging specialists, boating course lecturers and a host of others, all played a part in assisting us to make decisions.

Special acknowledgments go to: Daryl McGee and Val Chubb, for adapting the Mark 1 Gazelle yacht design to almost a Mark 2 and allowing us an input into additional strengthening of the hull; Bernie Perano, for modifying the hatches and for his initial tips on sailing; the Mana Cruising Club, who held our 10-minute forms, for providing facilities and for their guide books on Fiordland and Stewart Island; our daughter Raewyn Te Tau who monitored our telephone calls and kept track of our movements. Also to editor and publisher Carol Dawber for her patient assistance and guidance in getting this book published; Phillip Wickliffe for scanning the photographs; Major Joan Hutson and Lieutenant Colonel Moira Wright for checking drafts, and Noel Bell for allowing me to quote from the Mana Cruising Guides.

Theoretically I am *Starlight*'s captain, as I hold the Yachtmaster Coastal, and Yachtmaster Ocean Certificates. I do the navigation and chart plotting as well as looking after the sails, anchoring, radio and stores, and I also do most of the cooking. Norm deals with the mechanical parts and repairs. We share the steering, the deck watches and the decisions to go or stay. Many visitors mistake Norm for the captain but he tells them, "Wait until the Admiral comes on board." However it is all teamwork and our crew member, Sam, fitted in well and played his part in our adventure.

We three are Christians and members of The Salvation Army, and we were led to encircle New Zealand in prayer and to read the Bible at each place. This became a special mission and we were enriched, blessed and guided by many answers to prayer. God strengthened us, and our family, as we experienced tragic deaths and I had to come home twice for funerals and to support close family members.

If you, the reader, can get a feel of this adventure – can imagine the wind in the sails, the motor churning on, the sea swells, the coastline as it passes, the bays and inlets, the majestic fiords, the varied ports of call and the sense of being there with us – then the writing of this book, sharing our experiences with you, will be well worth while.

Mavis Millar (née Clark)
Porirua, 2005

Contents:

PART ONE – THE NORTH ISLAND

Bernie Perano shows Mavis how to attach the sails, 1 January 1981

1

The Dream

In all your ways acknowledge God and He will direct your path.

Proverbs 3:6

The waves rose high as *Starlight* rounded the Cape. The seas roared as we steered five miles further out from the land in an endeavour to miss the turbulent waters. There was no wind to sail our 24ft 6in (7.4 metre) trailer yacht so the 10hp Honda outboard motor had the big task of propelling the yacht up the four-metre swells to ride the contrary waves in between, cut through the white ribbon of broken water on the crests and slide down into the troughs. The sea was too rough for the Autohelm 1000, so we tackled the seas by steering with the tiller. Then Norm was seasick and had to leave me to handle the yacht.

Would I be able to steer *Starlight* through this kind of sea, I asked myself. What made the sea so very rough on such a windless day? I knew the answer. We were off Cape Reinga at the top end of New Zealand where two oceans, the Pacific Ocean and the Tasman Sea, meet head-on. From the lighthouse lookout, the turbulence caused by these currents can often be seen stretching north for several miles.

I steered around the worst of the turbulence and then headed south, about two miles off the land, with only a slightly calmer sea. Cape Maria van Diemen and a few headlands guided our progress along the Ninety Mile Beach. There was no shelter anywhere and I dared not go further off the coast as the notoriously-shallow Pandora Bank, just a few miles off the northwest corner of the island, was bound to have even greater turbulence.

Why was I in this situation? What was I doing here? Was it a dream or a nightmare? Did I have the skills to handle it? In theory, yes, but in practice it was a new experience. The hours ticked by as *Starlight* motored south. Would the outboard keep going? Norm was seasick again and retired to the cabin to recover. I could not ask him to help if the motor failed or ran out of petrol.

Earlier that morning we had left the shallow Parengarenga Harbour to sail or motor around the northernmost part of New Zealand in our sturdy trailer yacht *Starlight*. The winds had been mostly strong southwesterlies for the eight days we waited there, but now an intense high-pressure system was developing over the whole of New Zealand. Light winds and calm seas were predicted for at least five days, so we gave it a go.

What were we doing there anyway? It was our retirement dream - to sail around the coast of New Zealand in our trailer yacht. We had been planning this adventure for a long time.

I was born and grew up in Gisborne. I enjoyed swimming sports, surfing and lifesaving at the local beaches, fishing off the wharf and hiking over the surrounding hills, but had never had the chance to go boating. I floated like a cork in the water, relished the sea with its turbulent waves, followed the tides controlled by the moon and studied the stars that shone brightly at night.

Norm was born in Leeston but grew up in Blenheim. He enjoyed swimming and diving in the rivers. In 1947 he had the opportunity to join the crew on the *Wairau* as assistant engineer. This cargo ship and the *Echo* (both run by Eckford and Company) took cargo between Wellington and the South Island, mostly to Blenheim. They crossed the often-rough Cook Strait, navigated over the Wairau River bar and travelled up the shallow Opawa River to unload their cargo at a the big wharf-shed near the railway station. Norm had many interesting experiences in the five years he spent on these boats.

We met in Wellington. I was studying for a Bachelor of Science degree at Victoria University and Norm was a second engineer on the ships going to and fro. When he was in Wellington, his motorcycle would be slung off first and our courtship was often spent on it, exploring the roads around the capital city. After our marriage and the birth of our son in Lower Hutt, Norm wanted some home life ashore so he gave up the sea and became a motor mechanic. We shifted to Porirua in 1956 and put a deposit on a state house in 1958. The next year Norm went into the garage business at Paraparaumu.

All thoughts of boating were on hold as we cared for our four children, until one day a friend took us in his powerboat to Kapiti Island. An outboard-powered motorboat speeding across calm seas was quite different to the slow, diesel-smelling, roly-poly cargo boats that Norm had once worked on. The lure of the sea hooked us both. Before long we had bought a 13ft 6in wooden clinker boat to take us fishing around Mana and Kapiti Islands. Heaps of fishing and rough sea stories abounded as the years rolled by. Then after the family grew up, we sold *The Clinker* and bought a 15ft 6in Crestacraft fibreglass boat, *Amphitrite,* powered by an 80hp Mercury outboard motor. It just flew across Cook Strait in a calm sea on New Year's Day 1975.

We both loved the adventures of exploring the Marlborough Sounds, French Pass, Tasman Bay and Golden Bay. We completed courses for Boatmaster and Marine Radio Operator certificates, bought charts for these areas and gained lots of experience in weather patterns and tidal flows. Then we sold *Amphitrite* and bought a 17ft 3in Vistacraft fibreglass boat, *Twilight,* powered by a 135hp Johnson outboard. "He'll be off to Australia next," Norm's friends at Paraparaumu said with a laugh, referring to our offshore attempts.

In January 1980 we trailered *Twilight* to Auckland and explored the Hauraki Gulf areas of Waiheke and the other islands, venturing as far as Great Barrier Island. We carried 112 litres (25 gallons) of petrol in the main tank with another 45 litres in two cans. The weather held as we crossed from Coromandel to Tryphena Bay. "Yes, you can get petrol there," we were told, but not a drop was available.

We motored north along the west coast of Great Barrier Island in sheltered seas. Each bay with facilities told us, "You'll get some at Port Fitzroy". So we carried on. Our petrol supplies were getting low. When we got to Port Fitzroy, the attendant said, "We are out of petrol but it's coming soon". The barge carrying the drums of petrol from Auckland was only just approaching Tryphena. It took another four days to arrive and unload its cargo.

The service station was rationing the petrol and we were told that 45 litres was all we would be allowed, but we needed at least 90 to make it safely back to the mainland. Norm bought 45 litres, and while we were berthed at the jetty we saw several yacht owners coming with 4.5 litre or 9 litre cans for their small outboards. We waited until everyone else had been served, and then I asked, "Can I buy 45 litres too please?" The sympathetic attendant sold me the extra petrol.

We realised that if we were going to explore more offshore places we needed to go sailing. We discussed our plans with people in yachts anchored nearby, and invitations to come aboard arrived rapidly. We saw a variety of trailer yachts at anchor and later we looked over some on shore. Should we start small to gain more experience of sailing, or should we go straight to a comfortable larger boat? The debate continued for a while after we came home. The Noeleda, 22ft and 24ft Noelex, Trojan, Aquarius and other models were all discussed and evaluated. Size, cost, comfort, handling and other factors were considered.

Then one day Norm's friend Val Chubb, a boat builder, asked, "Have you found the boat you want yet?"

"Yes," Norm replied, "I like the Gazelle trailer yacht. I saw one called *The Wasp* at Evans Bay. It has a rounded hull with no skeg, just like a dinghy." Val's eyes lit up with surprise. "Daryl McGee has just bought the plug and it's coming up from Christchurch next week. I'll be making Gazelles here, just two doors from your garage." We asked for specifications, costs and details, and we were the first to order this 'sail-away' yacht from Val Chubb.

We sold the Vistacraft and added some savings to make up the difference in cost but we were unaware that a number of essential parts had not been included in the price. It was 'sail-away', but only just. Hand-rails, motor, petrol tanks, trailer, anchor, rope, compass, speedometer, inside fittings, upholstery, cupboards, wiring, lights and hosts more equipment soon bumped the price up to double the original quote.

The workers laid the fibreglass and Norm asked them to put more rovings and thicker fibreglass in the hull to strengthen it. He also specified a big wooden board to be glassed in right across the stern so the dive ladder and the outboard could be bolted to a solid base, and a heavy plate under the foredeck to hold the mooring cleat for the anchor. "I don't want to be anchored under Puysegur Point in a storm and have the bow pulled out," Norm said. "We want our yacht for cruising."

The colour was to be our choice. Lots of boats were white with a bit of blue. Not many were colourful. Our Crestacraft had been all white and could not be seen in the surf at Paraparaumu Beach when Norm had escorted a swimmer in a race from Kapiti Island. Air-sea rescue guidelines recommended red, orange, yellow and black as colours that stand out at sea, so we chose a bright buttercup yellow for both the hull and the deck.

Our family became interested in the yacht project, so we involved them in naming it. We all made out lists, bearing in mind that the yacht would be yellow all over, and that the name had to sound clear on the VHF radio. Eventually we all agreed on *Starlight.*

The yacht soon took shape and by Christmas 1980 it was nearly ready. However the boat builders were making three Gazelles, two of them for racing, so our project got a bit behind. With the help of our boatbuilder friend Bernie Perano, we completed the fittings, tested the electric winch operating the 900 lbs (410 kg) centre plate, put the rudder into its frame, fitted the gas stove and checked the rigging. There was a lot more to do too, but when we did the trials on Porirua Harbour, everything worked well.

After Bernie had shown us how to rig the mast and fit the sails, we launched *Starlight* from the ramp at Onepoto on Porirua Harbour, not far from our home at Elsdon. It was 1 January 1981. We had our annual holidays and we were keen to take *Starlight* across Cook Strait and explore the Marlborough Sounds, so Norm took our van and the yacht trailer home and locked it to a 'deadman' on the lawn. Bernie gave us a two-hour sailing lesson, showing us how to trim the sails, jibe, steer with allowance for drift or leeway and spill the wind. Then we put him and his family back onto Shelly Beach at Whitireia Park and by one o'clock we were off across Cook Strait, driven by a gentle 15-knot northerly breeze.

We took five and a half hours to sail to Tory Channel. The learning curve was steep and had only just begun, but over time we learnt our lessons, sailing in and out of various bays and coves from Port Underwood to Puponga. We soon clocked up more crossings over Cook Strait in the yacht than the seventy we had done in the power boats.

On one trip, returning from the Marlborough Sounds, we struck a 'bullet storm' coming from the south and turned back. We had left the shelter of the sounds and set the sails, but when we looked towards the south we could see a strong wind taking the tops off huge waves. We hastily dropped the sails, just off the entrance of Queen Charlotte Sound, and Norm started the motor. We tied everything down and turned back into the shelter of Ship Cove, delaying our return by a day. It was Sunday 28 October 1981. Bernie Perano was concerned about our hatch cover, which he knew was a weak point, and thought we might have foundered in the storm so he persuaded our daughter Carolyn to report us overdue. We were blissfully unaware of the concern as we sailed back across the strait the next day. We had no VHF radio in those days, no sail numbers and no name painted on the hull, and we were listening to 2YA radio.

The rescue planes were sent out twice to look for us, and the search wasn't called off until 3pm on the Monday when we arrived safely back in Porirua Harbour. Everyone in New Zealand who listened to 2ZB radio knew that Mavis, Norm and their daughter Raewyn had been lost or missing all day. The yacht was new then, and needless to say we soon attended to our safety recognition markings and communication systems.

On another trip from French Pass to Mana Island we experienced strong northwest winds and 40ft waves with close deep troughs as we approached the North Island. We sailed with the jib up and the 10hp Honda outboard going as well. Norm was steering a course for the south of Mana Island, keeping at right angles to the waves. Going down one trough the waves within it caused the yacht to broach. Norm was unable to hold the tiller on course and the yacht slid sideways down into the bottom of the trough. The waves broke on top of us and filled up the cockpit. Then, amazingly, the yacht made a big 'pop' sound as it rose up out of the sea. All the water drained out through the outboard motor well. The mast stayed upright and the sail was still filled. We realised that our narrow centre-plate had saved the yacht from tripping up as it slid down sideways. After we had battled these large waves for over an hour, Norm was able to steer us safely into the lee of the island.

On another occasion, during a trip to Queen Charlotte Sound we were tacking off The Brothers islands in Cook Strait when the rudder broke with a loud snap like a rifle shot. We went to Resolution Bay under motor and clamped it together for the trip back home. Another rudder was made, stronger this time, but over several years water got into the grain and eventually it broke as we approached Tory Channel in a rough sea. We retrieved the rudder and its twisted frame, then struggled with the 8hp outboard on the outside bracket to steer us through the entrance and in to shelter in Okukari Bay. Our third rudder was made by Bernie Perano. He used Oregon pine, cutting the wood slightly on the diagonal and gluing the two pieces together to give it strength, and this one has proven successful ever since.

We trailered the yacht to Lake Taupo and later to Auckland for a trip around Great Barrier Island with Ruth Pascoe, Sam and Eva Medland and their son Stephen. Our dream to circumnavigate New Zealand when we retired was becoming more and more a reality. "Perhaps we could take two years and call in to lots of places," Norm suggested. I thought about this and did not like the idea of living on the yacht during the shorter wet, cold days of winter.

"How about doing the North Island first during one summer, staying home for the winter, and then tackling the South Island later," I said.

We bought 30 nautical charts of the North Island and an electric winch to haul in the 17kg anchor and its heavy chain. We also bought an Autohelm 1000 which we named 'Fred', as it was considered as good as an extra crew member. I read 25 books and in 1984 I gained my Yachtmaster Coastal and Ocean certificates as well as a first-aid certificate. Norm passed only the compass part of the Yachtmaster Coastal. He had been busy at his garage and found that he did not have time to study.

Every time we visited ports, river mouths, bays or headlands we would note the entrances, shorelines and approaches. For many years we listened to the National Radio marine weather forecasts at 3am or 5am and the five-day forecast at 12:30pm. We noted the tides and observed the sea conditions at every opportunity.

Norm's brother and business partner, Peter, died in 1990 so in October 1991 Norm sold the garage business. About the same time, I retired from my position as a Senior Statistician with the Ministry of Education. We were now retired superannuitants.

In 1992 we went to Tonga for a month to teach learners to play brass band instruments. Norm repaired two of the King of Tonga's cars and we enjoyed swimming in the warm tropical reefs among the colourful fish.

In 1995 we fulfilled our other dream of travelling around Australia on our GL1200A Honda Goldwing motorcycle. It took four months to travel the

27,000kms with five others. We flew our motorcycles from Wellington to Sydney and then headed north, all four motorcycles towing small trailers laden with camping gear. Beryl and Ken Trail, Audrey and Dave Jones and Bob Thyne made up a fine team to share this adventure with.

We headed north to Brisbane and Cairns, exploring the Queensland coast, taking a cruise to Hardy Reef where we swam with the big bass fish and viewed the coral on the unique Great Barrier Reef. We enjoyed the colourful birds, the tropical forest and sugar-cane plantations, and we camped with our gazebo, barbeque and dome tents at a variety of places. Then we crossed the mountain divide to Mt Isa, Tenant Creek and Darwin. We rode south to Western Australia, Perth, Kalgoorlie and east across the Nullarbor Plain. We rode north from Port Augusta to Coober Pedy and Yulara, climbed Ayers Rock, then headed to Alice Springs and back south to Adelaide. We went on to Melbourne and Canberra via the Snowy Mountains. Finally back at Sydney, we put our motorcycles and trailers into a container for shipping them back to New Zealand. It had been a never-to-be-forgotten dream fulfilled.

We cared for my mother after my father died in 1993. We tramped several of the top ten tracks with my sister Joan Hutson and her husband Don. Between 1992 and 1996 we walked the Milford, Routeburn, Greenstone, Heaphy and Abel Tasman tracks and did the Tongariro crossing, as well as doing a host of other things.

Sam Medland heard of our dream to sail around New Zealand in our trailer yacht and asked if he could crew for us on a leg or two. In early 1996, he enquired about our plans. "Not yet while Mum needs us," Norm said.

Sam replied gracefully, "The sea will still be there."

It was not until October 1996 that Norm said, "It's time to GO!"

"Go where?" I asked in amazement.

"Our yacht trip around the North Island, of course," he said. My mother had passed away the previous month, and now we felt free to fulfil our dream.

Preparation became a priority. Earlier that year we had bought a 1992 long-wheel-based 4WD Toyota diesel van to tow the yacht. *Starlight's* trailer had to be replaced, and that was Norm's project. He designed and made up two rocker frames with three rear go-cart wheels and tyres in each frame as support for the hull and for easy roll-off launching. He welded a frame for the winch on the front of the trailer and made supports for the bow of the yacht.

Each weld was covered with stainless steel, using stainless steel arc-welding rods to prevent rust. I ordered a spray-dodger to be made, and then I checked the rigging and changed a number of fittings. We bought a new fire extinguisher, a mobile phone, an EPIRB, a Garmin GPS 38, a smaller mainsail and an 8hp Yamaha two-stroke outboard as a backup to the 10hp Honda four-

Starlight at Kapiti Motors, Paraparaumu, December 1981, with her new heavier hatches fitted. Clockwise from front left: Mavis Millar, Alexander, Anton and Bernie Perano, Raewyn Te Tau. Mavis is standing on the diving ladder, and at the right of the transom is the bracket for the auxiliary outboard stroke. I made two new lee-cloths and covers for three fenders. I ordered Telecom mobile phone coverage maps and AA road maps for the North Island.

The realization that the trip was going to happen soon was exciting, but there were still lots of things to do. Food and water containers had to be filled. Extra one and two-gallon petrol containers were purchased, along with a huge list of stores and equipment. Christmas came and went, and the weather was still unsettled as we made our final preparations. Tropical storms swept south to deluge the Coromandel and East Cape areas in late December and early January. Sam Medland and his family lost their tent while camping at Otautu Bay in the Coromandel area. He would not be home in Napier until mid-January.

We cleaned the house, mowed the lawns and emptied the fridge, then on 16 January 1997 we launched *Starlight* at the Onepoto ramp. While we were tied up at the floating platform a single side-band radio, donated by Glen Wood, was checked and found unrepairable, so it was discarded. Ron Hubbard gave us an almost-new VHF as a standby for our fifteen-year-old radio. Both VHF radios had good reception. I was fascinated with the GPS and took some readings at the ramp, entering the latitude and longitude on the chart with a pencil mark and recording the waypoint on the GPS.

At last, on Friday 17th January 1997, the weather report was favourable - fine and calm, with little wind. I drove over to the Mana Cruising Club and filled in a ten minute form. This took a little longer than ten minutes as I entered details of *Starlight*'s size and equipment; VHF radio, mobile phone number, litres of petrol and water carried, consumption of petrol by the outboards, and the contact person, our daughter Raewyn Te Tau. The club secretary filed it, along with a photo of *Starlight,* for reference in case of emergencies.

The sky became cloudy and the forecast was updated to a slight sea with a twenty-knot northwesterly wind rising. Still, we had done this leg from Porirua to Wellington Harbour some years before, and a northwest wind meant we would be able to sail. At 3pm we said goodbye to a small group of family and friends at the Onepoto ramp near the south end of Porirua harbour and we were off, motoring through the shallow channels.

At last our dream was becoming a reality.

2

Porirua – Wellington – Napier

Jesus, Saviour, pilot me
Over life's tempestuous sea;
Unknown waves before me roll,
Hiding rocks and treacherous shoal;
Chart and compass come from thee,
Jesus, Saviour, pilot me.

Edward Hopper

We motored between the marker posts of Porirua Harbour, using the 10hp Honda outboard in the well of the cockpit. We passed the Mana Marina, Paremata and Plimmerton, then keeping the reef in the centre of Karehana Bay to starboard we headed out to the open sea. We were following our first chart, NZ 4632, Approaches to Paremata. We steered south west and hoisted the jib. The northwest wind quickly filled the sail and we cut the motor long before crossing the bridge of seaweed from the headland to Mana Island. Our friends Ivy Paul and Margaret Bailey were looking out for us from their vantage point in Titahi Bay.

"The yacht fair flew as it sailed across the bay," they told us later.

Starlight was doing five knots (her hull speed is 5½ knots) with a back wind and only a jib up, sailing on a 210-degree compass course. We were heading for Wellington Harbour as our first port of call, intending to travel east and then north towards Napier. We soon passed Makara Beach and noted the lighthouse on Ohau Point. We rounded Cape Terawhiti in a slight sea at 6:30 pm, changing to chart NZ 46, Wellington to Patea including Cook Strait. High tide at Paremata was 5:24pm but at Wellington it was 1pm, with low tide there at 5:20pm. The tide was going with us, the wind was now northerly and freshening, and the GPS reading showed seven knots. The moderate waves also pushed *Starlight* as we changed course to the southeast.

We sailed close to Karori Rock and Norm photographed the old beacon on it. We had a good look at the newer lighthouse which is now on the mainland. The sea had a slight chop as we passed through the well-known Karori rip but *Starlight* handled it well. The wind gusts were about 25-30 knots as we passed Sinclair Head and then our course was to steer east, but the wind came from the north east, almost head-on, so we started the outboard and dropped the jib as we passed Island Bay. The sea became very rough and the wind was too strong for us to go up to the foredeck and tie down the jib. We noticed that some of the clips slid up and down the bottom of the forestay.

As we came abreast of the Wellington Airport in Lyall Bay, the wind gusted even more strongly, so we started the 8hp outboard motor on the outside bracket as well, and *Starlight* started to make headway. Even though we were only a short distance from land, the offshore wind made a very choppy sea, lifting spray off the tops of the waves.

Gradually we crept along the south coast of the North Island, but when we approached the Wellington Harbour entrance, winds exceeding 50 knots swept down the channel. Even with the two motors going we found it impossible to make headway into the main entrance, so we cleared the west ledge of rocks off Palmer Point and steered for shelter at Breaker Bay, in the lee of the cliffs under Beacon Hill. It was calm there as we dropped the anchor, no swell and little surf. We had sailed for five hours and motored for one and a half.

We reported our position to Beacon Hill Radio on VHF channel 62. "The wind is gusting up to 60 knots!" we were told. "And there is foul ground where you have anchored – it's not good holding there because of heavy seaweed". But our anchor held well. We tied down the jib and dinghy onto the deck with extra ropes, tied the three halyards to the rails to stop them pinging against the aluminium mast, rang Raewyn and prepared tea just after sunset.

The wind was very noisy as it whistled over us. We could see the street lights of Breaker Bay, the cars coming through the gap and two bonfires on the beach. We were serenaded by guitar music coming from the twilight picnickers as we had tea and settled down for the first night of our North Island adventure.

I took a GPS reading – we were 41 degrees 6.831 minutes south, 174 degrees 50.719 minutes east. We planned to read the Bible from cover to cover during our trip, and pray a blessing for the people at each place we visited. Encompassing New Zealand and praying a blessing on the people of New Zealand was our aim. We wanted to claim the Bible verse found in 2 Chronicles chapter 7, verse 14.

"If my people will humble themselves and pray, and search for me, and turn from their wicked ways, then I will hear them from heaven and forgive their sins, I will answer their prayer and heal their land."

That night we made a start with the first two chapters of Genesis, realising that we would see God's creation from the sea - a different perspective than from the land. Then we said a prayer for the people of Wellington.

We slept uneasily that first night. In the morning the wind had died down a little to a 25-knot northerly, but it was still gusting, so we pulled up the

Workers laying the fibreglass in the mould for *Starlight,* October 1980

anchor and left at 9am, motoring through Chaffers Passage at the north of Barretts Reef. This passage, with a shallow depth of about ten metres, is often used by small boats.

"We saw you take a short cut," the radio operator at Beacon Hill said when we called up on the VHF. We skirted the rocks at Dorset Point and kept to the port (left) side of the main channel in a very choppy sea. Soon we rounded Point Halswell, with a good view of the Massey Memorial, and headed into Evans Bay. We hoisted the jib and sailed, even though the wind was still gusting. We glided into a wharf near the Evans Bay Yacht Club and were welcomed by a trailer-yacht owner who arranged for us to use a nearby berth. Soon we were tied up with fore and aft ropes and spring ropes to the bollards on the narrow walkway. Our fenders were put in place and we felt secure enough to go to the clubhouse.

Here we were warmly greeted by many yachties, including some Gazelle owners and a number of 16ft-Hartley owners who had gathered for their Wellington anniversary weekend regatta. Among them were my second cousin Winston Hoare and his friend Derek Coffey, both from Palmerston North. They were racing Winston's Hartley, *Pronto,* but there were no races that day because of the strong winds. There were yachts on trailers all over the car park. The club welcomed us and gave us the use of the facilities, including showers and toilets. Norm borrowed a long lead to add to our 60ft one so that *Starlight*'s batteries could be charged. It was calm overnight and we slept well.

On Sunday the wind turned to a gusty southerly but the Hartleys raced all morning. There was not much rain, but the rough sea caused damage to some of these 16ft yachts - a broken gooseneck, a damaged rudder, a broken boom (Winston's) as well as one yacht upside down. The rescue boats were kept busy towing them in. There was lots of talking in the clubhouse that afternoon. A barbeque tea had been arranged and we joined in, chatting with three other couples who had large 28ft to 36ft keelers. Experiences were shared and helpful tips on sailing exchanged with Errol and Juanita Crosland of *Contention,* and Gary and List Baldwin of *Enya.* Another couple had swapped their yacht with an American and sailed from Seattle to Alaska. They seemed surprised at our plans to tackle the circumnavigation of the North Island. We said we had plenty of time and thought it might take four or five months to complete it. Our itinerary was flexible to fit in with the weather and sea conditions. After all, we would rather sail or motor in calm seas than strike rough ones.

The next morning the weather had calmed down despite a noisy, windy night and a choppy sea. The sky was clear and the sea calm. Norm fitted a new bracket for the fire extinguisher. I did some laundry and our clothes were fluttering in the breeze when our daughter Justine Lee and daughter-in-law Barbara Millar arrived at 1:30pm. We all went for a sail on the harbour in a light northwest wind. We used the old mainsail reefed down a little with the jib and found that the weather helm had improved. We waved to the keeler owners who were also out for a fine day's sailing, and we were all back near the clubhouse jetty by 6pm. The Hartleys had caught up on the races that had been cancelled, and had finished their series. They were all packing up in the car park delighted with the results.

That evening we shifted *Starlight* to a ramp near Greta Point, close to Swanson's rigging workshop. It was calm there. Monday had been a public holiday and so Tuesday would be the first opportunity to do repairs.

The forestay had strands pulled out and needed replacing. The clips on the jib had worn thin and nine of them had to be changed. The new smaller mainsail had come without batons, and new ropes were needed for the main runner. Barry Swanson was available to do the forestay but the mast had to be dropped. Port Nicholson Sails in the nearby loft supplied us with the clips and batons, and we replaced wool in the sails and bought Teflon spray to lubricate the mast and boom slots. The northwesterly winds were very strong with rough seas, and much the same conditions were forecast for the next day.

On Wednesday, a southerly change with light rain was predicted, so after our chores were completed we walked to the Kilbirnie shops to get fresh food supplies and nine litres of petrol.

Norm and Mavis Millar with their four children, January 2002.
Standing, from left: Lloyd Millar, Justine Lee, Carolyn Wickliffe, Raewyn Te Tau

We were back at Greta Point for tea. Then at 8 pm a light southerly wind came to rock *Starlight* so we motored to the shelter of Kau Bay near Point Halswell. We put down the anchor and, though it was calm there, we felt the swell as large ships were passing nearby.

The TV weather forecast was good for the next two days. A big high-pressure system was coming, bringing fine weather with light southerly winds easing then dying out. We rang Raewyn at 9pm to tell her that if the morning marine forecast was the same or better, we would be off. Our plan was to do the East Coast first, picking up Sam Medland at Napier and heading on north as the weather allowed.

The 5am marine forecast for Cook Strait was reasonable, with light winds and southerly swells easing, so we left at 5:30am. We called Beacon Hill on channel 62 as we motored past. A heavy southerly swell was coming into the harbour and it was like being on a roller coaster as *Starlight* went up and down the three-metre swells. We kept to the main channel but watched out for other larger boats coming in or going out.

"We'll have breakfast on the way," Norm said when we left. But now he didn't feel like eating. I had a bite to eat and wished I hadn't. We passed Moaning

Millie on our starboard side. This beacon at the south end of Barretts Reef has a red light on it at night, and whistles or moans as the waves bounce it.

Fred the Autohelm was working well as we passed Pencarrow Head and later Baring Head, both with lighthouses on them. We always made sure that one of us was on deck watching our progress, checking the chart and looking out for dangers when the Autohelm was steering *Starlight*. We headed into the four-metre southeasterly swells on a compass course of 106 degrees. By 9:30 am, Norm was seasick and retired to the cabin for an hour or so.

We motored on, passed Turakina Head, looking across at the Orongorongo Valley and the high hills of the Rimutaka Range, but keeping our course towards the east side of Palliser Bay. We arrived off Ngawi at 1 pm. The large swells created heavy surf on the stony shore and we could not see a sheltered spot. The fishermen here used large trailers towed by bulldozers to haul their boats out of the sea and thus avoided the strong southerlies.

We tried calling our friends on our mobile phone but they were not at home. Beacon Hill came on the VHF to see how we were progressing, and we told them we were off Ngawi and couldn't raise our friends.

"They have all gone to Martinborough in the Wairarapa for the Market Day festival," we were told. "There's hardly anyone left in the village, and it would be unwise to try and anchor there in this heavy southeasterly swell." We thanked them, heeded their advice and carried on.

"If we could just round Cape Palliser and head northeast we might get enough wind to sail, and then the southeast swell would be on our stern quarter," I said. The lighthouse with its many steps was easily seen from our yacht but we dared not go too close because of the rocks, reefs and seaweed below. In the past we had visited several beaches and bays along this coast and realised that most approaches were full of rocks and reefs with little shelter. So it was to be an overnight trip to Castlepoint or a much longer one to Napier.

This would be our first night at sea. Stories of fierce storms and shipwrecks occurring on this rocky Wairarapa coast, even in recent years, came to my mind. Our friends Ron and Diana Macintosh had endured a stiff southerly storm when travelling north along this coast in their keeler. The cargo ship *Tuvalu* was wrecked near Honeycomb Rock in 1967, and there was the much-publicised capsize of the 12.5 metre *Rose Noelle* off this same coast in 1989. Her crew of four men survived 118 days adrift in the Pacific Ocean in their upturned trimaran, only to be shipwrecked when it smashed onto the rocks of Great Barrier Island. These and many others tales of shipwreck along this coast made us amateur sailors fearful.

We passed Cape Palliser and turned to the northeast. The sky had been cloudy but now the sun shone brightly and the wind was a light southerly. The jib and small main were hoisted and we sailed at three knots for an hour. However when we got down to one knot we started the motor. The sails assisted our progress by about half a knot for a time, but eventually the wind dropped completely and we hauled them down. Using only the motor *Starlight* did five knots, with the four-metre southerly swells giving us an extra push. Neither of us felt like eating - just a cold drink or a cup of tea from the hot water in the Thermos flask, plus a nibble from our lolly boxes, was all we could manage.

The grandeur of the dark grey granite-like cliffs along the shore, the dense bush and forest in the valleys, the surf pounding the shores and the swells crashing on the rocks and reefs were impressive on the port side. The uninterrupted view of the Pacific Ocean on the wide horizon to starboard made us realise how vast was the expanse of sea we were travelling on. We took turns at sleeping and watching our course, with Fred doing his share.

At 7pm we were off the Kairingaringa Reef and saw the road leading down to the small settlement of Glendhu. As the sun was setting behind the hills in the west, a brilliant golden full moon rose over the horizon. It was now 8:15pm. The sea had calmed a little and the swells were down to two metres.

As dusk fell I took a GPS reading and confirmed our position as a little south of Honeycomb Rock. The light on the 57-metre-high hill behind the rock began flashing, one white light every ten seconds. It had been 18-20 degrees Celsius all afternoon, but the temperature had been dropping since twilight and we put on lots of warm clothing as we prepared for the night. We heard later on National Radio that the nearby town of Masterton had a cool overnight temperature of four-degrees Celsius.

Although it was night time, the moon shone like daylight. We could see every ripple in the sea, the land was clear but dark, and the waves breaking on the shore or reefs showed up as white froth. I went to sleep in the bunk at 9:30pm while Norm kept watch, snugly wrapped in a warm coat, gloves, scarf, woolly hat and a blanket ready in case he needed it. Fred was set to steer a 45-degree compass course.

At about midnight, Norm was carefully watching the port side and shoreline when he glanced over his shoulder to starboard and saw a large turbulence in the water. The waves were rippling over a huge expanse the size of a football field making a moderate chop, but *Starlight* was passing it by in calm water. No reefs, shoals or shallows were marked on our chart, but Norm remembered a hint from the lady at Little Ship Services at Evans Bay. "Watch out for an area off Flat Point," she had told us. "It has a shallow reef that's not marked on the charts." When I woke up at 12:50am, Norm told me about this awesome sight. We looked it up on the chart and found that we had been at this very place, off Flat Point. The combination of swell and tide had produced large splashes and swirls there.

I took over the watch at 2am and took a GPS reading. I could see the lights shining from the houses at Riverside Beach. We were within the range of the Castlepoint Light – three white flashes every 30 seconds – and for some time this guided our progress. The sky was clear with only a few stars as the moon was very bright. Norm came on deck again at 4am and he noted that the sea was calm with only a one-metre swell.

We approached Castlepoint at dawn, while the lighthouse was still flashing. The swell was making big waves at the entrance to the lagoon so we did not attempt to enter, but reported our arrival to the operator on the VHF radio and waited for more daylight. At 6am we rounded the protruding reef and anchored in the calm bay near the fishermen's sandy launching spot on the beach behind the headland, just under the lighthouse. We had been travelling for 24 hours and needed refreshment – a large breakfast and a two-hour sleep.

Then Norm went ashore in the dinghy to buy 27 litres of petrol at the general store. Some local boat owners had seen us, or maybe heard us on the VHF, and offered to take him there in their ute. When he came back, the tide had risen and the afternoon sea breeze had freshened to a northeasterly wind coming straight into the bay. Norm could not row the dinghy against it but had to push it through the surf, wading with the water up to his shoulders. The yacht was tossing us around as he came aboard. After he had changed his clothes, we decided to go and find shelter somewhere else. I hauled in the anchor at 1.15pm, and we motored out of the bay into a headwind and in moderate sea. We called the VHF radio operator reporting our decision to go.

"Heading for Napier – ETA sometime tomorrow," I said, unable to guess exactly when we would be there. Somehow we managed to fit in our Bible reading and prayer for the residents along this coast, thanking God for their help and kindness.

We kept motoring in moderate seas, with a 15-knot northeasterly head wind but in a two-metre southeast swell, until we came under the lee of Cape Turnagain at 8pm. Here the sea was a little calmer so we hove-to and had some tea. The wind had dropped and the sea was slight by the time we moved on, motoring again. I slept for three hours.

The full moon came up shortly before 9pm, shining just as brightly as it had the previous night. "Look back at the high cliffs of the Cape," Norm said when I woke up. It was a spectacular sight, with the moon reflecting off the cliffs like a silvery mirror. It could still be seen at midnight, though by then the cliffs were a long way behind us.

The night air was cool as I took my turn on watch. At 2am *Starlight* was off Black Head. The lighthouse had a long white flash every 15 seconds. By now we were steering a compass course of 30 degrees and still keeping well offshore. Norm slept for only a short time and took over the watch at 4am, and at 5:30am we saw a red-coloured sunrise as the moon dipped behind the hills to the west.

The Honda 10hp outboard stopped suddenly, so we used the Yamaha 8hp on the outside stern bracket. At 6am a light northwesterly offshore wind sprang up and we set the sails to supplement the motor. *Starlight* glided along at six knots.

I took a GPS reading as we passed Bare Island at 7:10 am. An hour later the predicted northwesterly winds had died completely. The sails flopped and were dropped. As I sat on the foredeck after fastening the jib down, I saw a number of dolphins swimming alongside us. I watched them in admiration as they frolicked across the bow. We both saw a flying fish leap out of the sea and fly about 100 metres before flopping back. The sea had turned a deep blue colour and was oily calm.

At 10am the sun was shining and the air was hot as we rounded Cape Kidnappers. It was time for sunhats and sun block. We made sure we kept clear of the reefs and the craypot floats. A few gannets from the colony on top of the cliffs flew around us, some diving for fish. Somehow Norm managed to sleep for two hours while I was on watch.

As we came closer to the shore we could see the many tall Norfolk pines growing along the foreshore and the brightly-painted buildings of the Napier business area. It was an impressive sight from the sea.

As we approached the marina entrance, a flotilla of small yachts came tacking out for their afternoon races. We were motoring so we gave way to their sails but it was also low tide, and we ended up stuck on the mud on the starboard side of the channel. We had to pull up the centre-plate and reverse *Starlight* into deeper water after the racing yachts had all passed.

At 1:30 pm I found the marina manager's office and he directed us to a vacant berth. I was exhausted, but a warm relaxing shower, a cup of tea, a short sleep and then a good meal restored our energies. We had mobile phone coverage again so I rang Raewyn.

"Guess where we are?" I asked her.

"Napier?"

"Yes, we're here. We did two 24-hour hops with clear moonlight nights." I added that we were much relieved to have got this leg behind us so quickly. It was Saturday, 25 January 1997.

3

Gisborne – East Cape

One golden dawning, one glorious morning,
When earth's dark shadows flee away,
Our voices blending in song unending,
In brightest realms of fadeless day.
Sidney Edward Cox

There were good facilities at the Napier Marina; water and power on the jetty, with showers, toilets and a large restaurant at the Yacht Club nearby. That evening we received a message on the mobile phone from Sam Medland, and we arranged to spend Sunday with him and his family. Sam and Eva were in their late 60s and had retired to Napier in 1994 after serving 30 years as full-time officers with The Salvation Army. We had shared camping and fishing trips with them over many years. When they arrived to pick us up at 9:30 am, it was raining. We joined the Napier Salvation Army Corps at their 11am and 7pm services and enjoyed delicious meals in between. We talked all afternoon. Sam, who has a Sunburst yacht and a small powerboat, is a keen sailor and a good fisherman and he wanted to spend a month or so with us on *Starlight.*

The next day was showery and we spent the morning doing chores. Norm was using a long screwdriver to straighten the flukes of the main anchor when it flipped over the side into the water. It was his big, special screwdriver and he quickly put on his wetsuit and scuba diving gear to go down under the jetty to retrieve it. But the sea was six metres deep, murky and muddy, and although he searched carefully he couldn't find the screwdriver. "You'll have to buy another one," I told him.

Sam and Eva came for lunch and returned our dry laundry. We listened to the five day forecast at 12:30pm and the marine bulletin at 2:10pm on Napier radio. The forecast for the next 24 hours was for slight seas, east to southeast 15-knot winds with a one metre SE swell, so we decided to leave the next morning. Sam took us shopping in his car. Our list included a new Honda 10 fuel line coupling, as ours was leaking fuel and causing the outboard to stop working. We also bought 36 litres of petrol, a yellow fish lure and assorted groceries. Sam gave us a variety of vegetables, including lots of beetroot, from his lush garden. That evening I took a GPS reading and marked it on chart NZ 56, Gable End Foreland to Cape Kidnappers. I estimated that it would take 12 hours at four to five knots in a northeasterly direction to make Mahia Peninsula at the northern end of Hawke's Bay.

Sam joined us as a crew member in the morning. Norm got talking to a local boat-owner who told him that there was good shelter at Long Point on the west side of Mahia, almost 60 miles away, so we planned to make that our next stop. It was not until 9:30am that we said farewell to Eva Medland and set off. We motored past the wharves and cleared the beacons on Pania Reef before the mainsail and number two genoa foresail were hoisted. *Starlight* sailed well at three knots in a northeasterly direction for three hours, but leeway and the swells were taking us more to the north. The wind eased often, so we dropped the sails and motored east, and when the wind came up again we sailed northwards. We motored east, sailed north then motored east again. I took some GPS readings to check our progress as we zig-zagged across Hawke's Bay. We had plenty of time to read our two Bible chapters and pray a blessing for the folk who lived in this area, and to thank God for friends and the helpful locals.

The sea became slight, the cloud lifted and the sun came out as we had lunch. Norm put out the new tuna lure and caught a 15-inch kahawai. Then he let out a longer line and caught a small 24-inch kingfish. Our tea was organised.

"A large solitary bull dolphin kept us company for about three hours," Sam recorded in his diary. "He was so close, I could almost touch him as I sat in the stern, taking my turn at steering."

Because of the strengthening easterly wind, we motored east towards shelter in the lee of Mahia Peninsula, but it was some distance away. At 7pm we noticed the clouds gathering and saw that a two-metre southeast swell was developing, making the sea moderate to rough. Time was running out. At 9pm I took a GPS reading which showed us nearing Long Point as darkness fell.

Norm called out as he was steering, "Don't show a light. I can see." Only the navigation lights had been turned on. Low cloud hung over the hills and with no moon or stars to guide us after dusk, Long Point was obscured. We steered a little more northwards to avoid the rocks. The visibility became diminished but we could just see some craypot floats as we passed them. We must be getting close to shore, I thought, so I went up to the bow with a big torch and shone it around. The light beam was swallowed up in the mist until I shone it upwards and there, right in front of us, was a cliff.

I shouted out, "Cliff ahead!" Norm quickly put the motor into reverse gear and I threw over the anchor in a hurry. *Starlight* settled in about four metres of water, the seaweed and rocks just visible underneath. Too close for comfort, I thought. Sam was uneasy in this situation, so after a short discussion we pulled up the anchor and motored further out from the shore to drop it again in deeper water near the floats. We noted that the sea was calmer here, with *Starlight* still near the lee shore. We enjoyed a fresh fish supper and a peaceful night after the 13-hour trip.

In the morning the clouds lifted, revealing the cliffs close to the shore about 50 metres away. Expecting another long day, Norm wanted to get going at 7am and have breakfast on the way but I wanted to have breakfast first, fill the Thermos flasks and then refill the petrol tanks from the two-gallon cans. Some of the rules we observe for fire safety are that no one smokes on board, there are no naked flames when we pour petrol, and the gas stove is always turned off at the bottle. We settled our debate after looking at the chart and finding that it would be a shorter hop to Gisborne. It was breakfast and chores first though.

The forecast was good and the sea was slight at 9am, and as we motored south Sam pointed out the volcanic lava rocks that made up Long Point. The surf on the reefs protruding south off Mahia Peninsula and north off Portland Island looked at first as if the passage was one continuous reef, but when we approached a calm path opened up. We saw a modern light at the north of Portland Island, replacing the old one that had been on the south end. The old lighthouse had been shifted to Wairoa and erected near the bridge where it is now a historical landmark. We remembered the fishing stories (and the ghost stories) told by our friends Doug and Vicki Thompson who were lighthouse keepers there in the 1950s. Those were the days when keepers manned the lights, but now most lighthouses are closer to the shore and automated.

We kept motoring in a northeasterly direction in moderate seas with northeast to east winds and one-metre southeast swells until we cleared Table Cape on Mahia Peninsula. Then, with both sails unfurled, *Starlight* glided at five knots in a nor-northwesterly direction for four hours, creeping closer and closer to the shore. Sam was fascinated by the GPS navigation system and quickly learnt how to use it.

At 3 pm I tried to call the Gisborne Harbour Board Office on channel 12, then on channel 16, but there was no reply. I looked up their telephone number in the *New Zealand Nautical Almanac* and contacted them from our mobile phone. They told us that their VHF radio was only turned on if they were expecting a ship. However they gave us permission to berth near the dredge in the inner turning basin.

By 6pm we were getting closer to Young Nick's Head, named after Captain Cook's lookout boy when he 'discovered' New Zealand in 1769. Here the wind became slight and the sails flopped, so we motored across Poverty Bay, easily following the beacons, and entered the harbour at 7pm. *Starlight* was soon tied up against the wharf. It was still daylight and the trip had taken ten hours.

We were berthed beside other yachts, right underneath the Gisborne Tatapouri Sports Fishing Club. Here we were given a tremendous welcome by the club, and made honorary members with the use of all their facilities – food, drinks, showers and toilets. Water and electricity were hooked up. The berth was free for the first week. The retired president of the club called the next morning with a typed list of suppliers and offered to take us in his car to get petrol or parts if needed. We thanked him but as the service station was just across the road (we needed 50 litres of petrol) and at that stage we did not need any parts, we did not take up his offer. We kept the list just in case.

While we were at Gisborne we took the opportunity to catch up with friends and relations. My cousin Donald Bugden and his wife Denise lent us a car to visit his parents Thelma and Stan Bugden, also Naomi Clark, Rose and George Slade, Jim Dunsmore, Colin and Jean O'Donnell, Ray and Trish Pilkington and their families. Some of them visited us, including Rose and George Slade who came for afternoon tea. Then Mark Slade and his son, Justin, came to see us later.

Many passers-by stopped to chat. One man remarked, "I've seen you somewhere before." Norm told him where we lived, and said we had owned a garage at Paraparaumu, we played in the Sallies band, rode a Goldwing motorcycle… "That's it," he interrupted excitedly. "I belong to that club too!" Peter Anderson and his wife Maureen had recently joined the Goldwing Club but Norm hadn't recognised him.

Peter also had a 27ft double-ender, *Caravelle,* moored in the basin. He took us to see his yacht and we talked and talked. He passed on his local knowledge of the coast from Gisborne to Tauranga, and we greatly appreciated it. "There's deep water two thirds of the way across from East Cape to East Island," he told us. "As you approach the gap between East Cape and East Island, you divide the distance into three and stay on a course a third of the way from East Island and two thirds from the main land, East Cape. You'll sail through in deep water." We found this a most useful tip. Peter also lent us his 1971 *New Zealand Pilot.*

On Saturday a large 60-ft launch from Dunedin came into the harbour with eight men on board. They had endured rough seas all the way from Wellington but were keen to do some big game fishing in this area. We assured them that there must be lots of big fish available here as the club had numerous models of very large tuna, shark, moonfish and other species mounted on the walls. We had been fascinated by this display.

We attended the 11am and 7pm Sunday services at the Gisborne Sallies, had a scrumptious lunch at the Bugdens and later on used their washing machine and dryer, as the weather was showery and unsettled. Auntie Rose gave us two large jars of pickles and the next day we bought some stores, filled a new two-gallon container with petrol and received an up-to-date weather fax from the club. Sam shared the Bible reading with us, and our prayer of thanks that day was for friends, family and locals who had generously given us hospitality and information.

The 5am forecast on that Tuesday morning was for slight seas, two-metre southeast swells and variable ten-knot winds, turning later to 15-knot northwesterlies. We left at 6:45am, after six days in port. We motored in slight seas, rounding Tuaheni Point and the reef before heading northeast. We passed Tatapouri Point at 8:15am and cleared Monowai Rocks at 10:30am, arriving off Gable End Foreland with its conspicuous cliff and lighthouse at 11:20am.

Norm and Sam Medland on *Starlight*
in front of the Gisborne Harbour Board dredge, 31 January 1997

We had been travelling at a distance of two to three miles off this rocky coast. Now we unrolled Chart NZ 54. This was a much larger one, covering the area from Gable End Foreland to Slipper Island on the Coromandel.

The tide had been going against us and *Starlight* was motoring at only three knots. The wind increased to a 30-knot northeasterly – on the nose – and the sea became rough. "What happened to the northwesterlies they predicted," I asked. We came into a slightly calmer sea in the lee of Moutura Bluff and topped up the tank with 18 litres of petrol. As we approached Tolaga Bay the northeast winds were pounding the sea towards the old wharf, so we motored to the lee off the northern cliff. The sea was so rough that I made sure I had the safety harness on as I dropped the anchor. The yacht rocked up and down in the swell but the anchor held. By now it was 3:45pm. We had progressed north but only by motoring, not sailing. Tea was cold salad and ham with hot water from the Thermos flask for tea or coffee. *Starlight* jiggled all night and I slept with my clothes on in the centre of the boat near the foldaway stove. Norm slept on and off, and at 11:30pm he observed lightning but later he saw the stars shining.

In the morning the bay was calmer with light northwesterly winds, but when we ventured out into the open sea the winds were strong northerlies. We attempted to travel northeast, using the motor as well as the sails, but two losing tacks and a strong tide against us made progress impossible. We gradually made it back into the shelter of the northwest corner, only to drop the anchor near the spot where we had been the night before. It would be a rest day, but all thoughts of going ashore were abandoned as rowing back in our inflatable dinghy would be too difficult. Sandy the VHF channel 61 operator called us up at 1pm and we reported our position, as well as our intention to stay there another night. I was able to cook tea and we had a comfortable sleep. Our prayer that night included thanks for the sturdy anchor and for Sandy's radio call. At least someone knew where we were.

On Thursday 6 February, Waitangi Day, we motored north in slight seas with little wind or swell from 9:30am to 1pm. We had clear skies, warm weather and lovely coastal scenery all the way to Tokomaru Bay. As we approached the wharf at Waima, on the north side, we saw that the low tide had exposed rocks and lots of seaweed. *Starlight* berthed easily and was soon tied up beside a rusty ladder which was also being used by a group of boys who enjoyed diving and jumping off the wharf on this public holiday.

The Tokomaru Bay shops were over four miles away – how could we get there? Sam started chatting to holidaymakers Brenda and David, who had a yellow van. They generously offered to take us and our cans to get supplies – AND they brought us back again. We bought bread, groceries and 22.5 litres of petrol, but as there had been no rain for weeks the garage was short of fresh water, so we went without.

Sandy called us at 7pm on the VHF radio with an updated weather report. "Strong southerly winds expected overnight," she told us. Since Waima was very exposed to this wind, we cast off and motored north for an hour around the headland into Waipiro Bay, where we anchored securely below a hill covered in trees. The chart for the area had an anchorage sign marked on it, so we felt comfortable about being in this spot. After dark the southerly arrived and blew strongly in the trees above us for about an hour but we were well sheltered and secure. We had hooked a kahawai on the way round, so I cooked it in a pikelet batter – this makes the fish very moist – for tea. Later we saw the East Cape light flashing, a white flash every ten seconds. Although we were 23 miles away, we were within its nominal range of 27 miles. That night we gratefully prayed a blessing for the kind people who had helped us.

The 5am marine forecast was for a 10-knot southwest wind, a one-metre swell and clear weather. We realised that the southerly had gone through overnight and we would get the tail end of it to push us north, ideal for a run to the East Cape. The dawn was breaking as we weighed anchor and prepared the sails. The wind was light at first so we motored, our progress aided by the swell and the tide. We watched the sun rise over the un-obscured horizon – a beautiful sight. The wind freshened so we hoisted the mainsail and the genoa. *Starlight* was soon sailing, gull-winged, up to seven knots. "As good as it gets," Sam commented.

Sam had worked on the East Coast as the full-time Salvation Army Corps Officer 25 years before, and now he gave us a running commentary of the places along the coast and the people he had met there. He'd run Bible-in-schools here, dedicated a baby there, stayed with those farmers, been fishing there, climbed that hill, helped this family, conducted Bible-study or a church service there. He pointed out Mount Hikurangi, clearly towering above the coastal hills, and we noted the bays and headlands as we sailed north. He was very entertaining as he remembered people and places. Usually our Bible reading and prayer was done at night as we were anchored or berthed, but that day we read our two chapters as we sailed along, and prayed for the people who lived along the coast.

It was fascinating seeing the landmarks from the sea. They looked different. We noticed hundreds and hundreds of seabirds flying past us about a metre above the surface of the water. Some were gulls but most were shearwaters, and they seemed to be going on a big migration. However, it may have been that the birds were taking advantage of the light southerly wind. There was still good VHF coverage and I spoke with Sandy twice.

The East Cape area is notorious for big ocean swells, rough seas and strong tides but we were fortunate to see it at its best. I took a GPS reading because the longitude here would be the farthest east we would go. The latitude was 37 degrees 42.027 minutes south and longitude was 178 degrees 34.030 minutes east. We took photographs as we drew closer to the Cape. The tide rip was with us as we sailed easily through the gap between East Cape and East Island, carefully following Peter's advice.

Norm in scuba diving gear

The Autohelm was adjusted to steer the yacht towards Te Araroa and then Hicks Bay. Sam stood on the bow as memories of the fifteen years he spent there came flooding back. From well out to sea he could clearly see the row of pohutakawa trees he had planted in the 1960s.

We noticed a number of Tiger Moth biplanes fly from the south, pass us and land on the beach in front of the hotel at Te Araroa. We thought it must have been a rally point. We sailed on until 2:30pm when we arrived and anchored in Horseshoe Bay, in the south end corner of Hicks Bay. Sam went ashore in the dinghy and contacted some friends in the houses there. We tried to call up the VHF radio at Tolaga Bay, but were too far away. However we did contact the radio operators at Waihau Bay and Whakatane, on channels 63 and 71.

Saturday was fine and sunny so we moved north to anchor by a reef near the Hicks Bay wharf. We put on our wetsuits and went snorkelling for over an hour among the picturesque corridors of seaweed, the beautiful colours, pretty fish, kina and limpets. It was another world down there. A few butterfish were swimming about but Norm thought they were too small to spear.

Later we anchored with the centre-plate up near the mouth of the Wharekahika River, dropped the hinged boarding ladder at the stern and tiptoed ashore to enjoy a good soap-up in the fresh water. We washed our clothes and spread them over the driftwood to dry. Then we walked along the beach and had a chat to two caravaners who told us of recent cyclones eroding the beach of much of its sand and heaping up large logs and driftwood. They gave us blackberry jam and homemade bread. Yummy!

By the time we arrived back, it appeared as though *Starlight* had run aground among the tumbling surf, but the tide was coming in. A big man came along on a horse and another local drove up on a tractor to express their concern. We thanked them and chatted for a while, explaining that *Starlight* was a trailer yacht and that the centre-plate was up. Then we waded into the surf with our dry laundry held up high and climbed back aboard.

Back at Horseshoe Bay, now called Onepoto Beach, we decided that this was a good sandy place to beach the yacht. While the centre-plate was raised up and the yacht was floating in shallow water, we placed four anchors out at different angles. It was about an hour after high water. Soon another local man came wading towards the yacht, very much afraid we would get shipwrecked but we assured him that *Starlight* was not a keeler and that the centre-plate, motor and rudder were all lifted up. We had purposely anchored there so that we could have up to ten hours on the hard sand. The tide went out a long way, and by 11pm *Starlight* was resting out of the water with the mast vertical.

Apparently some years ago a large ketch had sailed from South America across the Pacific Ocean to sight land at Hicks Bay. Her crew anchored her and went ashore for supplies and when they got back the tide had gone out. The ketch was stranded on its side, and all efforts to right it were to no avail. Sadly, the owners and the locals had to watch it break up in the surf and storms. We could readily understand the concern of those who spoke to us – they were not used to seeing trailer-yachts there.

The tide came in and out again so that *Starlight* was high and dry at 11:30am the next day. Norm scrubbed the marine growth off the hull and placed the four anchors in better positions. The west wind was very strong but we were sheltered in that snug corner, and our devotions, thoughts and prayers on this February Sunday were for the people past and present who had lived in the area.

While *Starlight* was high and dry on the sand, a young couple came and gave us some freshly caught cod fillets, a very much appreciated delicacy.

"Is there anything that you need?" they asked.

"Yes, can you spare some fresh water?"

"Not a problem," they replied. "We only use the cottage for holidays and the water tanks are full." They carried away two five-gallon plastic containers and soon came back bringing them, full and much heavier, in a wheelbarrow. I expressed our gratitude, had a good laugh at the sight and took a photo.

Sam arranged for his friends Bob and Vivian McConnell to pick him up and take him to Te Araroa for the day, to visit people and places he had known years ago.

Early on Monday morning another of Sam's friends, Don Corlett, came down to the beach with a message from the police for Sam to ring his wife. Our mobile phone was outside the coverage area so Sam went ashore to use Don's telephone, his mind full of all sorts of possibilities. Bad news? Serious problems back home? But it turned out to be our bad news. Eva had heard that a mentally-unbalanced man had gone berserk at Raurimu and had shot Norm's nephew, John Matthews, along with five others. We had already heard the news on National Radio but no names had been mentioned and we had no idea at that stage that the terrible massacre involved our own family.

We went ashore to ring Norm's sister Margaret Matthews for details, then phoned our daughter Raewyn to let the family know that we had been 'found'. I felt that I needed to go and open up the house for family who would come for the funeral later in the week. Don arranged for a courier van to pick me up at 6:30am the next day so I could return home via Gisborne. Don and his wife Josie also let us to use their showers and laundry facilities.

That night we prayed earnestly for all the people affected by the tragedy. I left Hicks Bay early on Tuesday morning and arrived home at Porirua the same evening, confident that Sam would help Norm with the handling of *Starlight,* the navigation and the cooking while I was away. Norm and Sam continued on with *Starlight*'s voyage in my absence, and the next part of the story is theirs.

There was a lot of interest in the 'stranded' yacht on the beach at Hicks Bay. The southwest winds were strong all day Tuesday, with northwest winds on Wednesday. Visitors to the yacht included members of the Pahuru family, and a group from Te Waha o Rerekohu Area School who came to the beach for a confidence course with Richard Katipa, the deputy principal. Sam knew Richard's wife Hera, who was the daughter of Tene Henare. Sam asked the teenagers their names and found out that he had taught most of their parents at Te Araroa or elsewhere in the area. He wrote in his diary, "Some names were – Hooper, Te Purei, Green, Chester, Haukamau, Hovell, plus others. I was introduced to them all. Of course, no one knew me. We'd been away for 25 years."

A strong southerly wind blew during the night and the 5am forecast for the next day, 13 February, was for 20-25 knot southerly winds. Norm and Sam weighed anchor at 7:30am and motored out to sea, but once in the open sea the winds became gale force, about 35-40 knots, and they had to turn back into the shelter of the bay. At 1pm the wind eased so they left again. Once around Matakaoa Point they had a fresh southeast breeze behind them with a big following sea. They were able to sail at seven knots, using a small jib and the smaller mainsail, until they came to the west side of Cape Runaway. Sam was

Inside *Starlight,* with the centre-plate up and padded to avoid accidents

overjoyed when he caught a kingfish near the Cape. They dropped anchor at 6:20pm in the calm lee of the Cape where there was no surf or waves, and had a good nights sleep.

Friday was a most pleasant day for travelling, with a gentle northerly breeze. The men weighed anchor at 10:30am and sailed southwest until the wind dropped, then motored, using the 8hp outboard.

At 11:30am they went into Waihau Bay. Red and green buoys as well as beacons marked the channel to the jetty where *Starlight* was tied up. Sam visited an old friend, Mrs Winnie Walker, gave her some kingfish and asked for fresh water. She was surprised and delighted to see him and they talked about their families and her recent 80th birthday.

At 2pm Norm and Sam motored out and carried on to Omaio Bay, where they dropped anchor at 6:10pm just inside the reef. Norm launched the dinghy and rowed ashore to telephone me, arranging to meet me at Whakatane the next day. Before he returned to the yacht, he spoke to several teenagers gathered round a driftwood fire on the beach. They were gazing at our yacht and were very curious, so Norm stopped to answer all their questions.

Starlight, with Norm and Sam aboard, was now in the Bay of Plenty.

4

Bay of Plenty – Auckland

Out of earth's sorrows into thy balm,
Out of life's storms and into thy calm,
Out of distress to jubilant psalm,
Jesus I come to thee.

William True Sleeper

It was early in the morning and still very dark when *Starlight* left Omaio Bay and set a course towards the glow in the sky from the lights of Whakatane. Norm and Sam had breakfast on the way. They started off motoring but the breeze from behind soon filled the sails and they made good progress along the eastern coast of the Bay of Plenty. They could see several bays lined with pohutukawa trees, called the New Zealand Christmas Tree because of their copious deep-red December blossoms. They thrive on the salty coastal shores of the North Island. Norm kept the 8hp outboard motor running and the sails billowing, "To get there fast," he said with a laugh. Sam took some GPS readings and plotted them on the chart. Their speed was 6.25 knots, at times reaching seven knots. He used the VHF radio to call the marine radio at Whakatane, but there were many other boats reporting in and the operators were busy. The Whakatane Coastguard has over 800 members and the radios are manned from 8am to 6pm all year round. Then the call came on channel 71 (they now use channels 60 and 84).

"Radio Whakatane standing by."

"*Starlight*, ZM7060, yacht from Wellington," Sam replied. "First time visit. Is there a bar to cross? Can we have a berth or mooring?"

Nick Bannan, the operator, answered all his questions as *Starlight* approached the river mouth, and he directed her crew through the narrow entrance. He could see them clearly and talked them in.

"Come more to the east, *Starlight*, more to the east," he called. "See the two white triangles, line them up. Come nearer the red buoys. You are doing very well." Norm listened to the instructions as he handled the tiller. Nick's help and encouragement was very reassuring as big swells came up under

Starlight's stern and broke on the nearby rocks, but she was right on course in the deeper narrow channel. They passed the statue of a Maori maiden on the rock on their starboard side, and soon entered the calmer river channel.

The friendly harbourmaster, Brian Spake, met them at the ramp and showed them where to tie up at the wharf, pointing out a mooring in the river to go to later on. The minimum fee of $10 was for a week, even if you only stayed one day. The Whakatane Sports Fishing Club manager Kevin McCracken was also helpful, offering free showers, toilets and laundry facilities. Hospitality was overwhelming. Boaties were amazed at our journey, surprised at us going so far in a trailer-yacht, and their comments ranged from "stupid, mad, silly" to "brave, adventurous, courageous, good on you."

"We are water gypsies," Norm told them. "We anchor where we like and travel only when the sea conditions are right." He explained how he and Sam had waited six days for the weather at Hicks Bay before moving on.

Whakatane's many attractions included an aquatic competition of swimming and dragon boat racing, jet ski racing around Whale Island and, for keen swimmers, even a five-mile race from the island to the beach.

That night I rejoined *Starlight* and we shared experiences before moving onto the mooring for the night. My few days at home had been busy, as the deaths at Raurimu had been very traumatic for the families involved. There was huge media coverage on TV, radio and newspapers. I was able to help at Margaret and Paul Matthews' house where many visitors, flowers and messages came expressing sympathy for the loss of their son John. I also opened our Porirua home so the Christchurch family members could stay overnight. The celebration of John Matthews' life was held on Friday 14 February at 11am in the Salvation Army Citadel at Tawa. The family and many friends gathered to share their grief and shock and to comfort those most distressed. It had been a tragic loss.

After the service, I took some visitors to the ferry and others to the airport. The next day I caught a plane to Auckland, and while *Starlight* was negotiating the Whakatane river bar, I was flying low over the Coromandel in a small 12-seater plane. I landed at Whakatane and went to visit Betty and Lionel Freeman, who had shifted there from Napier. Betty was my contact for researching the Millar-Freeman family history and we had much to talk about. Finally I was able to contact Norm by mobile phone.

I re-joined the yacht at 7:30pm, and our devotions that night were a sober reflection of the recent events and a thankful prayer for those we had met. The events of those few days made us more aware than ever of the need for the healing of our land. I was happy to be back on *Starlight* and to continue on our journey by sea around the North Island.

On Sunday Sam made contact with the Salvation Army at Whakatane. The Corps Sergeant-Major Jim Kennedy, a lay pastor, came in his car to take us to the 10:30am service and we enjoyed a time of worship and fellowship. Jim led the service and spoke of living life to the full. Afterwards, Jim and his wife Kath invited us to their place for lunch and then we went next door to see the 12-metre boat Graham and Margaret Dixon were building and outfitting inside a huge shed. Their yacht *Lively Lady* was eventually launched in February 2001. Graham gave us useful information on how to approach the marina at Tauranga.

John Boyd and his wife Kathy were the musicians at that morning's service. He called at Jim's house and gave us tomatoes, eggs and potatoes. We went back to the yacht at 3:30 pm and moved out onto the mooring as the launches were returning to their berths at the wharf.

Monday was a hot day. We left *Starlight* at the wharf with the battery charger hooked up to the power supply to recharge the yacht's batteries, and walked to the nearby shops. The 10hp Honda outboard had earlier stopped. "No ignition," said Norm, and he went looking for parts. We needed eighteen litres of petrol, and Sam bought another lure for catching the big ones. I bought a few groceries and we all enjoyed a cold ice cream. A fishing boat had berthed beside *Starlight* and proceeded to unload its catch, including some large tuna and a round one-metre-in-diameter red-coloured moonfish, a type we had never seen before.

"Must be plenty of fish around here," I commented. We had enjoyed our stay at Whakatane. A yachtsman lent us *Royal Akarana Yacht Club Coastal Cruising Handbook*, a guide to the northeast coast of New Zealand and the anchorages from Three Kings Islands to Cape Kidnappers, and we found it very useful. At every port and bay, the generous sharing of local knowledge and hospitality overwhelmed us.

Again our Bible reading and prayer reflected our gratitude and we asked God for a blessing on the people of the area.

At 6:20am on Tuesday we were ready for the next leg of our journey. There was just enough light to see the entrance – lots of rocks at low tide with the channel near the east side of the river. The calm sea, small waves and light wind surprised me as we passed effortlessly through the entrance. *Starlight*, powered by the 8hp outboard, rode out in grand style. There was a slight following swell and a light 10-knot southeast wind that turned to 20 knots northeast, strong enough for sailing. We set a 270-degree compass course, heading west, and noticed that the smoking, misty trail from the active volcano on White Island was visible on the horizon for a while. Sam was pleased with the kahawai he caught, but it wasn't the big one he still hoped for.

Our forward berth in *Starlight*

We sailed at four knots along the coast towards Makatu Point, arriving off there at 11am. We could see Mount Maunganui in the distance. Rain had been predicted in the afternoon, and at mid-day some drops began to fall. The cloud got thicker and misty rain set in around 2pm as we rounded 'The Mount'. Chart NZ 5412, Port of Tauranga, with a scale of 1:10,000, gave us the essential guide to following the buoys outside the port and then into the channels, but it provided no details of the marina. The chart showed the way to the main wharves for big cargo boats.

We cautiously steered towards the green buoys that led away from the wharves to starboard, crossed the shallow estuary and entered the marina at 3pm on a very low tide, following Graham Dixon's useful advice. We approached an empty berth. I was on the bow ready to tie up at a finger jetty, but there were no posts to grab hold of so I jumped, just as the bow jerked away from the jetty. In I went, up to my armpits, still holding the rope tightly. Sam heard the splash and yelled, "Man over board!"

He and a passer-by hauled me out, but Norm had not seen or heard me go overboard and wondered what all the fuss was about.

Afterwards Sam thought he should have called out. "Woman overboard," so he looked up a pamphlet on boat safety. The correct procedure is to call "Man overboard!" whether it is a man, woman or child, so he had actually made the right call. I changed into dry clothes while Sam made me a hot cup of tea.

Norm went looking for the marina manager, who re-allocated us to berth G9. This berth cost us $6 per day with use of all the facilities, shared by hundreds of crews from the many other yachts and launches in this large marina. Shortly afterwards we were invited on board a 50ft Salthouse yacht, built out of New Zealand kauri and recently fitted out for missionary work in the Pacific Islands. It had a luxury main cabin with a private toilet, and all the woodwork was curved, polished kauri. It was a grand yacht.

Later, Norm was talking to a security officer about our 'man overboard' experience when they saw a man fall off the back of a launch into the sea. He was jammed between the boat and the jetty, with his head submerged, and they both rushed to pull him out. No harm was done, but he was a very wet and sober man after his unexpected dip.

It had been raining most of the afternoon and we took the opportunity to collect fresh water running off the boom-tent. That night we had a quiet sleep with no worries about the anchor not holding or a sudden change in the weather. In the morning it was still raining, and after lunch we put on our wet-weather gear and walked three kilometres to the Tauranga shops. We bought our usual eighteen litres of petrol and some groceries, and had the LPG gas bottle refilled. We also found a cheap and tested 240-volt electric jug at the Sallies' Thrift Shop to use when we were connected to mains power in the marinas. A taxi took us back to the yacht where we relaxed and read books for the rest of the day.

Sam's friends Ian and Grace Ellis called on Thursday morning and took us on a tour of new expensive housing estates. We had lunch with them while our many wet clothes were washed and dried in their machines. The next day, John and Norma Turner invited us for tea and then took us to a seawater thermal pool for a relaxing soak. I had known Norma when we were both teenagers. John was involved in sailing a 51-ft yacht, *Sarah Jane,* which took twelve or more young sailors at a time on cruises to give them sailing experience.

Diane Dinnan called and took me to visit her mother Maureen Lindsay at a rest home. They had been our neighbours some years ago, but Maureen was very frail and did not know me. Diane's beautiful home at Welcome Bay had a wide panoramic view of the Tauranga area, and her husband Michael gave me some of his homegrown tomatoes. These hospitable people, and many others, made our stay at Tauranga memorable, and our prayer was one of gratitude and thanks.

Norm was still trying to start the Honda 10, but couldn't get it to go, and in the end he rang our son-in-law Ed Lee at Upper Hutt to get a coil and other parts couriered to Auckland. On Saturday 22 February we paid $24 for the four days we had been in the Tauranga marina, packed up and set off at mid-day. We motored for an hour and a half and then set the sails, and had good running on several port and then starboard tacks for the next six hours. We were heading for Mayor Island, but Sam was convinced that we were heading away from our destination. Norm thought he should be steering for hills on the distant coast, about 90 degrees from our true course. I marked a GPS reading on the chart, checked the required compass course, then I pointed out the south end of Mayor Island. All the tacking had confused Norm and we had to correct our error.

After the northwest wind dropped, we motored the last one and a half hours to reach the southeast cove in Opo Bay by 8pm. We anchored in this tiny volcanic bay with many other boats; yachts, trimarans, luxury cabin launches, fishing boats and another trailer-sailer all sheltering there for the night. I counted eighteen boats. Some had big-game fishing rods and large armchair seats on their decks. Because the swinging area was very tight, we dropped a heavy brass folding fishermen's anchor over the stern to avoid the risk of bumping into another boat close beside us. Then we made sure that the kerosene riding light was hung in the rigging.

The bush, trees and lush undergrowth came right down to the water's edge, but we could see houses and buildings nestled among the pohutukawa trees. We had heard that to land here required a fee of $5 per person, payable to the Mayor Island Trust Park Board which represented the Maori owners. We stayed on board. The overnight lights shining on the boats and the full moon overhead made a picturesque scene, but a noisy generator which went on until 10pm, two very late arrivals and then loud music on one of the boats made sleeping difficult. However it was calmer inside the cove than it would have been outside.

Most of the boats had gone when we woke up in the morning. Off to catch the big ones, we thought. The weather report was for slight seas, 15-knot northeast winds but poor visibility – time to get going.

When we went to weigh anchors, the stern one was stuck hard and fast. Norm put on his scuba gear and dived down in ten metres of water to retrieve the anchor, and found that it had gone through a hole in the rock and got stuck underneath. Fortunately it was a folding anchor so he folded it up, pushed it back through the hole and brought it on board before we hauled up the main anchor at the bow.

The water was calm, unpolluted and very clear as we set off that morning, motoring north along the east coast of Mayor Island. We noted rugged cliffs and a number of caves, and identified the edge of an extinct volcano. The mist lifted briefly and it became very hot.

"Isn't the spray-dodger good," Norm kept saying. It kept off the wind, spray and now the heat from getting into the cabin. The space between the dodger and hatch cover made an ideal chart table to hold the current chart in place with the help of blue-tack.

We left Mayor Island behind and motored at five knots, steering a 280-degree compass towards Slipper Island. We changed to Chart NZ 534, Mercury Bay to Mayor Island. Sam caught a kahawai soon after we left, and later both Norm and Sam caught tuna at the same time, but the struggling fish jumped off the hooks just before they were landed. The BIG ones got away after all.

The visibility became hazy and we couldn't see any land. The compass course of 330 degrees needed checking with the GPS, and we corrected our course to steer 260 degrees, then 280. We recorded more frequent GPS readings for a while. We were surprised to see many dolphins, and there were also flying fish, stormy petrels, shearwaters, young gannets and other sea birds. Then the Autohelm started to steer the yacht all over the sea, going badly off course, so Norm disconnected it and used the tiller. We kept clear of some small islands with reefs between them, and then out of the mist our destination, Slipper Island, appeared straight ahead. We anchored near a beach in South Bay at 5:45pm.

It was a well-sheltered and peaceful place. We saw cattle and geese grazing on a nearby farm. The mobile phone had coverage, so we rang Raewyn and Sam rang Eva to report our position. As the weather was very hot and sticky, we decided to go swimming around the yacht and to the shore, then snorkelling around some rocks on the point. Then we all shared the cleaning of the growth off the hull. After dark another yacht came in to anchor near us. Just as well we had the riding light shining, we thought.

Fog and mist surrounded us on Monday morning so we delayed our departure until 9:40am when most of the fog had lifted. The sea was glassy calm and there was no wind. We motored north, passing Pauanui and Tairua headlands with trees and houses on the port side and Shoe Island on the starboard side. The visibility became clear enough to see the Alderman Islands, a wildlife sanctuary, about eight miles away to the east. All the islands appeared to have tall steep bare rocks and cliffs in clear relief like sentinels on a painted blue ocean. We soon identified Hot Water Beach on the Coromandel, where hot water oozes out of the sand at low tide, and the isolated Castle Island that looked like a haystack about two miles to the east of us.

We tested the Autohelm, but it still would not keep us on course, so it was tiller steering again. We passed many coves and rugged headlands before we turned into Mercury Bay. Sam reflected on all this fine warm weather and compared it to his family's tenting holiday at Otautu, on the western side of Coromandel, the previous month when Cyclone Drena hit the area and did a lot of damage.

I changed to Chart NZ 531, Great Barrier Island to Mercury Bay. We followed another boat in to Whitianga at low tide and came in between the red and green buoys outside the new marina. The notice at the entrance said to call up the office on channel 73, and when we did so they gave us berth B5. It was easy to find and we were tied up at 3:40pm after a six-hour trip.

The marina, built two years earlier, had all the usual facilities plus a lift-out crane, and the charge was $11 per night plus a refundable $20 for a security card. There were boats of all kinds moored here from various parts of New Zealand. Since the shops were close by, we walked to them to get stores and 45 litres of petrol. We bought chicken and chips and a salad for tea, and finished off with an ice cream each.

The next day, Norm had a look at Fred the Autohelm to find out why it had steered the yacht suddenly to port and then stopped working altogether. Sam went to fill the dive bottle, which had been used for pumping up the inflatable dinghy and then twice for diving. I did the washing in the automatic machines at the marina's laundry. It was teamwork all the way.

It was a very hot day and in the late afternoon we walked to Buffalo Bay beach for a swim. There wasn't much surf but we enjoyed the cool water, and collected some pipi for tea. Sam and I strolled back along the beach but Norm kept to the shade since he had a bit of sunburn on his chest. He struck up a conversation with a visiting English couple who had hired a campervan. They had bought a fishing rod and, within minutes of casting it into the sea, had hooked a two-kilogram trevally. They told Norm that they didn't know what to do with it.

"My wife will fillet it for you," he offered.

"No trouble," I agreed back at our yacht, and a few minutes later two fillets of fish were ready for Phil and Kath Phillips' tea. They came from Hampshire and were over-awed by the ease of catching fish in our country.

Sam wrote in his diary, "Norm is priceless as far as striking up conversations with total strangers. He gets to know some interesting people." We were thankful for the people we met and the variety of experiences we enjoyed.

The strong incoming tide and light southwest wind meant that we had to motor as we left Whitianga the next morning. "Heading for Great Mercury Island," we told the Whitianga Coastguard on VHF radio channel 87. Soon the wind strengthened and we were sailing out of Mercury Bay at five knots in slight seas. Then the wind changed to northwest, the seas became moderate and we were tacking but making no headway, so we motored for three quarters of an hour to get around a headland. Another sail, with only the mainsail up, gave us enough speed to glide into Mercury Cove by mid-afternoon. We read the instructions in the cruising handbook and followed a yacht ahead of us to drop anchor among several other boats already there. A luxury house was under construction nearby, and noisy chain saws and a generator disturbed the otherwise idyllic scene. We compared the sandy beach, and the soft grass growing on the flat land above it, to Mayor Island's rugged terrain.

Sam had caught another kahawai. These fish swim near the surface and readily take a lure, trolled at about four knots, about fifteen metres behind the yacht. They range from fifteen to twenty inches in length and need to be bled quickly so that the flesh has a better taste.

After dark, a large boat came very close to us. All we could see was two white lights over one red one, indicating that it was a barge. We heard the cargo, presumably material for the builders, being unloaded onto the jetty nearby and it left soon afterwards. There wasn't much room for manoeuvring.

Before the sun broke through the low cloud, I photographed the scene in the early morning stillness. The weather report was for slight seas and light winds – good conditions for exploring. We glanced at nearby White Beach with its fine sand, before motoring north for half an hour. Then we caught a northwest breeze and *Starlight* sailed to Coralie Cove, on the eastern side of the island, where the shore was rocky with high steep cliffs. We dropped the sails, anchored, put on our wet suits and snorkelled amongst the rocks and seaweed. We saw plenty of kina (prickly sea-eggs) but not many fish. It was a relaxing day. By the time we had finished our tea of sweet corn cobs cooked in the pressure cooker, potato chips and eggs, there were five other boats anchored beside us.

Norm finally found the trouble with Fred the Autohelm. He unscrewed the casing and found that a nut from the gyrocompass had come off and rolled out of position. The nut was re-attached, but it had made a short in two circuits on the motherboard. Our Mr Fix-it soldered two small pieces of speaker wire across to re-join the circuits, using a 12-volt soldering iron, and the job was done. Fred worked better than before and never gave us any more trouble.

It was a warm, pleasant night and we used only light sheets to cover us instead of the sleeping bags. The riding lamp was hoisted overnight again. There was rain overnight but the weather was clear in the morning, with the forecast for fifteen-knot southeast winds. We listened carefully to every forecast, then wrote it down before it was forgotten. The marine forecasts start at the Bay of Plenty and go north and then south along the west coast, back north along the east coast and then start on the South Island. The five-day land forecasts start at the north of the North Island and work south. We had been used to listening to the Wellington-Kapiti-Cook area forecasts and it took some adjusting to tune in to the forecasts at our new, further north locality.

We left Coralie Cove at 10am, negotiated around the rocks at the entrance by motoring for quarter of an hour and then hoisted both sails. We sailed north, avoiding the rocks and Never Fail Island off the north of Great Mercury Island. We headed northwest and noted Cuvier Island, a wildlife sanctuary, to the east and Great Barrier Island to the north. Soon we were approaching Cape Colville, at the north of Coromandel Peninsula. We sailed with a following wind and moderate seas, but near the Cape the sea became rough because the wind was against the tide.

The wind increased to 25 knots from the southeast, and *Starlight* sailed at nine knots with the two sails gull-winged. This made the rigging shake and the strain was obviously too much, so we dropped the genoa and the yacht was travelling at six knots as we passed the Cape. We turned to go south along the western coast but the gusty wind coming down the valleys made this course impossible. Instead of heading south for Otautu Bay we steered southwest towards the Motukawao Group, known as the Happy Jack Islands, and entered Elephant Cove. We had covered 40 miles and by now I was using Chart NZ 532, Approaches to Auckland.

"One of the best sailing days yet," Sam declared. "Far more challenging than just motoring all day." Because no fish had been caught on the lures that day we cooked bacon, eggs and pancakes with lettuce salad for tea. That night, with the anchor holding firm and the yacht secured in the horseshoe-shaped cove, we withstood a gale of over 40 knots.

We stayed put all the next day because there were strong 40-knot northeasterly winds, rough seas and heavy rain. The VHF radio reported more gale warnings for the area so we changed the genoa for a smaller jib, shifted the yacht to another more-sheltered anchorage under a cliff, caught a shoal snapper for tea and had a rest day. The mobile phone had coverage and Sam rang his wife at Napier and his daughter Christine in Auckland to say that we would be there soon and that he planned to return home by bus. The rain eased at 5pm, and when the clouds lifted we saw the glow of the Auckland lights over Waiheke Island. We had reception on our small TV so we watched the evening news and saw the weather map.

We left Elephant Cove at 7am on Sunday 2 March, sailing and motoring. It was my 65th birthday and Sam and Norm joked all morning about celebrating it with a tin of baked beans. This was Norm's idea of cooking a meal for me, but I was looking forward to buying a cooked chicken when we got to Auckland as a real birthday treat.

The calm sea was a surprise after the storm. There were lots of yachts and boats out sailing or motoring. The sunshine warmed us as we passed to the north of Waiheke Island, south of Rangitoto Island and entered the Waitemata Harbour, carefully following the beacons and keeping clear of big cargo boats. But we passed through hundreds and hundreds of small sandflies or blackflies – clouds and clouds of them. Norm used up all the fly spray, and the yacht became black with their dead bodies.

I called up the Westhaven Marina on Channel 13. They told us that berth M56 was available until 5 March, and gave us a security gate number. We arrived at 1:45 pm, but since the office closed at 2pm on Sundays, we had to wait till Monday morning to pay the $10 per day berthage and get a key for the laundry and shower facilities. Water and power were available on the jetty, so Norm immediately hosed down the decks, sails, buffers and other equipment to clean off the dead insects. The marina, catering for over 1400 boats, was close to the Harbour Bridge and the road was noisy with heavy traffic.

"Wow, what a lot of money is tied up in all these expensive boats," Sam commented.

Sam's daughter Christine Ellis and her children came to the marina to meet us and see the yacht. He showed them how to use the GPS to find the latitude and longitude and then mark it on chart NZ 532. I used the shower at the Ponsonby Cruising Club (50 cents in the slot) while Norm rang his brother Dave who came for us in his car. We found a supermarket, then picked up Dave's wife Ofelia and his daughter Janice. We all celebrated my birthday by sharing a cooked chicken tea aboard *Starlight*.

The next day, Sam said a sad farewell to us. He had enjoyed being on board and wished that he had more time to go further. He had been a keen yachtsman, learning navigation and chart reading, handling the tiller, anchor and sails, filleting the fish and doing his share of the cooking. We appreciated him as a great and useful mate, taking his turn at every aspect of the journey.

"I have kept well all the time and praise the Lord for a safe trip, His protection, goodness and blessings," Sam wrote in his diary. We shared a last Bible reading and prayed for the people of Auckland, the largest city in New Zealand. We also prayed for Sam's safe return to Napier by bus. It was a seven-hour trip, a very short journey in comparison to the many hours he'd travelled by sea during his five weeks on board.

Our progress around the North Island had been slow compared to the faster keelers, but we had expected to wait for the weather, and so we had.

Thank you, Sam.

5

Whangaparaoa – Bay of Islands

Thou burning sun with golden beam,
Thou silver moon with softer gleam:
Thou rushing wind that art so strong,
Ye clouds that sail in heaven along,
O praise Him, O praise Him, Alleluia!
Francis of Assisi

The days we spent in Auckland were varied. Sometimes we visited friends and relations, other days we took folk out for short sails on the harbour or to a nearby island. We seemed to walk for miles along the foreshore and wharves each time we went to Queen Street or the supermarket. We also enjoyed lots of activity in the marina and on the harbour each day.

My brother John Clark and his wife Mary came with the Honda 10 parts that had been posted to them. Norm was able to repair the outboard with the new coil, but found that the steel petrol tanks had rusted up inside because four-stroke motors do not have oil mixed in the petrol. The rust flakes had caused the carburettor to block up. With Dave's help we were able to get two tanks steam-cleaned, and while we had a car for transport we also bought 31.5 litres of petrol.

On 6 March we shifted *Starlight* to another berth, Y11. It cost less ($8 a day) as it was a working jetty and outside the security gates. There was a mast lift here and many boats were being repaired. I decided that two sails needed a wash, so I spread them out on the jetty, scrubbed them clean and rinsed them. How to dry them was the question.

"I know, I'll put them up the mast as if we're sailing," I told Norm. "We won't be going anywhere, the yacht's firmly tied to the jetty. It'll be fine." The warm sun and light winds soon dried them, but not before a conscientious security guard, who rode a bicycle around the marina, spotted the sails and came to tell us to haul them down. Evidently no one is allowed to put up sails inside the marina, even for drying purposes. Another rule was that no laundry was allowed to dry on the boats. Everyone had to use the washing machines and dryers at $2 a time.

Norm scrubbed the hull and cleaned out the water containers. We bought a five-gallon plastic petrol tank with fittings, new sail numbers for the smaller main and genoa, and Chart NZ 4212, Hokianga Harbour. Since Norm and I had been suffering from insect bites, we slapped on antihistamine cream and bought some more fly-spray for below decks.

We were moored beside *Tethys,* a 38-ft Orca yacht from Seattle, USA. We soon got to know Nancy Erley, the captain, and Kaci Cronkhite, the first mate. They were on their second all-women circumnavigation of the world. On each section they took two other women aboard and taught them the skills of sailing. The crew paid for their tuition and on-board expenses, and received an International Sail and Power Association (ISPA) certificate on completion of the cruise. Nancy and Kaci's schedule took them to exotic places. While they were in Auckland they were repairing the yacht's refrigerator and replacing the rigging. Their American 110-volt power system was not compatible with New Zealand's 240-volts so they needed an inverter. Norm lent them our battery charger, 60-ft lead and a double three-pin plug so they could charge their yacht's batteries and use NZ power tools – a sander and some drills which operated on 240 volt power.

On the next Sunday morning we went to the Vietnamese fellowship meeting at the Salvation Army Congress Hall in Queen Street. Envoy Christian Nuygen, who was leading this service, remembered us from his time as a cadet doing out-training at Porirua. We shared greetings – our English being translated by Christian – with the Vietnamese gathered there. Some had previously lived in Porirua, and all had been refugees, with horrific stories of surviving ethnic cleansing and being rescued after their boat sank in the China Sea before going to Korea and then to New Zealand. They called our country 'The Promised Land'.

My brother John and his wife Mary, with friends Justine and Michelle, came for an afternoon sail. All around us were yachts, launches and powerboats enjoying the sea. It took three hours to sail with a 15 to 20-knot southwest wind to Motuihe Island. We came to the lee of the island, dropped the anchor and backed on to the beach with the centre plate up. Our crew climbed down the stern ladder and went ashore to stretch their legs and buy ice creams at the little shop. Mary had brought a quiche and we all enjoyed a picnic tea on board. Then the tide began to drop and the slight surf made the yacht groan on the rough shelly beach, but we were soon off again.

The journey back was in a moderate to rough sea with the wind against the tide, so we motored using our repaired Honda 10hp outboard. The young women sat in the dinghy on the bow and thoroughly enjoyed the roller-coaster ride even though they got drenched in spray. John and Mary had a 16ft Hartley trailer-yacht, and rough seas usually meant a good soaking so they appreciated our dry cockpit. John, who was a keen sailor and a 'purist', soon had the mainsail up and we tacked into the wind for a time along the Motukorea Channel. John was a doctor in general practice and Mary was his practice nurse, so they gave me practical tips on minor ailments and first aid. Everyone was delighted with their afternoon outing.

The next day we discovered that the yacht's speedometer was not working. We suspected a paddle had broken while we were on the beach, but when we examined the tube that went through the skin fitting into the sea, we found that it was only a small shell jammed in the paddle causing the trouble.

We had visits from Tony and Margaret Rogers, who took us to see their home at Hobsonville and their ketch berthed at Westpark Marina. Then Sarah (née Slade) and Tim Workman, who had recently arrived from England, came with their children Joshua and Amelia for a two-hour sail with us on the harbour. Our son Lloyd, with Linda and Tristan, also had a cruise, motoring under the Harbour Bridge and back. We even had a concerned yachtsman who came to look over our itinerary to make sure we would be safe, and to check our competency in seamanship. Did we really know what we were doing? He went away satisfied.

We went by bus to Kelly Tarlton's Underwater World and Antarctic Encounter, a must for nautical folk. Another day we visited the Maritime Museum near Kings Wharf, noting the America's Cup KZ7 yacht on a stand nearby. All the time we were listening to weather reports. On Tuesday 11 March, strong southeast winds rattled the boom tent and there were reports of Cyclone Gavin progressing south from Fiji to affect New Zealand's weather. Strong winds and high seas were predicted. We put car tubes in the bow and stern mooring lines to act as bungy cords, took down the boom tent and stored the two dry sails in the cabin.

For the next two days the heavy rain, strong winds and high seas continued as the cyclone hit the outer gulf and carried on to pass over East Cape. There was no chance for us to go further north yet. We wondered how long we would have to wait, but we agreed that high seas were not for us in our small yacht. On Thursday our long-time friend Shirley Stanton rang us on our mobile phone to express concern for our safety. She was expecting us to call in somewhere near her home on the Whangaparaoa Peninsula.

"Don't come yet, because of the cyclone," she implored.

Someone else needed the berth at the working jetty, so the marina office arranged for us to use X75 for $8.50 per night. This was within the security zone but it did not have a finger jetty, so we backed *Starlight* between the posts onto the X jetty. On Saturday we went to a family wedding blessing. Norm's brother Dave had married Ofelia a few weeks earlier in the Philippines, and this was a chance for his New Zealand family to celebrate with the couple. Millars, Grays, Bennetts and some of Dave's workmates attended. Dave and Ofelia were delighted that we were still in Auckland for their big day. There were lots of speeches and I was pleased to welcome my new sister.

We were able to visit the Crump family at Glenfield on Sunday, and then we prepared to leave as the rough weather had abated. At 10:15am on Monday 17 March we left Westhaven Marina, motoring for a short time in the Waitemata Harbour. We soon set sail, using the working jib and the small mainsail, and made good progress along the Rangitoto Channel. Here we had a southwest wind behind us and a moderate sea with a cloudy sky, and *Starlight* did seven knots. Team New Zealand's two Merit Cup 12-metre yachts left at the same time, match-racing in preparation for the forthcoming America's Cup. They soon left us behind, and we could see them practicing on the proposed course.

After three and a half hours travelling, we gradually approached the peninsula wondering if we were near the Wade River entrance in the northwest corner or near the new marina at Gulf Harbour, 'somewhere on the south coast'. The tide and wind had brought us about halfway along the peninsula and the chart showed several small bays but there was no marina marked on it. As we sailed closer we saw a bay that might possibly be the one. The headland obscured the bay, but gradually we could see a breakwater. It was a bay we had visited back in 1980 when it was only a sand and stone beach. Imagine our surprise when we started to see multi-storied apartments, all brightly coloured in cream-orange tones. Then more and more apartment blocks came into view as the bay opened up. As we came closer we found the entrance to the marina – a narrow muddy channel at low water – so we motored in and found an empty berth.

The new marina was well equipped with showers, laundry facilities, a café, a boatlift and many boats on stands being painted, repaired or cleaned. We paid $28 for two nights at our allocated berth, H73. There were condominiums under construction on the waterfront, with berths for boats out front and car garages behind. Some were five or six storeys high with observation towers, and most had good-sized balconies with views of the marina. We heard that each unit cost $500,000 to $700,000. A golf course was planned nearby. Was this luxurious accommodation planned for the America's Cup visitors, we wondered? Extravagantly, we bought our tea at the nearby café.

The next day was spent with Shirley Stanton, who had been our bridesmaid in 1952 and had kept in touch over the years. She took us all over the peninsula in her car, then to the shopping mall, and we had tea at her unit in The Peninsula, a retirement village where Shirley and her late husband Gordon had settled many years earlier. Shirley is a good friend, but we couldn't entice her to sail with us.

Our progress north continued towards Kawau Island, one of the larger islands in the north of the Hauraki Gulf. Once a busy mining settlement, the island is rich in history. In the 1860s it was the home of New Zealand's former colonial governor, Sir George Grey, who developed the stately Mansion House and its exotic gardens. About ten percent of the island is now public reserve land administered by the Department of Conservation.

Using the working jib and the small main we sailed in moderate seas with a following west to southwest wind, doing six knots. We arrived at Mansion House in the early afternoon and tied up to the jetty with springs fore and aft because of the blustery winds. We walked for an hour along one of the tracks, looked at Mansion House and saw wallabies and peacocks. Later we anchored in Harris Bay, further along Bon Accord Harbour. We found sheltered, shallow water where we had to lift up the centre-plate.

The next port of call was Whangateau Harbour, a very shallow estuary leading to Point Wells where we hoped to visit Peter and Gaye Cowan. We contacted them on the mobile phone and Peter told us to follow the markers in. The water was very clear and surprisingly deceptive, deeper than we thought as we crossed the sandy bar at high water. White wooden stakes marked the channel but it was difficult to tell the deep water from the shallows. We tied up at the jetty that Peter had built some years before when he had a launch. We knew Peter when he was the Solarc battery salesman and had lived near us at Paremata. Like us, he had often used his launch to cross Cook Strait and to cruise the Marlborough Sounds. Peter and Gaye had retired here to the north of Auckland, and we enjoyed their hospitality for a few days.

When the tide went out our yacht rested on the mud, giving Norm an opportunity to scrub the hull. The Cowans gave us a small fender, some homemade jam and *Northland Coast*, a cruising guide which covered the area from Cape Rodney to Cape Kerikeri. One stormy day they took us on a driving tour of Warkworth, Sandspit, Leigh and Omaha. The nearby Goat Island is a marine reserve and very popular for scuba diving but no fishing or anchoring is allowed.

After attending the Sunday morning service at the local Methodist church, we listened to the forecast. The thunderstorms had eased and a fifteen to twenty knot southwest wind was forecast for Monday, just what we needed for a run towards Whangarei. So we said farewell, motored out at half tide through the narrow entrance and anchored for the night at Omaha Cove with eighteen fishing boats, all looking resplendent in the calm water under a full moon.

After the 5am marine forecast on National Radio we had a quick breakfast and made an early morning start. There were still a few squally showers, but the weather was otherwise good with light winds, no swell and a fifteen-knot southwest wind predicted. The sun rose over Great Barrier Island and sent warm rays to cheer us on our way. We passed Cape Rodney and Goat Island, then motored almost to Bream Tail before deciding to go to the offshore Hen and Chicken Islands.

A calm, deep-blue sea and a few short showers made for a pleasant journey as we passed Sail Rock and headed for the south side of Taranga Island (the 'Hen' of the island group). We took photographs, from the nearby Witches Cove, of the steep rock formations called The Pinnacles, and enjoyed our lunch before setting off for the Marotiri Islands ('the Chickens'). The southwest wind sprang up, gently at first, so we hoisted the sails. The wind grew stronger as we rounded the Chickens and there was no sign of shelter even on the north side, so we kept sailing towards the mainland. By now we had moderate to rough seas in a fresh 25-30 knot southwest wind. We were heading west, with lots of waves spilling over the bow, but *Starlight* sailed well, sometimes heeling 20 to 30 degrees. The spray-dodger kept most of the water off us.

"Isn't the spray-dodger good!" Norm remarked again. We looked for some shelter under the lee of cliffs just north of the entrance to Whangarei Harbour, but found nowhere to anchor safely, so we dropped the sails and punched into the sea and wind with the motor going, struggling to make headway towards the harbour. At last we passed the spectacular steep headland, followed the large red and green buoys marking the channel, rounded Marsden Point where the oil refinery is located, and anchored in the shelter of Marsden Bay at sunset. There were other boats moored in the shallow three or four metres of water. I was very exhausted but it was nothing that a good sleep couldn't fix.

It was a long way to the Town Basin the next day, fifteen miles of winding but clearly marked channel. Motoring against the tide took three hours. As we approached the town basin we called up on VHF channel 64 and the friendly marina manager, Lou, asked, "How big are you?"

"Only 24 feet," I replied.

"You will fit into the narrow berth, number 37," he told us. "It's just been vacated by its owner who is repairing his boat on the hard." It was a tight squeeze, with just enough room to place the small fender Peter had given us between *Starlight* and the next big yacht. The berth cost $48 for the week.

The Town Basin was crowded with ocean-going yachts and launches, travellers from all over the world. The area also boasted that it was the cheapest place in the world to get repairs or refits done on any small or large boat. International sailors were resting, repairing or cleaning their boats, washing bedding and replenishing stores after their long sea voyages.

On Wednesday 26 March we joined other yachties doing exactly the same sorts of housekeeping chores. While we were there we visited Norm's brother Bill and his wife Alison, my cousin Iris and her husband John Platt, my auntie Hilda Clark, Ruth Pascoe and her mother Thelma, Irene Pyle and her daughter-in-law Colleen, as well as meeting and visiting with other yachties. A tour of the fabulous and renowned Clapham Clocks museum was a must. Established in the 1940s by Whangarei resident Archibald Clapham, this amazing museum housed a large collection of timepieces including antique clocks and cuckoo clocks. We also inspected the rebuilt Quayside area at the town basin with its stylish cafés and restaurants, art galleries and gift shops. We saw the Museum of Fishes, Di's Dolls and other attractions, admiring the blend of colonial-style architecture and modern landscaping. Because it was Easter we joined in the services on Good Friday, the Saturday street drama and Sunday services at the Whangarei Salvation Army. On Monday we took Bill, Alison, Ruth and Iris for a picnic cruise. We went down the harbour hoping to do some fishing but instead enjoyed a sunny day motoring among the beacons, keeping out of the shallows.

The Sydney Congress Hall Band was visiting New Zealand and a concert had been arranged for that Tuesday night in Whangarei. As Norm and I play the cornet and trombone, this was a bonus. Afterwards the band's Corps Officer Major Derek Tyrell, who had a 24-ft keeler and sailed it on Sydney harbour, came to visit our yacht. Another visitor who came for tea was John from Seattle, USA, who was berthed next door at number 36 in his 32-ft keeler *Vahevala*. There was much to share.

Having completed our chores, we said farewell to our hosts and set off on the afternoon of 2 April to carry on cruising. We motored down the channel with the easterly wind against the tide, looking for the next calm anchorage. The Royal Akarana Yacht Club's handbook showed an anchorage at McLeods Bay in the lee of the high Whangarei Heads so we steered in that direction, but the centre-plate bumped into some soft sand as we went over a large shoal. It was rudder and centre-plate up as we traversed the one-metre shallow waters to find the anchorage. During the night a light westerly wind sprang up and the boat rocked a little.

The next morning we followed the beacons out, motored then sailed north towards Tutukaka. The two-metre southeast swells were crashing on the rocks at the entrance. We used chart NZ 5212, Plans between Whangamumu and Omaka Cove, with a scale of 1:12,000. It was very detailed, and by following the beacons and markers we arrived at the marina at low water. There was a new office, and pile drivers were installing posts for several new larger berths to cater for 40-70ft pleasure boats. Tutukaka Marina is used as a base for tours of the Poor Knights Islands, a very popular destination for scuba divers.

Settled weather was forecast; slight seas, a one-metre easterly swell easing and 10-knot variable winds. Before setting off we obtained a pamphlet about the Poor Knight wildlife sanctuary showing the restrictions on anchoring and fishing. We set a northeasterly course, motoring with a half-knot lift from the sails. We enjoyed the deep blue sea, clear sky and a small swell. This part of the Pacific Ocean was renowned for its particularly clear water and prolific underwater life. As we approached the rocky islands, we saw many reefs, spectacular arches and steep shores but noticed very few landing sites. However we had heard that there were a few anchorages available, albeit in very deep water.

We skirted the south end of Aorangi Island, marvelling at the rock formations on Arch Island and the very high steep cliffs. The powerboats and launches used by diving parties were dwarfed by the huge rocks and towering cliffs above them. We observed many caves, colourful rock formations, large numbers of birds nesting or flying about and copious seaweed clinging to the rocks. The water was blue and sparkling as we motored north up the east side of the island. We had almost encircled Aorangi and Tawhiti, the two main islands of the group, before we entered Nursery Cove and settled on the mooring there. Then we donned our wet suits and snorkelling gear for a swim amongst the colourful fish. The water was clear down to six metres or more. Tropical-looking black and white striped fish swam close to me and some even nipped my gloves. Fishing was not allowed here – no wonder they were so tame. We found this a unique and exhilarating experience.

After tea we settled down for the night. Although the sea was calm, the slight swell caused a choppy surge as it hit the rocks and bounced back towards *Starlight.* We had been warned about this but it was too far back to the marina for us to make the trip in daylight. No problem for the fast powerboats and launches that only did day trips, but we were on a different kind of vessel.

Sleep was fitful as the yacht rocked unevenly, so at first light we cast off and headed all the way to Cape Brett which we could clearly see 25 miles away. We motored and sailed with a light westerly wind. A one-metre easterly swell on an oily calm sea, a clear sky and warm mid morning sunshine made it possible to do shifts at the helm so that we could each catch up on some sleep. We passed under Cape Brett at 12:30pm and saw the 'hole-in-the-rock', a large cave-like arch of rock in a small island at the entrance to the Bay of Islands. It had deep water through it and was wide enough for a launch to go right through.

We saw several fishing boats and a tourist cruiser pass through it but I had doubts about whether *Starlight's* mast could fit under the arch so we gave it a miss. We went on to anchor for the night at Oke Bay, which had a sheltered beach.

Bay of Islands is well named, as there are lots of small islands dotted around in enclosed sheltered waters. Chart NZ 5122, Bay of Islands helped us negotiate the rocks and reefs around Rawhiti Point and we passed cautiously through the Orerewai Pass rather than going a little further north to the Albert Channel.

A light wind sprang up with a slight sea. It was ideal for sailing so we hoisted the genoa and mainsail. Doing four knots was pleasant as we passed the Paramena Reef Beacon which has two black balls on it. Quite a few yachts and fishing boats passed us, heading out, as we sailed down Rawhiti Channel on a course towards the houses in the distance. It was Sunday, and the VHF radio Channel Three reported on a big game fishing contest where game fish were caught, tagged, measured for length and girth and then released.

We had heard about the lagoons at Motuaroha (Roberton) Island and thought it would be worthwhile visiting. However we were unsure which island it was, so while Fred the Autohelm was steering a steady course we both stood up on deck to identify the islands as we passed by. *Starlight* had been sailing in open seas with no reefs or obstacles, so we felt quite comfortable leaving the tiller.

Suddenly we heard a "Ho, ho, ho, WHOO…!" A small powerboat was anchored right in our course and we had not noticed it because our big genoa hid it from our view. When the men started yelling we realised what had happened. Quickly Norm jumped down to the tiller, flicked off the Autohelm and steered away from the wind while I dropped the genoa as fast as I could.

"Sorry," we yelled. *Starlight* spun around, missing the stern of their boat by less than three metres. Our centre-plate caught their floating lines and zing went their reels while my heart lurched into a fast bump, bump, bump rhythm. One nylon line got tangled around our centre-plate and then the outboard motor propeller. We quickly dropped the mainsail to slow the yacht down. It must have given the fishermen a big fright, but they were probably very relieved to have lost only a bit of line instead of having a dreadful collision. They went on fishing undeterred, and we proceeded on our way subdued and shaken. The lesson we learnt that day was ALWAYS keep a good lookout.

We floated around for a while until we freed the fishing line, then motored to an anchorage in the south bay of nearby Roberton Island. Part of this island is a wildlife sanctuary and we were also interested in its unique geographical features. The gaps in the cliffs on the northern side allow the tide to fill lagoons on the south side, and these are full of marine life and very popular with snorkellers. We launched the dinghy, rowed ashore, walked along the sandy beach at half tide and climbed a lookout to take photographs of the terrain. Our friend Gordon Stirling had lived there many years ago so we visited his former house, still standing at the other end of the bay. It had been usefully converted into a backpackers' hostel.

When we arrived back at the yacht, Norm put out a stern anchor to avoid swinging and I set some fishing lines. I caught a small snapper and a trevally. Fresh fish for tea was a treat we had not had since Elephant Island. We used the riding light here. In the morning we had a visit from one of the tourist launches which cruised the islands. The many tourists crowded on the top deck gave us cheery waves as their craft glided past.

Later we cruised and sailed around to Opua, near Russell, which is an international port of call for ocean-going yachts. The jetty was full but there were lots of moorings nearby in shallow, muddy waters. The weather was overcast with an increasing northwest wind, and rain had set in, so we chose to anchor in the sheltered Te Wahapu Bay off Pahia. We contacted our friends Pauline and Peter Jesperson of Kerikeri, using our mobile telephone, to let them know we would be there the next day. The question on our minds was could we navigate the Kerikeri Estuary?

The weather did not ease the next day, but we continued with our plan, motoring against the gusty winds, heavy rain and moderate seas to pass through the channel between Moturoa Island and the mainland. This was well marked with beacons. It took us into the Kerikeri Inlet, also well marked, but the tide was out and there were mud banks everywhere. Fortunately the *Northland Coast* had sketches of the area, detailing the Western Kerikeri Inlet, the upper Kerikeri River and the Kerikeri Basin. We kept a close lookout for sandbanks and shallow muddy areas, passing beside and almost touching the marker posts. We turned at Junction Beacon into the upper Kerikeri River and wound on until we arrived at the jetty near the historic Stone Store. The river ended with a weir across it and just near the jetty, right in the middle, was a black beacon marking a boulder bank now exposed at low tide. We tied up to the jetty but found a notice stating that berthing was temporary, for unloading only.

After school Pauline and her three children came to visit us. The weather had cleared so we took them for a ride down the river and back again, admiring the luxurious houses among the lush bush. We were able to use a nearby mooring and tie *Starlight* between the posts. We found out that the nearby tearoom was an agency for the local authority, and paid the going rate of $6.00 a night. We rowed our dinghy to the jetty and tied it up among the dozen or so others. Pauline invited us for tea, and we slept in a large double bed in a room attached to the garage rather than row back to our yacht in the dark. Pauline had lived with us for six months at Porirua when she was a teenager and we had always kept in touch.

After we had caught up with our laundry and shopping, Pauline took us for a walk to Rainbow Falls which had lots of fast-flowing water. We saw Hone Hika's Pa and Kemp House but the Stone Store was under repair and not open for viewing. Pauline's house had a panoramic view of the area and I soaked in the sunshine while I enjoyed my breakfast from their balcony the next morning. She and Peter had gradually demolished a small cottage and built over it a large four-bedroomed house with a study, two bathrooms, an octagonal lounge, and a dining room and kitchen, complete with a huge deck giving superb views of the valley and inlet. It was all made from Douglas Fir milled locally.

We had an excursion to the Puketi kauri forest and to Rewai's authentic Maori village, and we visited our friends Murray and Pauline Taylor and looked over their lemon and kiwifruit orchard. Later in the day we took Peter Jesperson for a ride down the river. After three nights ashore we rowed back to the yacht with our fresh supplies and slept on board. The weather was improving and the showers clearing, so we decided to move on, and the following morning Pauline and her children came to the jetty to bid us farewell. It had been a very pleasant and interesting stay.

We motored down the Kerikeri inlet at half tide and found it much more attractive now that there was less mud showing. We headed out into the northern part of the Bay of Islands, where we encountered light winds and only a slight sea with a half-metre easterly swell.

Our visit to this coast had so far been most rewarding, there was so much to see. We found wonderful hospitality, a variety of places to visit, interesting rock formations, sheltered anchoring places and good fishing. No wonder the region is popular with the boating fraternity. At each place we visited we read two chapters of the Bible and prayed a blessing on the people who lived there. We thanked God many times for the friends and the local folk we met. We were grateful for their help, local knowledge and hospitality, and for the wonderful opportunity to see so much of this coast from the sea. We saw places we would have been unable to visit by road or on land.

But there was more to come. The far north beckoned us.

6

The Far North

For the beauty of each hour
Of the day and of the night,
Hill and vale and tree and flower,
Sun and moon and stars of light,
Father, unto thee we raise
This our sacrifice of praise.
Folliott Sandford Pierpoint

We left the Bay of Islands in a slight sea with a half-metre easterly swell. Starlight cruised comfortably in the light winds. We rounded Cape Wiwiki, keeping well clear of the rocks and islets, then motored north. We passed between the Cavalli Islands and Matauri Bay, then spotted the settlement of Tepene on the hillside. Still keeping the distance off the coastline, we noted Flat Island to port and Stephenson Island to starboard. By now we were in a squally shower of rain, and we approached Whangaroa Harbour entrance carefully after consulting the relevant charts and books. We read in the *New Zealand Pilot* that it was important to distinguish North Head from the more prominent False Head, with its sharply defined cliff face, about one and a half miles further west. We turned to the southwest and found the narrow but deep entrance between the North Head and South Head that led us into this fascinating fiord-like harbour.

Just inside the entrance we noticed a disused turret and gun emplacement on Kingfisher Point. We wondered why it was there, but later found out that Whangaroa Harbour was used by the United States Pacific Fleet during World War Two, and this point, so close to the narrow entrance, guarded the fleet. Thankfully there were no hostilities and Whangaroa Harbour was left unblemished. South of the point, which also had a light on it, was Kingfisher Cove. We saw a wharf which serviced a licensed fishing lodge where meals, laundry and shower facilities were available for those anchoring. But we motored on. We were astounded and overawed by the distinctive basalt rock formations and the lush green foliage. Mount St Paul, a cupola-shaped dome 213 metres high, dominated the eastern side of the harbour while Mount St Peter, a similar dome of 168 metres, was prominent on the west. We went further up the harbour in a light shower, making for the main settlement, and anchored among other boats in a sheltered spot just north of the jetty.

We reported our arrival to Dolly on VHF Channel 62, and she told us that the VHF range faded around North Cape. It constantly amazed us how friendly these radio volunteers were as they monitored fishing vessels and pleasure craft, day after day, ensuring their safe return to base and welcoming visitors. Our mobile telephone had coverage and we rang our daughter Raewyn, back at Porirua. She and her children also kept track of our movements, noting our progress on a map of the North Island.

The next day we tied up at the Whangaroa Game Fishing Club's jetty to welcome our visitors Ian and Loreli Hayes, who came for lunch. Norm's brother Jim had told us to contact them. They lived on a farm at Tepene and had a launch, *Horo,* moored nearby. Ian told Norm about the boat-building industry across the bay at Totara North. Norm knew that the kauri-timbered scow *Echo*, well known in the Marlborough and Nelson regions, had been built at Northern Wairoa, Dargaville in 1905. The other ship he had worked on as second engineer, now named mv *Wairau,* was originally built here in 1900 as the topsail schooner *Ronga*, also made of kauri. Later on the masts were cut down and *Ronga* became a cargo motor vessel.

Obviously a visit to the shipbuilding facility was a must for Norm, so after our visitors had left we moved *Starlight* to the Totara North jetty. Norm walked to the mill and was amazed that such a small timber mill and boat slip could build these sturdy ships. He knew that if the *Echo* or *Wairau* needed a plank replaced, permission would be required to fell a kauri tree to supply the timber. Not so in the earlier times when kauri was a shipbuilder's regular source of timber. In the years between 1850 and 1909, the many mills and shipbuilding yards at Whangaroa produced over a hundred ships – schooners, brigantines and ketches – which sailed the high seas and ended up in all corners of the globe. The mv *Wairau* was one of them.

We bought petrol, oil and fresh bread, then motored on to Pekapeka Bay, just west of the entrance, in more showery weather. There was a Department of Conservation hut for nature lovers, and part of the area was a reserve with picturesque bush right down to the water. Spectacular blocks of stone piled one on top of the other lined part of the shore. The tops of the bluffs had been weathered to form bulbous pedestals that looked ready to topple at any moment. One formation, called 'Duke's Nose', particularly caught my eye. The towering bluffs and vertical cliff faces, formed by ancient volcanic activity, made the landscape resemble a miniature fiord.

We chose to anchor in a sheltered cove near the head of the inlet. In the evening we saw five canoeists glide by. They were part of an outdoor adventure

Turret at entrance to Whangaroa Harbour – dark clouds approaching

group based at the DOC hut. If we had gone ashore there would have been much to explore – large waterfalls, thick bush tracks and evidence of early settlements at Lane's Cove. The unspoiled beauty of this region is hidden from road travellers, but such a short distance by sea reveals a unique and idyllic scene. No wonder the trampers and canoeists revel in their isolation.

But the days were getting shorter, with sunrise at 6.50am and sunset at 5.50pm. Daylight saving had long gone, and on overcast days it was almost dark at sunset. We needed to move on to encompass the North Island before winter came. It was April 15. Almost three months had passed and we had not yet reached the west coast.

Our next hop was to Mangonui Harbour in squally, fickle weather. *Starlight* sometimes sailed at two to three knots, and at other times we were motoring. Norm reset his lures for trolling, as he had not caught any fish since the Bay of Plenty. We entered the narrow entrance of Mangonui Harbour at 2:30pm and approached the commercial wharf, but it was school holidays and the wharf was crowded with more than twenty keen fishers, all catching fish. An energetic boat owner told us not to tie up near the bridging jetty, as strong tidal rips and rocks at low tide would hem us in. However he found a space for *Starlight* at the end of the main wharf by a low platform.

"That platform will be covered by the sea at high water," he warned us.

"Not a problem," we told him, grateful for his help.

We walked to the Four Square supermarket and then to a shop built on piles over the sea. The sign on its roof promised "World Famous Fish and Chips". Bluenose fish was weighed and cooked here and it was fresh, hot and tender. Four pieces of fish and some chips cost $8.90, and we finished this most delicious meal with an icecream.

By the time we got back to the wharf, we had to wade across the small platform to get aboard *Starlight*. We cast off and found a sheltered corner in the shallow harbour, away from the swift tidal flow. The cruising guide showed an anchorage at Butler Bay, and there we met Bob who had lived permanently on his yacht for twenty years. He came to our aid and told us that the mooring next to his boat was available – just what we needed. We hooked on, and realised that we were opposite the historic wooden house built by Captain William Butler in 1847.

We had friends living in the nearby town of Kaitaia. Where was the closest anchorage, we pondered. Should we go into the shallow, muddy Rangaunu Harbour? Would we find a suitable jetty or place to land? We rang Rob and Jenny Bartlett who told us that they were taking the next day off work and coming to Mangonui with their children, Ashley and Andrew, and their two friends Nerisa and Grant, to go fishing. Imagine their surprise at hearing that we were there. They gladly accepted our invitation to go sailing and fishing from our yacht.

They arrived at 9am complete with fishing rods, bait and a lunch-basket. The weather was fine with a light wind in Doubtless Bay so we motored out and then sailed using only the genoa. The sea was slight, but too bouncy and uncomfortable for the four children, so we went back to our mooring for lunch – filled rolls and a smoked kahawai. Rob had brought some squid bait and soon six rods were dangling over the side in somewhat shallow but calm water. The harbour was teeming with fish and we could see that those on the wharf were getting good catches. Soon we were hauling in lots of shoal snapper, the rods bending regularly with the tugging fish. The children were well behaved and very excited about catching so many fish, and I filleted more than fifteen medium-to-large snapper for them to take home. It was an experience never to be forgotten, a special and satisfying day.

We left the next day at 9am and *Starlight* sailed easily in a fifteen-knot southwest wind across Doubtless Bay to Cape Karikari, but then we had to motor against a rip tide and contrary winds to negotiate the many rocks and islets. We set the sails again and took a compass course for Houhora Harbour, gladly missing our planned call into Rangaunu Harbour. The 240-degree compass heading took us a little north of Perpendicular Point, a clearly-identified cliff face rising to Mount Camel (235 metres). Both were easily seen as we approached from the east. After we dropped the sails again, we motored close to the northern shore until Mount Camel was abeam, to avoid a large sandbar outside the entrance to Houhora Harbour. We consulted the Royal Akarana Yacht Club's handbook to find details of the depths and beacons, then followed the marked channel to berth at the main wharf near the settlement of Pukenui.

Norm took an empty two-gallon petrol can ashore, assuming that there was petrol available at the local store. A fisherman read his thoughts. "Take my car," he said. "Here's the key. The service station is five kilometres down the road."

What wonderful hospitality from Bill. Norm couldn't believe his ears, and gratefully accepted the offer. We later anchored among the many moored boats, and while we were anchored I caught a shoal snapper for our tea. The peaceful harbour was surrounded by low hills and at low tide we could see massive low-lying sandbanks drying out.

A lot of boats went out the next morning for a fishing competition organized by the Houhora Fire Brigade. We heard their chatter on the VHF radio and then called Maureen McMillan, the Far North Coastguard Radio operator on channel 60, to report our position and intention to stay a few days as the weather was unsettled. We went ashore, used the shower and laundry facilities at the nearby motor camp, then bought some stores. Later on we motored to the new Houhora jetty where a new clubhouse was under construction for the Houhora Big Game and Sport Fishing Club. It was well-sited, with a magnificent panoramic view of the harbour and entrance. While we were there we noticed many fish swimming in and around the new piles, and Norm spied a large John Dory, round and flat with a black thumbprint on its side. He quickly grabbed his spear gun and soon had it caught in the prongs. Too easy, I thought, but as John Dory is a choice fish, it was also too tempting.

Very soon the boats were returning with their catches. Three tuna weighed in at 24.6, 10 and 11 kilograms respectively, and a large launch, equipped for big-game fishing, berthed with lots of flags flying to indicating their catches. They had been to the Three Kings Islands, 28 miles northwest of Cape Reinga, for a five-day fishing trip. They had caught two tuna and tagged three marlin, three skipjacks and three sharks. They told us that mooring there was all right apart from the swells or winds, but coming back they had experienced eight hours of very big, rough seas. This information put all thoughts of going there out of our minds. It was too far and there was no shelter for our small yacht.

The birds around us were often undisturbed by our presence, with a cheeky seagull or two landing on the deck or perching on the danbuoy, but the most friendly was the resident white heron at Pukenui so I photographed it.

While we were at Pukenui we found that one of *Starlight*'s batteries was flat. Norm looked for a power point to use for his charger but there was not one available. A local resident, Laurie Anderson, offered to take the battery to his home for recharging. Another local couple, John and France Cousins, kindly

The display of 480 potties at the Wagener Museum, Houhora

invited us for a roast dinner and a refreshing shower. They had a powerboat and were very interested in our trip. What overwhelming hospitality.

The next day we moved to the south side of the entrance and anchored there at low tide in order to visit to the Wagener Museum, the Subritsky Homestead and the nearby motor camp. The museum was a privately-owned collection of lamps, Maori artefacts, artworks and other miscellanies, with 480 chamber pots hanging from the rafters. I wondered why anyone would collect so many. The Subritsky Homestead was another example of an original pioneer home, built in 1860 and complete with furnishings from the period. After we had looked around these attraction we motored to the eastern side of the harbour to see and take photographs of the wrecked scow *Pearl Kasper*, now only a shell of rotting timbers. Norm remembered the scow in the 1940s, when it carried cargo between Wellington, Nelson and Golden Bay.

Laurie returned the fully-charged battery on Monday and told us about Dick Grimes at Henderson Point, who gave a detailed weather report seven times a day on VHF channel 74. We wrote down the times. Dick also listened on VHF channel 16 and on his SSB radio.

Norm glued the front hatch and other spots to stop some leaks, while I walked to the shops to top up our food supplies and to post a book, *The Northland Coast,* back to Peter Cowan who had lent it to us. We had now covered the area from Cape Rodney to Cape Karikari on Northland's east coast. It was another sector of our journey completed.

At 7:30am on Tuesday the weather report was for slight seas, southwest winds rising to 20-knots, no swell and fine skies with a little cloud. It was time to move on. We motored out of the harbour and turned northwest along the coast and we soon had both sails up, filled by the slight southwest wind, with *Starlight* gliding gracefully over a light blue sea. Dick's weather update at 9:30am reported ten-knot southwest winds and he also gave temperature, sea conditions and local weather as he saw it from his lookout. We called him on VHF channel 74 and told him our plans.

"You've picked a dicey time of the year with changeable weather," he commented. "And I can't see you yet." A little later we came into view and he said, "What a pretty sight!" Norm talked with him on the VHF about our dream of sailing around New Zealand. He also told him about our trip around Australia on our GL1200A Honda Goldwing motorcycle in 1995.

"I envy you," Dick said. "But jealousy will get me nowhere." Norm promised to visit him one day on the bike, and a few months later we did just that and took photographs of him and his radios. He said to keep in touch with him using channel 16 if we needed to.

The sail all the way to Parengarenga was a dream. Fred was steering perfectly in Great Exhibition Bay. The slight swell created surf that broke on the long sandy beach, and more than 60 gannets flew and dived about us. The dazzling white sand hills with tufted marram grass could easily seen from the sea. Locals had told us about a long sandbar at the entrance with a wreck on it, and this was also well described in the Royal Akarana Yacht Club's *Coastal Cruising Handbook*. As we came closer we dropped the sails, started the outboard and raised the centre-plate, then took a wide sweep around the Koteonepoto spit. The bow of a wreck was protruding boldly from the sand. "*SEA...*" was all we could read of its name. It was a stark reminder of what could happen if a vessel got too close to a reef or sandbar.

We motored into the deepest part of the entrance channel. Ahead of us was the black stake that marked the end of the sandbar east of Dog Island, but as the tide was fully in we could not see the extent of the shallows. We turned south into the Kauanga channel, following the diagrams in the cruising guide, and headed towards the wharf at Paua Peninsula. We could see a large shed on a hill behind the wharf, but the wind blew strong and gusty so we decided not to tie up there. We moved a little further south and anchored near a moored fishing boat, hoping for deep water. The southwest wind was still gusting and making the water choppy.

"Strong runs of tide can be expected here," the book said, but it was the best shelter we could find. As the tide dropped we could see lots of mangroves, reefs, sandbanks and mussel farms in the shallow harbour. There would not be much room left to anchor at low tide. The bird life inside the harbour was prolific. There were more gannets and a variety of seagulls and land birds. Swallows darted swiftly about and dozens of large, graceful, magnificent swans entertained us. We were fascinated by one swan with a damaged wing. It tried to fly but only flapped, and never got off the water.

The wind eased in the evening and the temperature dropped so we put on our tracksuits and cooked a hot evening meal. The cabin was cosy. The full moon shone brightly as the tide came in filling the mudflats, giving us a splendid view of the sparkling water and the surrounding low hillside farms

The next morning we tried to send a message to Dick on the VHF, but could not raise him. I suspected that either *Starlight* was outside the VHF range, or the VHF station that had notified us of a temporary closure for aerial maintenance was still closed down, or maybe the aerial was out of action due to damage by a jerking lure. Norm hooked up our spare VHF radio to an aerial hoisted halfway up the mast, and we heard Maureen on channel 60 and some fishermen talking. It was obviously still receiving so we reported our position to Maureen, but there was no contact with Dick on 74. It puzzled us.

The marine weather forecast at 5am was for rough seas, strong southwest winds, rain and hail showers. We decided to stay put inside the harbour.

As we were motoring towards the Te Hapua wharf, two barges went past full of people going to the White Sands to protest against the mining of this precious silica sand. Banners and flags said, "Not For Sale", "No Mining", "Enough". There was also a television crew present. We spoke to some folk ashore and they told us that the 80-year lease was up and had not been renewed, but the taking of sand was still going on, leaving huge holes and unsafe caverns beneath the diminished sand hills. The protestors left their notices behind, embedded in the sand.

We met Jewel Sucich, the owner of a small shop. She did not stock many supplies, as a posting box nearby had replaced her lease for NZ Post services and people did not call so much. Her husband Matt, a mechanic and an oyster farmer, was preparing the stakes that held the spat. The stakes are placed so that they get covered with seawater as the tide rises. Rock oysters can grow quickly in the warm waters, often ready for harvest in just under a year. "They're best in June," we were told.

Rain set in and our anchorage north of the wharf became rather precarious. The wind came from the northwest then turned south-southwest. The tide went out and we bottomed in shallow muddy water. So did the other permanently-moored boats, but in the morning the stronger wind was blowing the yacht towards the shore and onto a rocky shelf. We had to move out quickly, but there seemed no safe or sheltered places. Any possible anchorages had rocks, reefs, exposed sand or mangrove bushes in shallows. The two wharves were both exposed to the southwest wind. Then we saw a launch anchored in the lee of the white sand hills in the entrance channel, so we tried this spot. The wind was gusting to 40 knots but the sea was not rough, and eventually after a light shower it calmed down to 35 knots, still southwesterly, then to ten. In the late afternoon a fishing boat came in and anchored beside us, which made us more confident of our position.

The locals had warned us that the southwest winds could last all winter and that the west coast had huge surf and large sandbars extending many miles out from shore, far too dangerous for our small yacht.

"Go back along the east coast or get your trailer and go home by road," they told us. This, along with the forecast of more rain and strong southwest winds, made me anxious, then fearful. An intense feeling of despair set in. I couldn't eat lunch. Tears filled my eyes. I had no faith in our ability to go on, nor did I have any hope of better weather. Norm tried to cheer me up. "There's often a good spell of settled weather in the wintertime," he said, "And we have plenty of time."

My fit of despondency lasted only two hours, the time it took to think it all through. It would take Norm almost a week to go home, hook the yacht trailer onto our four wheel drive van and tow it to Parengarenga, and the weather could have changed by then. I decided I could wait.

We spent the next few days waiting for the weather to improve. The National Radio, mobile telephone and VHF reception improved and we even got channels 60 and 74 again. Dick thought we must have been out of range when we couldn't get him earlier. We thought that as the VHF relied on a clear line of sight, maybe a hill was in the way.

"There's gold in them there hills, blocking the radio waves," Norm joked.

Northwest winds and then more southwesterlies were predicted for Kaipara, with rough seas and three-metre swells. Norm waited patiently for slight seas and perhaps light northerly or easterly winds so we could travel south along the west coast. Our Bible reading and prayer time for the people in this area included asking God to give us wisdom, guidance and knowledge for the next leg of our journey.

We found a shallow lagoon on the north side of the channel with about two metres of clear water. It was sheltered under a bluff, on which stood the Perpendicular Point leading light. The other leading light was on the north side of the harbour entrance at Ohao or Coal Point, a little to our east. Both lights twinkled merrily at night. We put out two anchors and expected the hull to bottom at low water. Norm scrubbed the hull while the yacht was in a foot of water. There was heavy rain overnight and we were thankful for it as we caught nine litres of rainwater off the boom tent.

Three wild horses nibbled the high tide grasses early the next morning, but they did not stay long. We repositioned the anchors so that *Starlight* would sit flat on the sand for a few hours at low water, and it was nearly 4pm before we walked up the steep hill behind the anchorage to look at the view of the inner harbour. We saw many lines of oyster farms, almost filling the northeast channel. We found a path that led through some scrub and manuka bushes to a house, and there we met Marion Brown, whose family has been involved in rock oyster farming for many years. Her husband Winiata was employed by the Department of Conservation and Forestry. Access to their home was precarious at times, and only a four-wheel-drive vehicle could get through by land.

From her front lawn we found ourselves looking down on our yacht. "I saw you come in the other day," she said with a smile. She lived very frugally – no electricity, bare bulk stores, kerosene lanterns, battery-operated TV, a gas stove and a wood burner that provided hot water for showers. The wild rabbits ate any vegetables she tried to grow, and the diesel generator needed repairs. She told us that the wild horses drank the water from the streams but it contained too much sulphur for people, who had to rely on rainwater held in tanks for their supply. She said that keeler yachts rarely came in, as the inlet was too shallow except in the entrance channel. She also told us that the easterly and northeast winds brought rain, big swells and rough seas, making it almost impossible for boats to get out again. She offered us a cup of tea but as the sun was setting we did not linger. We thanked her for her kindness and hurried down the path just in time to board *Starlight* before the yacht floated.

The next day we berthed at the Te Hapua wharf again, bought some frozen mince, bread rolls and a few tinned goods and then walked along the dusty road to see the local Ratana church. We found it well-appointed and very neat, and we also glanced at the local cemetery on the nearby hill. But the road that led to the wharf was poorly-maintained, with rubbish strewn each side from years of untidy travellers. Norm asked for some plastic bags from a nearby house and we soon had them filled with bottles, paper, rags, cartons, old clothes and even shoes. We pulled out a big sack from a bush and filled it too. A few locals passed by in their cars and gave us cheek, and much to my embarrassment Norm told them, "We're from the Ministry of Works."

By the time we arrived back at the wharf we had several bags of rubbish and we piled them high on the only rubbish drum around. The road certainly looked different. Then we had to quickly vacate the jetty, as an oyster farmer wanted to load a barge. Back to our sheltered lagoon we went. Two days later we motored back to Te Hapua to try to get 22.5 litres of water, some bread and

18 litres of petrol as we had used quite a bit going to and fro. Jewel gave us some water but had no bread or petrol. Later she offered to take me to Waitiki Landing on the main highway leading in to the cape. We got ready and put our cans in the boot of her car, but the sixteen kilometres of narrow, winding road was much further than I had expected. I was able to buy some bread and I filled the cans, and her car, with petrol at the last service station on the highway. We chatted all the way back. She had worked sixteen years earlier with a team planting pine saplings that were now fully-grown and ready to be felled and logged. She had to drive carefully, aware of the logging trucks taking up the road or coming onto it from side roads.

"Why would she do that for us visitors?" I asked Norm later, but he had overheard her saying, "Fancy these tourists cleaning up our road." It seemed that one good deed deserved another, and we were very grateful.

With our stocks replenished, my spirits renewed and the weather improving we prepared to move on. While we were anchored near the lagoon we heard the forecast predicting light easterly winds. This could bring a huge swell into the entrance, making it difficult to leave. The locals had told us, "You'll never get out of here if the wind turns to the east." However a high-pressure system was coming over New Zealand with light winds, slight seas and settled weather for the next five days. While we were anchored in the channel overnight, a slight swell from the east came into the entrance, indicating that an easterly wind was on its way. The 5am extended forecast for Brett and Kaipara areas was for slight seas and very little wind, so we set off at dawn.

The sun rose at 7am behind a bank of cloud, with glorious colours of red, orange and purple as well as golden rays in a fan. We motored north and at 8am we passed the North Cape by skirting around Murimotu Island, just off the cape, and the reefs extending from it. I took a GPS reading and observed the lighthouse on the summit of Murimotu Island. Further on I took another GPS reading off Surville Cliffs, the most northern point of New Zealand. We were at latitude south 34 degrees 23 minutes, longitude east 173 degrees one minute. It was 30 April 1997.

At Tom Bowling Bay the sea was oily calm, deep blue and glistening in the bright sunlight. It was alive with fish splashing and birds diving. We had three lures out but caught nothing. There was no wind and little swell as we cruised on with the current assisting us. We heard Maureen on the Far North VHF radio, channel 60, at 9:30am but had no reply when we called her up. We managed to talk with her at 11am while motoring in Spirits Bay and she gave us the updated weather reports, all good but not much wind. She told us to contact her again down the west coast. We had an early lunch and drew close to Cape Reinga. We were still in calm water and we could see the lighthouse on top of the cliff with cars and buses parked near it. The tourists walking to the famous signpost looked so small from our distant position.

We could see the reef extending north from the Cape, and the turbulence on the other side. We had planned to head west, then south to face the dreaded West Coast, but instead of going west we headed north, trying to avoid the turbulent sea.

The waves rose high and the seas roared as we steered five miles further out from the land. There was no wind to sail with, so the outboard motor had the huge task of propelling the yacht up the four-metre swells to ride the contrary waves in between, cut through the white ribbon of broken water on the crests and slide down into the troughs. The sea was too rough for our Autohelm, so we had to tackle it by tiller steering. Then Norm got badly seasick and had to leave me to handle the yacht.

I steered around the worst of this turbulence and gradually turned west before heading southwest. We were in a very rough sea about two miles off the land. It was a new experience, and the hours ticked on slowly as *Starlight* motored south. Would the outboard keep going? Norm was seasick again and retired to the cabin. Not much use asking him for help if the motor failed or ran out of petrol, he was too ill to cope. We were in three to four metre southwest swells, but *Starlight* handled the waves well, taking them on the quarter as we punched and rolled over them. I gave Cape Maria van Dieman a good clearance of two miles to avoid the turbulence there. There was no shelter anywhere and I dared not go further off the coast as the notoriously-shallow Pandora bank was just a few miles off the northwest corner. It was bound to be even rougher out there.

At 2:30pm I marked our position on Chart NZ 51, Tauroa Point to Cape Brett, as three miles off Scott Point. Our course was 120 degrees and only a few headlands guided our progress along Ninety Mile Beach, whose actual length is 60 miles or 96 kilometres. Motupia Island, 58 metres high, was conspicuous and we could see The Bluff, 11 metres high, clearly from three miles out but the rest of the coastline was low-lying sand dunes.

I carried on. Gradually the swells reduced and the sea became moderate. Norm recovered and came on deck at 4pm, so I was able to rest for an hour. With the evening drawing to a close and the sun near setting, we set the Autohelm to handle the steering and before darkness fell, I checked our position and marked it on the chart.

As we set a course of 135 degrees heading towards Tauroa Point, we noted several lights that confused us. One had an irregular sequence and it turned out to be a tuna fishing boat. Another very bright light looked like a sports stadium or some high tower on the shore. There was no moon to light our way that night. The sea showed up as dark shadows of waves and ripples, and the shoreline was a dark grey blob. A GPS reading at 10:35pm confirmed we were on course, and we took turns to rest.

Norm saw the Tauroa (Reef Point) lighthouse flash – two white flashes every ten seconds – even though it was a long way off. It had a nominal range of eighteen miles, but because it stood on a 65-metre cliff it could be seen a lot further away. It was very comforting to be guided by its regular flashes. Later, while I was on watch, I saw the lights of the Ahipara settlement in Shipwreck Bay. The sea was almost calm and the chart indicated a safe anchorage, but I was unsure about anchoring there in the dark. The weather report was for calm seas and little wind so I carried on, changing course to give us about three miles of distance off the light. The very close and bright beam coming from this lighthouse was reassuring.

Chart NZ 51 covered the large area from Cape Brett to Tauroa Head. We used Chart NZ 41, North Cape, for a short time, then NZ 42, Hokianga Harbour to Manukau Harbour. The gap between the two was filled in with AA road maps and Chart NZ 4212, Hokianga Harbour. We passed Herekino Harbour, about nine miles southeast of Tauroa Point, in the dark. Any thoughts of entering it were passed over as we had no charts or data. To tackle it in the dark would be foolish, even if we did have the information, and by 4.15am our GPS reading had us well south of the harbour. We pressed on.

At dawn I took a reading that showed us four miles off the sandy coast, so we altered course and headed for the entrance of Hokianga Harbour. The sand hills on the north were clearly identified, but the swells made huge breakers in the shoals extending more than three miles from the shore. Our charts were consulted, so was the GPS, and then it was up to Norm to read the sea, steering *Starlight* in the deepest parts where the waves break the least. His experience of the sea all those years ago gave him a feel for this tricky manoeuvre. The chart showed the deepest sea near the south entrance and so we slowly made our way towards it. *Starlight* rolled over the almost breaking waves and into the next calm patch, and not one drop of water splashed over us. Soon we were through the entrance heading for the wharf at Omapere. It had been a long 27-hour overnight hop.

As we went to berth a man called out, "Give me a rope!". After he'd helped us to tie up he asked, "Have you been in here before?"

"No," we replied.

"Well, I watched you come in from the balcony of my house and you were right in the middle of the channel." He was impressed, and we felt a sense of relief and assurance that we had done our best in an unknown situation. Gordon and Eileen Franks offered us beds, showers, laundry and lots of local knowledge. They were boaties too, and told us that the entrance could at times be calm enough to row across.

After a two-hour sleep and a light lunch, we visited them to use their laundry and shower facilities, topped up our petrol tanks with 43 litres from the nearby service station, but declined the offer of accommodation ashore. Gordon and Eileen took us to the lookout at the top of the hill behind their house, on Highway 12. We could see Omapere and the Hokianga Harbour from there. Their advice was to go further up the harbour, because the current flowed swiftly near the entrance, and anchor near Opononi, so we thanked them gratefully, cast off and motored upstream in this beautiful harbour.

It was 1 May 1997. The weather reports were still good, a huge high covering the whole of New Zealand bringing settled and fine weather with calm seas all around the country. Amazing – this was a most unusual weather pattern.

At 5pm we anchored a little upstream of the Opononi jetty, beside two moored launches. This settlement became well known in the summer of 1955-56 because of a friendly, tame and playful dolphin called Opo. Visitors came from far and near, parking became congested and shops ran out of supplies. Children loved to frolic and swim with Opo, and there was even a song composed about the Opononi dolphin, but sadly it was found dead from an unknown cause. A statue of Opo is a permanent memorial of that magical summer.

Our mobile phone was within range, so we rang Raewyn to report our arrival. Lloyd rang us from Taupo and Pauline Jesperson from Kerikeri. She was anxious to know our progress and keen to drive over to see us the next day. We were unable to contact anyone on the VHF radio, however. Perhaps we were out of range?

The next morning we were motoring a short distance towards the jetty when the Honda 10 outboard motor sheared a propeller pin. Norm promptly started the 8hp Yamaha and *Starlight* glided into a berth. He was able to renew the pin right there on the jetty, just one of the many repairs he carried out during our trip, and while he worked on it I was able to buy groceries at the Four Square shop.

Pauline and her friend Michelle arrived at 10am in her four-wheel drive and took us for a tour of the Waipoua kauri forest. The 2000 year-old Te Matua Ngahere and the 1400 year-old Tane Mahuta are giant trees among the many tall kauri. On the way back we stopped at the entrance to the harbour and took photographs of the surf on the North Head shallows.

Tourists could catch a ferry from Opononi on the south side and go across to the 300-metre high sand hills on the north side. Sliding and tobogganing down these sand hills were very popular sports. Fishing charters, bush walks, canoeing and kayaking were some of the other activities available in the area. At nearby Rangi Point incredible shapes, huge sculptures and massive sand canyons had been carved out by the natural erosion of wind, shifting sand and rain. It's amazing to see what nature can do with a bit of sand given a lot of time.

We went back to the yacht for a quick lunch and a cuppa before Pauline had to go. Then Norm and I decided to explore the upper reaches of this narrow harbour. The light wind filled our sails for two hours as *Starlight* gently slid along. It was pleasant sailing. The skies were clear blue with a few white puffy clouds and we sailed on, enjoying the green hills and valleys on each side. When the wind dropped we motored, passing the township of Rawene. We saw the ferry crossing the harbour and bumping on the shoals as the tide was low. We went into The Narrows as far as the beacon, turned around and then headed back downstream to anchor at Opononi in the twilight. I cooked a meal of lamb chops, potatoes and vegetables – a delicious treat at the end of a lovely day.

We consulted the charts and the tides and decided to leave at 7am the next morning and head for Manukau Harbour. This would mean missing out the Kaipara Harbour with its many shoals and bars, as well as the long haul of 28 miles to get to the town of Dargaville. We decided that was just a bit too far, and that we needed to make progress south while the fine weather lasted. It was already May and the shorter days, cooler temperatures and winter weather would soon be with us.

I wrote a letter to the Porirua Salvation Army Corps care of the Corps Officer, Lieutenant Mark Ennever, telling them of our progress. He read out part of it at the next service and told them we had taken over three months to go UP north but going DOWN south would be much quicker! The congregation didn't blink an eyelid or laugh, just accepted his pun.

I woke up at 5:30am and saw the stars shining but an hour later thick fog had engulfed the harbour. We weighed anchor at 7am but, as the visibility was poor, we tied up to the jetty. There were people there waiting to catch a bus to take them to Rawene and onto the vehicle ferry, then by road again to the town of Kohukohu on the other side of the harbour, so that they could play sport. We chatted to them for a while until the scow *Alma* tooted us – they needed the berth. We cast off and motored very slowly towards Omapere while I stood by the mast looking through the mist for landmarks. We tied up at the Omapere jetty but the fast outgoing tide and surge from the sea swells made the mooring ropes jerk and the yacht bang against the posts as the fenders missed their places.

We found out later that our daughter Justine Lee had sent a letter and a Mother's Day greeting to "Starlight, care of the wharf or store at Omapere." It arrived just after we left. On the back she had written, "Starlight is a 24-ft trailer-sailer yacht sailing around the North Island, calling in for supplies at Omapere or Opononi (my guess)." The envelope was returned to the sender with lots of different post office marks on it, and is a treasured memento of our trip.

While we were bouncing against the Omapere wharf a local boat owner warned us, "There could be a fifteen-knot tide running at full moon." This would be hard to fight against, even with our two motors going flat out.

He also said, "The best time to go is when the horis are out".

"What do you mean?" I asked, puzzled.

"See those horizontal beams under the wharf? When the tide uncovers them, it's the best time to go." Apparently the current was slack then and had stopped running. We thanked him for this useful bit of local knowledge. By 10am we had had enough of banging against the wharf so we cast off, coiled in the ropes and stowed the fenders just as the fog started to lift, and cautiously motored out of the harbour. The waves and breakers were clearly visible. *Starlight* cleared the swells without a drop of water over the side, and at 10.25am we slid into the deeper calm water of the Tasman Sea.

Our stay in the far north had been full of interest. The people we met were friendly and helpful. Many of them lived in isolation, far from the services of cities or towns. We prayed for these folk, asking God to bless and guide them as they lived and worked in this mild climate some call 'the winterless north'.

As we left, we made contact with Northland Maritime Radio on VHF channels 16 and 71, and asked them to pass messages to Maureen and Dick telling them of our progress. The operator told us to contact Auckland Maritime Radio when we got to Manukau Harbour.

At times we may have thought we were on our own as we sailed or motored around the far north, but we had been assisted or watched over by local people, VHF operators, National Radio, cell-phone communication, several charts, the GPS, the *New Zealand Pilot,* the trusty outboard motors that had kept on going and a sturdy yacht. Our confidence and experience was growing but we knew we needed to be as alert as ever to the weather conditions. We had to watch out for obstacles, rocks or reefs, and the ever-changing sea, particularly on this dreaded West Coast.

7

Hokianga – Porirua

God moves in a mysterious way
His wonders to perform;
He plants his footsteps in the sea
And rides upon the storm.

William Cowper

Looking back at the entrance to Hokianga Harbour we could see that the fog and mist was still lingering there, but we were motoring in clear skies. The sea was moderate with a small swell; nothing like the expected big swells and rough surf. We were surprised and certainly not complaining.

Starlight slid over the waves with ease. There was a light easterly wind beyond the breakers and we soon had the sails hoisted. *Starlight* made four knots on a slight sea, but not for long – the wind soon dropped and we were motoring again. The fog had delayed our departure and we were three hours behind schedule, but I was pleased that we had been cautious in the fog.

"Don't worry," Norm assured me. "We have plenty of time. We are retired, no work to go back to." The Honda 10 outboard in the well of the cockpit was purring and *Starlight* was making good progress on a southeasterly course in slight seas with no wind.

Chart NZ 42, Hokianga Harbour to Manukau Harbour, was unrolled. This was an update of a 1908 British chart with random soundings taken in 1976. A note read, "Mariners should navigate with caution when approaching the coast." It was not very detailed, with a scale of 1:290,000, and it was in fathoms but it was the best we had. The *New Zealand Pilot* was also consulted, and we kept a good three miles off the coast with a careful watch out for reefs and other disturbances in the sea. We passed a few craypot floats, and observed grey cloud over the land. The out-going tide of about one knot to the north was impeding our progress, and a southwesterly swell of one metre with a light southeast wind sprang up right on the nose. The sea became joggly but we motored on. We had a good lunch and took turns at resting.

We identified the Maunganui Bluff and steered towards it to have a closer look. After this we steered a 140-degree course then veered to 130-degrees. At 5pm Norm put eighteen litres into the petrol tank and I checked our position to find we were nearly halfway between Hokianga and Kaipara harbours. We saw various high hills between the clouds and identified beach settlements, river mouths and gullies from the charts and maps. At 5:40pm the bright golden ball of sun sank below a clear horizon and we changed course to 150 degrees in order to clear the shoals and shallows outside Kaipara, as we would be passing the harbour entrance in the dark. We caught, filleted and cooked a kahawai for tea and at 9:20pm I took another GPS reading. We were almost nine miles off shore and we changed our course to steer 140 degrees. Fred the Autohelm was steering accurately and well.

While I was on watch I noticed a large, bright star rise over the eastern hills, and from its position I realised it was the planet Jupiter. Its rays ran along the surface of the sea, almost touching our yacht, and as the hours passed I was able to follow its course as it climbed higher in the night sky. It was a really awesome sight, not easily seen at home. We identified many of the other planets: Saturn, Venus and Mars, and the stars Sirius and Canopus along with the constellations Orion, The Southern Cross, The Scorpion, Pleiades (the Seven Sisters) and Regulus in Leo. They were particularly brilliant on clear moonless nights. Sunrises and sunsets were also vivid at sea, especially if there was little cloud and a clear sharp horizon. Sometimes we saw the moon rise and set over the water or over the hills.

The southwest swell increased to two metres in a moderate sea. *Starlight* rode the waves well, but there was not enough wind to sail. I slept for two hours but I was on deck at midnight, and by then we were nine miles off the entrance to the Kaipara harbour and not a breaker to be seen. We had cleared the shoals. We steered a 130-degree course, and I checked our position at 2:40am and 5:00am. The slight wind dropped overnight and the sea became calm. The Honda 10 kept going so long as the petrol was topped up and the clear light shining from the Piha lighthouse that stood on a high cliff guided us for over twenty miles.

At daybreak we were six miles off the coast, but our route was well within the twelve-mile limit as marked on Chart 42. Now I changed to the more detailed Chart NZ 4314, Manukau Harbour and Approaches, as we headed towards the shore. We approached Piha Beach as the sun rose just after 7am, and we altered course to take a closer look at the well-known Lion Rock, then we steered away off shore. Piha Beach is very popular with surfers, but the under-current can be treacherous at times. At 9:30am we were near the shoals and breakers of the Manukau harbour entrance, about five miles off shore. I was suffering with intense headaches and a double dose of Panadol did little to ease the pain. I was not much use on deck.

Norm steered *Starlight* over the swells and into the deeper water where the waves were not breaking so heavily. We went through this turbulence for over two hours, making slow progress. Gradually we came around the North Bank shoals and into the main channel, but we were making little headway against the strong out-going tide even with the two outboard motors both going at top speed. It was a fine Sunday morning and as we passed the Ninepin Rock light we noticed many fishermen surfcasting. Nearby was a small bay where a powerboat had anchored, and as we were running low on petrol, we thought it wise to stop there until the tide had turned.

"How's the holding?" Norm called to the fisherman in the runabout. "Okay," was the reply. So we dropped the anchor and it held fast. I was still unwell. Besides the headaches I had nausea, weeping eyes, chest pains, aching limbs and exhaustion. I was not seasick but I had lost my voice, and the pain relief we had on board was ineffective. This puzzled me but we slept for three hours while we were at anchor, and when we carried on I felt a little refreshed.

The tide had turned so we motored easily into the channel, noting the South Head cliffs with an old signal station on top. The high hills on the north side were part of the Waitakere Ranges. The detailed chart helped us avoid the Huia Bank and guided us around Puponga Point, and we anchored off the old wharf at Cornwallis at 4:10 pm. We rested and enjoyed a hot cooked tea after our long trip of nearly 34 hours, and I felt much better.

We telephoned a friend, Judy Corlett, and she offered to take me the next morning to get petrol and stores from nearby Titirangi. Judy was a midwife and had to call into her office to catch up on paper work, so while she was busy, I wandered around the shops and walked into the chemist. There, much to my surprise, was a back wall filled with a large window instead of the usual shelves, dispensary or office. Through this wide window I could see a breath-taking view of the harbour's blue water framed by large trees, bushes, and shrubs. I will always remember this spectacular natural scene.

While I was away Norm chatted to the friendly fishing folk on the disused wharf.

"Doesn't matter if we catch anything or not," they told him. "We just like the atmosphere, the fresh sea air and the tranquil surroundings." Some also fished at night but only at high tide, and we soon found out why. The tide dropped very quickly exposing large rocks and stones. We moved *Starlight* to a nearby mooring for lunch and a rest but returned to the wharf later. We had been invited to Judy's place, where we met her son and daughter and enjoyed a scrumptious feed of roast chicken and baked vegetables. We were back at the wharf at 9:30pm and, using the shore lights and a torch for illumination, found our way back onto the mooring in the dark.

The next day we used the detailed chart to navigate the Wairopa channel and follow the many markers all the way to the wharf at Onehunga. It was full tide. Large cargo boats regularly used this marked channel and tied up at the main wharf. We entered the fishermen's harbour with the red port light on our left, but then, as I was standing on the bow ready with a mooring rope, I spotted another marker.

"There's a big black buoy ahead," I shouted. Norm, at the helm, did not respond. He didn't hear me and he didn't see the buoy. We passed it on our starboard side and I saw that it was red. It should have been passed to port. The fishermen who watched us arrive told us later that they were at first anxious, then curious to see if our keel would get stuck in the mud, but we had our centre-plate up. The high tide had also covered a fence line, but fortunately for us there was plenty of water over it. Keelers or trailer yachts rarely sailed in this harbour because there were too many mud flats. It was exactly the opposite on the Waitemata Harbour, on the other side of this narrow neck of land, where thousands of pleasure boats and yachts ply the deeper harbour.

We started to tie up to a jetty beside a ladder, the nearest one to the shore. The Auckland Port Authority assistant harbour master saw us and came running along the jetty.

"You'll be all right there," he told us. "See the harbour master tomorrow, he's at a meeting today and there's no charge for the first one or two nights." He didn't tell us how big the rise and fall of the tide was, but we could tell that it was considerable so we used extremely long springs and mooring ropes, and decided there should be plenty of slack. We went off shopping.

We bought petrol, gas for the stove and groceries. We wrote out twelve postcards to send to family and friends. I had a haircut and Norm bought a second-hand hat. It was a long walk and it took us some time to find the service station, so by the time we got back to the wharf at 5:30pm, the tide had gone right out. What a surprise – *Starlight* was stranded on the mud. She was leaning over, away from the jetty. The drop in the water level here was over five and a half metres, much more than at Cornwallis. The two ropes attached to the stern were about half a metre too short and the weight of the yacht had pulled the starboard stern cleat right out of the gunwale.

What were we going to do? I could not jump from the ladder to the deck, but Norm managed to. He threw me a rope and I tied it to our purchases and lowered them one at a time down to the yacht for him to stow away.

What about cooking tea, I thought? It was obviously not going to be possible on board, so we went to the nearby pub to buy a cooked meal. We used their telephone, watched the weather forecast on their TV and talked to other patrons. Some of them were fishermen and recognised us from 'the yellow yacht'. They gave us hints about going into other bar harbours like Kawhia and Raglan. "You'll get in there okay, but you could be stuck there for days if the weather turns bad," we were told. But a high weather pattern was still hovering over the whole of New Zealand. It was a most unseasonal situation. The barometer was reading 1035 millibars, much higher than normal, and rising.

One short man, who was playing pool, kept coming up to Norm to shake his right hand vigorously while still holding the pool cue in his left hand. Each time he told Norm some new fact about fishing or the weather, then went back to his game. Eventually he told us the name of the boat he was on and offered to give us a weather fax in the morning. Norm found this unusual behaviour very amusing.

The tide began to rise and by 8:30pm *Starlight* was floating high enough for us to to get aboard and renew the mooring ropes. Our visitors David and Lorraine Smith had to wait for us before taking us to their home at Otahuhu for supper, but when we got back again about 11:00pm the tide was full. We found *Starlight* floating beside the jetty and we got aboard her easily. The next day Norm inspected the Honda 10 outboard and found that the fuming exhaust gases were being emitted not only from the propeller shaft but also from two small breather holes underneath the head of the motor. In the past we had sometimes smelt petrol fumes and assumed that it was lack of air going into the motor, so we had lifted the covering to allow more air into the intake. But apparently on our long hauls the fumes were being sucked into the cabin where we slept, and as I could sleep longer than Norm, I got more exhaust gases into my lungs. My headaches and illness, Norm theorised, were symptoms of carbon monoxide poisoning.

"We need to get a bigger, better motor, especially if we have to go out of here against a swift seven-knot incoming tide," he explained. I was all for it, especially if a faster and more powerful outboard would fit onto the outside bracket. The latest *Trade & Exchange* newspaper advertised a 15hp Yamaha outboard for sale for $2,100, so we rang the owner and arranged for him to bring it to us in the afternoon. It was a nearly-new 1996 model and had done only ten hours running.

In the meantime, John and Mary came for lunch. They and their family were very interested in our travels. They talked of their sailing experiences around the Bay of Islands in their 16ft Hartley over Anzac weekend. Their outboard motor let them down and they found it difficult to sail back to where they had launched. Their outboard was now being repaired, and I gathered that they would rather have had a reliable motor.

The two-stroke Yamaha 15hp outboard was a good buy. The owner Paul Simpson took Norm into Auckland to buy a new petrol tank and a connection, and we also needed a new cleat and some resin to do the necessary repairs to the deck. They returned at 5pm, noting another very low tide with a four and a half metre drop.

We decided to replace the erratic and unreliable Honda 10hp with the new long-shaft Yamaha, so we rang Lloyd to come and get the Honda that evening. We hauled it up to the wharf using a halyard, and lowered the 15hp the same way. We spent the next morning fitting the Yamaha into the well but found that it fumed and did not run well in there, and nor did it propel the yacht properly, so we fitted it to the outboard bracket on the stern and used the halyard again to transfer the 8hp outboard into the cockpit well. Another task on Norm's repair list was the starboard stern cleat. He used two-pot epoxy resin to fibreglass a block of wood onto the gunwale to hold the new cleat. I was kept busy preparing the yacht for the next leg by cleaning it and removing the rubbish, filling water containers, checking our stores, unrolling and checking the next charts, consulting the tide-timetables and listening to weather forecasts. At 11am we were asked to move from our place by the jetty to make room for the fishing boat *Compass Rose,* and we tied up on the outside of it.

Mark Bamford, the owner, was from New Plymouth. He gave us a sketch of the harbour there and told us to use his mooring, but he thought there would be room in the marina now that the tuna fishing boats had gone. We were pleased to get this local information and very grateful.

Five days of good weather at Onehunga was more than we could expect. "How long can this high pressure system last?" we asked each other. At 2pm we set off for the Manukau Harbour entrance when the tide was halfway out. The 8hp outboard in the cockpit well fumed and cavitated, so we started the 15hp Yamaha on the back bracket. It went well and pushed the yacht along at six knots, lifting the bow a little. We telephoned Lloyd, told him what had happened and asked him to swap the 8hp for the old Honda 10hp, and we arranged to meet him at Cornwallis that evening. It was 3:30pm when we got there, so we anchored close to the boat ramp in the shallows and as the tide dropped *Starlight* settled in the soft mud. There were no rocks in sight. Lloyd and his four-year-old son Tristan came in the evening and we swapped over the motors easily. The 10hp went back into the well and he took the 8hp back to his home at Waitakere. After this we had black sand all over the yacht, so another clean-up job got underway. Then as the tide came in, *Starlight* floated and we went onto the mooring.

David Smith had sold Norm some lubrication additive to put in the petrol for the Honda 10. He explained that it would lubricate the top rings and give the motor a longer life. Four-stroke outboards have a sump for oil, like a car, and normally do not need oil mixed with the petrol the way two-stroke outboards do.

"Use a mix of 1:100," David advised Norm, so he topped up the petrol tank with the additive. The petrol tanks for the 15hp Yamaha were topped up with outboard motor oil, also in a 1:100 mix.

So many people had helped us, given us advice and local knowledge. We had learnt quite a few lessons, especially about the tide rise and fall, in this shallow, expansive harbour. While we were there we had read several chapters of the Bible and prayed for the more than a million people who lived in the extended Auckland metropolitan area.

The weather forecast was for easterly ten to fifteen knot winds. Maybe we would be able to sail again? The sea was calm but the tide was rushing in against us. We decided to head out of the harbour against the tide, using the two outboard motors. We left Cornwallis at 6:15am on Friday 9 May and headed for the Manukau Harbour entrance. There was a slight sea but a strong rip at the heads. With both motors going, *Starlight* was pushed along at seven knots but she moved only slowly ahead against the tide. We noted that there were no breaking waves to the south so we went through this channel and were in calmer waters in just over an hour. It was a remarkable contrast to the turbulent seas we had encountered a few days earlier. The easterly wind came up and soon we were sailing at five knots.

Norm called up Auckland Maritime Radio on channel 71 to report our leaving Manukau Harbour and heading for New Plymouth, with our ETA in approximately 24-30 hours. We had breakfast while the yacht sailed steadily. I took a GPS reading at 9:30am and marked it on Chart NZ 43, Manukau Harbour to Cape Egmont, and we set a 175-degree compass course towards New Plymouth. We heeded the advice of the fishermen and decided not to go into the two harbours on the way, so our course took us off the coast into deeper water. Here we found a steady light wind of ten knots, with a slight to moderate sea on the port stern quarter that gave us a comfortable sail.

Starlight did a steady three to four knots, and I took GPS readings every two or three hours. The fickle wind dropped just after mid-day and we were motoring again, but this time we used only the new 15hp Yamaha on the outside bracket. It pushed the yacht along on a 140-degree course at a steady pace of seven knots with the bow weighed down.

At 1:35pm Norm caught a skipjack tuna on a yellow lure, then two more. Was this because we were well off shore or because we were travelling faster, we wondered? They were black with fat round girths, about 24 inches long and with a lot of meaty flesh. Norm was delighted with his catches.

There was not much to see. The coastline was only a faint grey blur, but at 3:50pm we looked to the south and were surprised to see the tip of Mount Taranaki, also called Mount Egmont, rising above the horizon like a white tent. It was a majestic sight from as far away as Raglan. We altered course to 170 degrees, and just after dark we saw the new moon set in the west with only a few stars in a cloudy sky. We were able to eat our meals and have hot drinks of Milo from the Thermos flask as we journeyed on through the night.

During his watch, Norm saw two torpedoes racing towards the side of the yacht. It gave him quite a start for a moment. White froth and phosphorus lit up two long tube shapes under the surface of the water. They were heading swiftly towards the bow, but the shapes were dolphins greeting us in the night. That was a sight he will always remember.

At 2:40am a steady easterly wind sprang up and we cut the motor, hoisted the sails and headed south towards New Plymouth. It was pleasant sailing. For some time we were eighteen miles off the coast in the Taranaki Bight, as the land curved inwards towards the Cape.

The mountain was obscured by cloud when we arrived at 7:15am. I reported our arrival to Taranaki Coastguard Radio on channel 61 and then called the harbour board to arrange a berth but there were only a few private ones available. We tied up in an empty berth with lots of heavy dangling lines. "That fishing boat could come back any time," a fisherman told us, so we made enquiries and telephoned an owner who was prepared to rent out his berth to us. His yacht was away being repaired.

I was alert and feeling fine after our 25-hour trip. No fumes, no headaches and enough energy to clean the yacht, fillet three tuna and bottle four jars of fish in the pressure cooker. We gave some of the tuna away to Goldwing motorcycle friends Colin and Viola Berry.

The fine weather broke into strong, cold southwest winds and rain. The stationary high had finally moved off New Zealand after a record fifteen days – what a miracle it had been for us. The latest weather forecast was for storms in many parts of the country, and the marine forecast was for rough seas, three to four-metre swells and 25-35 knots winds with heavy rain. Looked like we would be here for a few days, we thought, so we walked to the nearby motor camp for hot showers and used their laundry facilities. We both slept well that night.

On Sunday 11 May we rang and found out that the services at the Salvation Army started at 10:30am. We rushed to get ready and two fishermen gave us a lift to the hall. Captains Bruce and Marilyn Tremain looked after us all day, and special meetings at both New Plymouth and Stratford kept us busy until nearly nine o'clock that night. We had not been able to contact the owner of the berth who had offered to give us a key to the security gate. We had missed him at the yacht club – it was closed and the patrons had gone. We walked along the breakwater and found that the gate to the marina was locked and there was no way could we get to our yacht. We called and shouted but although other boat owners knew of our plight in not having a security key, they did not hear us yelling.

"What are we going to do?" I asked Norm.

"Let's go to the police station and see if they can locate the owner or find a key for us," he suggested. We hitched a ride from two sightseers who dropped us off at a nearby corner.

"We need a bed for the night," Norm said cheekily.

The polite duty officer heard our story, then said, "Wait a minute." He rang the port authority who held a key, then we were taken in a police car to the port office. A port official took us back to the wharf in a little jeep and let us into the marina. I noted his telephone number and had to use his services again two nights later as we had been locked out again. It was not until Friday that we were able to share the key with another yacht. The owner of the berth we were using had given his key to the skipper of *Elle*.

While we waited for the weather, everyone on the marina was friendly and shared experiences. They told us to be aware of a recent rash of thefts from boats at the marina, but no one knew how the thieves were getting in. Later we were sent a newspaper cutting which explained how thieves had been caught red-handed after rowing from a beach to board and loot a boat.

The crew of *Cho Cho San* shared their yachting experiences, gave us encouragement and had plenty of tips for the next leg. "Watch out for shoals and rough water along the coast," they warned us.

Friends made us feel welcome. Colin and Viola arranged a gathering of eleven Goldwingers to have a meal together at the Stratford RSA and we shared our experiences and talked about the next rally to be held on 20-21 June at Wanganui. Gordon and Thelma Smith invited us to their place for a meal and a tour of the Pukekura Park. Mervyn and Phyllis Smith came to visit us on board for morning tea, bringing fresh homemade scones. We visited Gordon and Joy Muir and shared our news of our trip as well as catching up with the latest news on the Millar family history.

On Friday, Neil Ritchie from the *New Plymouth Daily News* interviewed us. Both Neil and the photographer were interested in our small yacht adventure, and their report was published in the Saturday paper.

The next morning we had a visit from the berth owner's partner. She told us the charge was $15.00 per night. I wrote out the cheque for $105.00 (for seven nights) without querying the cost, but I thought it was rather high since

Mavis with Phyllis and Merv Smith, visitors at New Plymouth

there were few facilities. A few days after we arrived home there was a letter in the mail from her apologising for her mistake. The fee should have been $10 a night, and she enclosed a cash refund of $35.00. What an honest person.

The week in New Plymouth had flown fast. The latest weather forecast was for a small high coming over New Zealand and the next two days were expected to be good, with light northeast winds and fine weather. Two other yachts were preparing to leave the next day, one going to Waikawa Bay in the Marlborough Sounds and the other to Nelson. So we prepared to leave too.

The 5am marine forecast was for variable winds and slight seas at Raglan but in the Stephens area, light north and northeast winds were expected to build to 15-20 knots later. Colin and Viola came to say goodbye and wish us good sailing and promised to return the key to the berth owner. New Plymouth was yet another port of call where friends and locals gave us hospitality and useful advice. We remembered them all in prayer each time we had a Bible reading, and thanked God for their kindness. We also prayed a blessing on all the people that lived there in the Taranaki region, under that unique inactive volcano.

We left at 8am in slight seas and very little wind, motoring near the shore, checking the GPS and changing course regularly. Some dolphins visited us and frolicked for a while. We passed Cape Egmont Lighthouse at noon, noting the two-metre southwest swell, but there was still no wind. Fred steered south then southeast for us as we travelled two or three miles off the coast, and Norm caught six kahawai on his lure. Well done.

Later on we noted the area clearly marked 'fishing and anchoring prohibited' on Chart NZ 45, Port Taranaki to Patea, and saw the two black beacons on the hills either side of Oaonui that marked the limits. Looking southwest towards the horizon, we could see the lighted gas on the Maui A oil platform over fifteen miles away. The gas pipeline ran all the way to the shore where we could see the gas works. The nearest town was Opunake, and the caution on the chart read, "Vessels are warned not to anchor within the gas pipeline area and fishing vessels are prohibited from anchoring and fishing within the limit line area. The gas pipeline contains flammable gas under high pressure. Any ship damaging them would face an immediate fire hazard." Strong words that needed to be heeded, I thought.

At 5:30pm a slight northeast wind rose so we set both the genoa and the mainsail. The sky was overcast with no rain, and we were soon sailing goose-winged at four knots in a slight sea, the swell giving us a kick at the stern. The town lights of Manaia, Hawera, Patea and Wanganui were visible that evening. We had thought of calling in to Patea or Wanganui, but decided to head for Kapiti Island instead. For most of the night, stars and the moon were our illumination. We took turns at sleeping and recording our position as the 140-degree compass course took us offshore by more than 20 miles. At 7am we were off Foxton Beach, then we saw the settlements of Otaki and Levin. We were heading straight for Kapiti Island.

We arrived off Kapiti at midday. We were familiar with the lee of the island as we had spent many happy hours fishing there in our clinker and power boats. The island is a bird sanctuary, with good fishing reefs and underwater seaweed forests for scuba diving. The dense bush on the leeward side made this area an attractive place, but the seaward side has high dark cliffs and looks quite different. There was a possible anchorage in the lee of Kapiti but as *Starlight* was sailing well at five knots with a good northeast wind and a following sea, we were reluctant to stop.

The weather forecast for the next day in the Cook area was for strong northerly winds and rough seas, so we decided to keep sailing and head for home. We would be there in about three hours.

We rang our family and friends and told them to expect us that afternoon. Ken, Raewyn and family had been having a guessing game as to the date of our arrival. Raewyn thought about 2 June (Queen's Birthday weekend) but Ken had guessed 17 May. He was the closest to 19 May, which was when we actually got there. These guesses they had made told us how intensely they had followed our progress and how much they looked forward to seeing us home safely.

We had lunch on the way and swiftly passed Pukerua Bay, entering the headland into Plimmerton at 2:15pm. The course into Porirua Harbour is well marked by day with sets of two white triangles, and by night with two red, white and green tunnel lights. We sailed right up to the end of the first two markers but as the wind had died down, the sails were dropped and we motored for the last part. It was low tide. We glided passed the Mana Marina, beside the boats moored to the posts and around the starboard markers as we approached Porirua. I looked eagerly for our house on the hillside at Elsdon, and there it was among the trees, houses and town building. Our yellow-roofed home beamed a bright welcome home. I had looked forward to the sight.

We were alongside the Onepoto jetty by 3:30pm. It had been a 31½-hour leg, the best of our trip. Ken and our six-year-old granddaughter Talitha were there to catch the ropes, and others soon arrived. Boat-builder Bernie Perano, Dora and Jim Stoneham, our lookout person Ivy Paul and, in the evening, more family. Carolyn and Phillip, Raewyn, Ezra and Ezekiel came down, Ken brought our van but we decided to stay at the jetty overnight and wait for the high tide in the morning before retrieving the yacht. We read our next two Bible chapters and prayed for the people who lived along this coast as well as making a prayer of thanks for safe passages and to a faithful, watchful God who had cared and guided us on our journeys.

We had completed our dream of sailing around the North Island in our Gazelle trailer-yacht *Starlight,* and it had taken us four months and two days.

The story of our trip was published in the *New Plymouth Daily News* and in the local Porirua *Kapi Mana News,* complete with coloured photographs of us both on board. People often asked us, "What's your next trip going to be? Are you going to go around the South Island?"

"That WOULD be something to write about," my brother John encouraged.

"We need to get up courage for that," we told them. We knew that the South Island circumnavigation would take longer and that the seas along the coast would be more challenging. For now, all we wanted to do was to be safe at home, to rest, relax, reflect and ponder the world of the sea, shore and sky, including the ever-changing weather patterns.

Who knows what the future will hold?

PART TWO – THE SOUTH ISLAND

Starlight and trailer on our lawn at Elsdon, for maintenance of the centre-plate. On the right is our clinker 14ft 9ins double-ended cabin boat, *Goldstar*

8

Getting Ready

Eye hath not seen, nor ear heard, neither have entered into the heart of man, the things which God hath prepared for them that love him.
1 Corinthians 2:9

We had navigated around the coast of the North Island in 1997, and that had taken over four months. All thoughts of sailing around the South Island were on hold. There was the unknown coastline to consider, the changeable weather, the risks involved in travelling at night. Could *Starlight* withstand the punishing sea? Would we be able to hold on to body and soul? We had asked ourselves these and other questions before tackling the North Island, and found that we could answer most of them in the affirmative. But we had only sailed a third of the way, the rest of the time was spent motoring in calm seas. There was no doubt that our trailer yacht *Starlight* could tackle anything the sea gave to us, but could we?

Each year we grew older and each year we wondered if we could still cope with the rigours of life at sea. Our greatest fear was the treacherous ocean swells, then the fury of the big surf at various places like Puysegur and Nugget points. There were also the long distances between places to shelter on the West Coast of the South Island. We needed to drum up a huge heap of courage. Would we ever be able to tackle it? Maybe never, we thought.

In 1998 we made plans to visit Ireland and Norway. Norm's great-grandparents had come from these countries in the 1870s, and I was into family history research. I had contacts in County Down, Ireland and Toronto, Canada for the Millar roots but had none for the Anderson and Thorsen families who came from Norway.

We flew to Hawaii on route to Toronto, then on to London where we bought a second-hand campervan so we could travel through Ireland and Scotland and on to Europe. We found relatives in County Down, Ireland but none in Vennesla or Fjotland, in the south of Norway. We knew that a brother of Gundvar Anderson had immigrated to Wisconsin, USA and the family had kept in touch with them, but we did not know if any of the family had stayed behind in Norway so we left a letter at the Lutheran church in Vennesla explaining who Norm's ancestors were. Then we headed north, travelling for a week towards the Nord Kapp. We were inside the Arctic Circle for a few days – it was summertime there and the sun shone 24 hours a day.

After we came home to New Zealand, we received a telephone call from Norway that enlightened us about the descendants of a sister who had stayed behind in Norway. "Your great-great-grand daddy and my great-great-grand-daddy, the same great-great-grand-daddy," Arthur told us. "I know it all. So sorry you did not find me." After this call, we exchanged letters and photographs and then later on we found Church records and archives on the Internet and on Latter Day Saints micro-fiche and films that filled in more details.

We sold the van in London, flew to Toronto and bought another for a tour of North America. We visited relatives in Canada, Boston, Wisconsin (they were Norwegian descendants) and in Seattle. Altogether we travelled 9,000 miles in Europe and 6,000 miles in North America. It took us five and a half months and we used up most of our spare cash.

When we arrived home *Starlight* was still sitting on the trailer on the front lawn, waiting patiently for the next trip. Our friend Ivy Paul had been hoping to go with us to Ireland to visit her husband's relatives but was unable to travel. Norm had said before we left, "If you don't make it to Ireland, we will take you overseas when we get back." What he was promising was a trip over the seas of Cook Strait in *Starlight*, so in January 1999 we went to the Marlborough Sounds for two weeks. The yacht sailed well in spite of having been high and dry for over eighteen months.

Did we still want to circumnavigate the South Island? We needed at least a year to think about it. What about going in the year 2000? Not then, as there were too many activities planned for the millennium. I wanted to be home to celebrate the turn of the calendar with family, to see the last sunset in the west for 1999 from Titahi Bay and the first time the sun rose in the east from a nearby hill for 2000. We did both of these things, but each time the horizon was obscured by cloud. Other millennium celebrations soon filled the calendar and it was September 2000 before we began to think again about sailing around the South Island.

We realised that if we were going to do it, it had to be done soon before we grew too old. Norm was 70 years old and I was 68. We had been retired for nine years and had fulfilled a number of our hopes and dreams, like the motorcycle tour of Australia, our overseas travels in a campervan, tramping ten of New Zealand's top tracks, as well as taking ski trips to various snowfields, scuba diving and snorkelling. Then there had been the trip around the North Island in *Starlight*.

There was still this one dream to fulfil, of sailing around the South Island. If it had taken four months to do the North Island how long would it take to circumnavigate the South? We calculated at least six months, and that meant that we had to leave well before December if we were going to do it in the summertime. However, our friends told us that the best weather in the Fiords was often in the winter. "Not in the colder temperatures, nor in the shorter daylight hours for me," I told Norm.

Which way to go? East or West Coast first? After a few inquiries into current directions, swells and weather patterns, we decided to go via the Marlborough Sounds, Tasman Bay, Golden Bay and then south along the West Coast. We agreed that we'd rather get the worst over first. There would be more ports or shelter on the eastern coast, we thought, and perhaps calmer seas and less swell. Preparation was essential. We had sold the 15hp Yamaha outboard and the 10hp Honda was unreliable. Norm sought advice.

"You need at least a 25hp motor for a yacht to get in and out the fiords," a yachtsman told him. Norm bought a 15hp Honda four-stroke outboard, which had only ever been carried on the stern of a large powerboat, for $1,200. We also bought a nearly new 10hp Honda four-stroke for $2,000. It was the same model as before, so we had plenty of spare parts. We put the 10hp in the well and attached the 15hp to the outboard bracket on the stern. We checked our petrol cans. We would need to carry more fuel, but how much? I wasn't sure.

The centre-plate needed inspection. Norm dug a hole in the front lawn, put *Starlight* on a frame support and pulled the trailer out from underneath her. He dropped the centre-plate, scraped and painted the bit below the hull and then lifted it up into the cabin so that the top end could be done. He filled the hollows inside the centre-plate with ten litres of oil to prevent the inside of the steel case rusting.

A heavy wire attached to an electric motor lifts the plate vertically (although it may be also be winched by hand) through a series of pulleys, and a supporting chain attached three inches in front of the cable tilts the plate. This chain locks the plate into the fibreglass housing and jams it in a firm position, then the chain is padlocked so that the centre-plate will not rock or thump in a turbulent sea. We usually travelled with the centre-plate in this three-quarter-down position. We also carried a strong board that could be fitted between the top of the centre-plate and the frame of the lifting wire, just in case of an extra heavy sea. This was to prevent the centre-plate staying up in the event of a 360-degree roll. Gazelle yachts have a good record for righting themselves again, but we needed to be sure.

Powell and Rae Lewis inside their yacht at Mana Marina

In the meantime I completely cleared out all the gear in the yacht, putting it into the garage for checking. Then I cleaned the inside, getting into all the corners and storage compartments. I washed and checked the sails, and found them all in good order. I made two new lee cloths and covered the fenders with new waterproof cloth. I sewed new zips into two lifejacket coats that had been given to us, and I washed and dried the carpet.

Earlier in the year I had bought two books, *A Boaties' Guide to Fiordland* and *Stewart Island Cruising Guide*, both produced by the Mana Cruising Club. Both had details of places where we could anchor in various wind or weather conditions. Peter Foster lent me his copy of *New Zealand Pilot* and I borrowed some South Island charts from Ron Perano and Powell Lewis. Over the years we had accumulated ten charts of northern South Island areas but I was still short of some, so we purchased them. I now had 40 charts, but there was a new one for Stewart Island which had not yet been printed. Perhaps it would be available by the time we got there.

I ordered maps for Telecom mobile phone and VHF coverage as well as AA land maps for the South Island. I bought a calling card to ring our daughter from a landline if the mobile was out of range, and I also obtained the recently-released *Nautical Almanac* for 2001.

While I was cleaning out the yacht I felt a drop of water fall onto my cheek. Where was that coming from? I told Norm about it.

"There nothing to leak in that part!" he exclaimed. On further examination he found that the moisture had come from the compass, which was only half full of liquid. This leak had to be dealt with, and there wasn't enough time to send to Auckland for a bottle of special replacement fluid. Then Norm remembered that a compass could work well on half vodka and half water, which would not affect the compass card, so he went to the local bottle-store.

"Do you sell vodka?" he asked the lady in the store.

"Yes. Do you drink vodka?"

"Oh no," he replied, "It's for the compass. Can you spare me a litre?"

"What a waste!" she commented, but she sold him some. Back home he mixed the vodka and water and carefully filled up the compass after patching up the tiny crack in the housing. It would have to do. We also carried a trampers' Silva compass, and the GPS gave a very accurate speed and direction reading as well as the latitude and longitude. My Casio watch could also record barometer, altitude, temperature and bearings, so we would be well covered if our floating compass card failed.

Sam Medland heard of our plans to sail around the South Island and indicated his desire to do a leg with us. Which part? What date could he join us? Where would he start? How long could he sail with us? I told him that we were planning to do the West Coast first, then the Fiords and Stewart Island and then sail north along the East Coast. He and his wife Eva had arranged to go to Christchurch to visit their son Stephen and his family in the New Year. Sam wasn't sure when he could join us, so we decided to wait and see.

What else was there on the list to be done? I checked everything for wear and tear; the rigging and sheets (sail ropes), the rails, the LPG gas bottle, the porta-loo toilet and the chemical for it, the GPS and batteries, the large supply of long ropes, the springs, mooring ropes and anchor ropes. I also inspected the five anchors, replenished the first aid kit and medications, checked the flares, the EPIRB and the five fire extinguishers, made sure the VHF radios and the Autohelm worked. I bought a replacement gas stove, a new 3-kg LPG bottle and a second-hand camera. Then I cleaned out the containers for the 67.5 litres of fresh water we carried on board and I packed bottled, tinned and freeze-dried food as well as yeast and flour for bread making. I sorted out and packed pots and pans, cutlery, utensils, pressure cooker, towels, sleeping bags, pillows, summer clothes and waterproof gear. The clothes for cooler weather went into a small backpack.

The list seemed endless but it all fitted into its allotted place. It was like shifting house. We had to be independent and as self-sufficient as possible, and I was sure I had missed something out. Did I mention the nine torches and lots of spare batteries, and the box of 32 cans of fruit, meat and vegetables, all wrapped in waterproof material as a reserve food supply?

Norm checked and repaired the inflatable dinghy, then blew it up tight to test it. He made a long shelf above the quarter berths for the long oars, pole, gaff, fishing rods, boat hook and dive flag. He checked the outboards, bought 113 litres of petrol and a litre of engine oil. He fitted a new car radio and two new car batteries and he packed two transistor radios – one was a Venturer with several channels and a direction finder. We were assured that the VHF repeater stations would cover the Fiords, so we did not worry about a single sideband (SSB) radio.

Time was marching on. The more we prepared and planned, the more confident we became, especially as people gave us useful hints and encouragement. It was not easy to overcome our fears of the unknown, but we were going to give it a go, even if we had to stop halfway and come home by road and ferry or by air.

December arrived and the weather was unsettled. We kept up our daily routine of listening to the early morning marine forecasts and the mid-day long-range land forecasts, concentrating on the South Island areas. There was still the laundry and vacuuming to do, the fridge to clean out and the lawns to mow, then the final loading of the yacht. At last *Starlight* was on the trailer waiting to go.

On Wednesday 13 December, I drove to the Mana Cruising Club to fill in the important ten-minute form. As we had missed the 11:30am high tide at the Onepoto ramp, the manager offered to let us use their ramp and by 5pm we were almost ready. We had a much-needed last hot meal at home, and after that we hooked the trailer onto the four wheel drive Toyota van, the dinghy was flung onto the deck and we were off down the hill.

We arrived at the Mana Cruising Club ramp at 7:30pm, and lifted the mast and rigged the boat with the help of Clive Stephens and Glen Woods. Other family members came to watch and help. Ken and Raewyn Te Tau came with our grandchildren, Talitha 10, Ezra 6 and Ezekiel 4. Our other daughter Carolyn Wickliffe came too, as did Yvonne Stephens and her grandson Jesse, aged six. They all took a great interest in the launching.

The yacht slid off the trailer smoothly while willing helpers on the ramp jetty held the mooring ropes. Then Norm and I took the excited and noisy children for a short ride on *Starlight* to the wharf outside the clubrooms. It was half tide when we tied up there using three mooring ropes and several fenders. Norm took the van and trailer home, locking the trailer to a deadman in the front lawn, and Clive brought him back to the yacht. In the meantime I sorted out the gear inside *Starlight*, made up the bed on the double bunk and had a hot cup of Milo ready by the time Norm returned. We flopped into our bunk at midnight.

In the morning it was raining, then drizzle and low cloud with a 35-knot wind and very rough seas offshore. I clipped the number three jib onto the forestay and tied it down securely while Norm threaded the four lee cloths on to the rails. There was not much hope of leaving that day after all. I wrote out the last of our Christmas cards and posted them, then bought some nibbles (sweets and nuts) at the nearby supermarket. After tea I wandered into the clubrooms and chatted with Sue and Wayne Roberts, Ron Macintosh and Jim Gibson. They shared interesting sailing experiences and gave me excellent hints.

Friday was another very wet and windy day with poor visibility. Norm went home by train, taking a small TV that didn't work, a stainless Thermos that wouldn't keep water hot and coming back with a few 'forgotten' items like car tubes which could be useful as extra fenders or cushioned seats on the cockpit benches. I put the slats into the small mainsail and threaded it onto the boom, cleaned the deck and tied new red and green ribbons on to the port and starboard stays (we use these ribbons to assess the direction and speed of the wind). I checked the marine forecast on the VHF channel 68 at 1:33pm. The wind strength was dropping and the rough sea easing but drizzle was still forecast for Cook Strait.

We met our friend Peter McChesney walking along the marina jetty. He had just arrived after a solo crossing from the Marlborough Sounds. The sea was rough and the visibility poor, but his 34ft keeler had handled it well, he told us. Then he invited us on board.

"Come and see my shower." This should be good, thought Norm.

Earlier in the year Peter had invited us to go on his yacht *Nagu* and be part of the spectator fleet watching the America's Cup race at Auckland. He had motored out to the marked course and we had lunch at a good vantage spot, then watched the race from a distance as well as viewing it on Peter's TV screen. While we were waiting for the race to start I spoke with Jim Taylor, who owned the small trailer yacht *Just In Motion*, about roller reefing on the forestay of a trailer yacht. He and another yachtsman on board suggested a downhaul to control the foresail from the cockpit.

Throughout the race Peter had to keep his motor going, steering backwards and forwards to maintain his selected position in the spectator fleet, as no boat was allowed to anchor. We observed the hype and excitement of many sightseers on a variety of large or small boats. Then, after the New Zealand yacht won the race, we motored back amid the turbulence of the race boats and the spectator fleet. It was a never-to-be-forgotten experience.

We knew he had a toilet on board but hadn't seen a shower. When we boarded his yacht at the Mana marina he showed us a one-litre plastic milk bottle with four small holes in the cap. This surprised us immensely.

"Can you have a shower with that?" we queried.

"You fill it partly with hot water from your kettle then top it up with cold, soap yourself well with a flannel then pour the warm water over you by holding it up above your head. Squeeze it if you want more pressure," he explained. "I guarantee you'll have some left in the bottom afterwards." We were amazed but quick to see that this device would be useful to us too. Thanks Peter.

The tide was well out at 7:30pm when family and friends called. Among the visitors was our friend Ron Hubbard who had donated a VHF radio before our North Island trip. Yes, it was still working and used as a standby.

"We could be off in the morning," we told them all.

The 5am National Radio marine forecast was for northerly winds easing to 15 knots, sea becoming slight, then variable winds in the afternoon but drizzle patches for the Cook Strait area. We woke up at 8am and prepared to leave. Two other yachts were also leaving that day, but we were not sure what time. One skipper had said that 6am was too early for him and 9am was more like it.

Norm went to pump up the flattened car tubes from the two air bottles but found they were empty. He had had them tested at Elsdon but had forgotten to fill them. Fortunately we were able to carry them to the nearby Mana Dive shop where they were filled with 3000 pounds of air – another delay. It was not until 11:30am that we cast off. We telephoned Ivy Paul who once again wanted to watch us from the balcony of her Titahi Bay flat as we sailed away. We also rang our daughter Raewyn Te Tau, our contact person, to say we were off at last.

It was Saturday 16 December 2001. We did not know when we would be back, maybe in less than six months. Or would this trip be longer?

Once again we planned to read some chapters from the Bible and pray for God to guide us on each leg and to bless the people at all our ports of call. Our aim was to encircle New Zealand in prayer for the healing of the nation.

Starlight with sails unfurled in Marlborough Sounds, 1981 – no name and no sail numbers

right: Bernie Perano building the teak-based heavy main hatch and installing the screw-down front hatch

Bernie Perano (standing by stern),Sarah Perano, Jenny Perano (standing) Elsie Hughes, Anton, Alexander and Eugene Perano, with Mavis on board *Starlight* at Shelly Bay, 1 January 1981. The National Radio masts are on top of the hill behind at Whitireia Park

Starlight ready to leave Onepoto ramp, Porirua Harbour, 17 January 1997

Fresh water delivered in a wheelbarrow by locals while *Starlight* is resting on Horseshoe Beach, Hicks Bay

above: Norm on East Cape, looking over East Island, with a small launch going north through one of the deeper channels.

right: Sam Medland with a kingfish caught in the Bay of Plenty.

Norm going ashore at Castlepoint Beach (behind the lighthouse) – surf pushed the dinghy ashore.

Mavis taking a GPS reading near East Cape, 7th February 1997

Mavis with Peter and Gaye Cowan on Peter's jetty at Point Wells, Whangateau Harbour

below: Sam Medland with his daughter, Christine Ellis and her children Jonathan, Michael and Rochelle at Auckland

Reflections of boats berthed at Gulf Harbour, Whangaparaoa

Former Governor Sir George Grey's Mansion House at Kawau Island

Sails being washed and dried at Westhaven Marina, Auckland

below: Sam Medland with John Turner (holding the danbuoy) at Tauranga. The hinged diving ladder and rudder are pulled up

Mavis with Peter and Pauline Jesperson and their children Lisa, Mark and Joanna, at the Kerikeri jetty

Kerikeri Stone Store, yachts and jetty at full tide

Mavis with Jewel Sucich at Te Hapu Wharf, Parengarenga Harbour, on 29th April – note the reefs exposed at low water

Pauline, Michelle and Mavis overlooking the North Head shallows at the entrance to Hokianga Harbour.

Starlight in the shallow lagoon near the entrance to the Parengarenga Harbour – note the white sand on the spit and the distant hills

Rocks towering above launches
at Poor Knights

right: Thick fog at Opononi jetty, Hokianga
Harbour – Norm gets 10 litres of petrol

Motoring in the swells off the Hokianga harbour entrance

Alison and Bill Millar, Iris Platt and, in front, Ruth Pascoe with Mavis at Whangarei, ready for a cruise along the harbour on 31st March

Basalt rock formations – Duke's Nose and cliffs - in Pekepeka Inlet, Whangaroa Harbour

The Bartlett family and friends catching fish in Mangonui Harbour.
Clockwise from front left: Nerisa, Ashley, Mavis, Andrew, Jenny, Rob, Grant

Starlight stuck on the mud at low tide, Onehunga wharf, Manukau Harbour

Norm with tuna fish caught on a lure on the way to New Plymouth

Looking through the security gate at the Taranaki Marina

The tide flows in from the gap to fill this lagoon on Roberton Island, Bay of Islands.

Port Taranaki marina gate and ramp

Norm repairing a damaged stern cleat at Onehunga

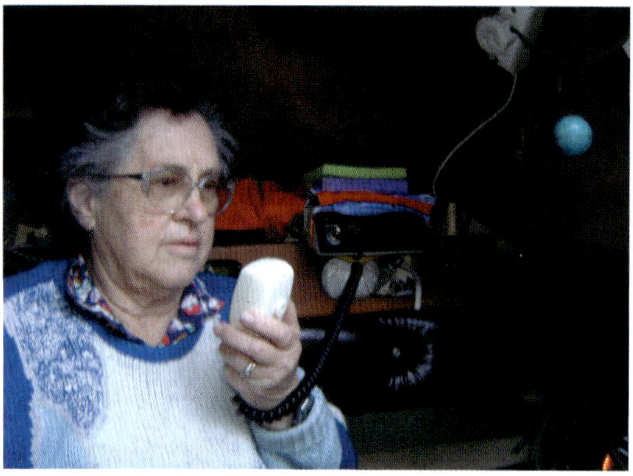

top: Sailing towards Mana Island, 19th May 1997. *centre*: Inside *Starlight* - Mavis on the VHF radio, Norm at the table. *bottom*: Approaching Cape Reinga, lighthouse on point and reef with surf extending northwards

top left: Mavis cutting Norm's hair at Westhaven Marina, Auckland. *top right: Starlight* before the spray dodger was fitted. *bottom: Starlight* on the Onepoto Beach, Hicks Bay, at low tide

Ken and Talitha Te Tau and Bernie Perano welcome us home at Onepoto jetty, Porirua Harbour – 19th May 1997

Norm scrubbing the hull at the Onepoto ramp

9

Marlborough Sounds – Nelson – Golden Bay

The earth with its store of wonders untold,
Almighty, thy power hath founded of old,
Hath stablished it fast by a changeless decree,
And round it hath cast, like a mantle, the sea.
Robert Grant

At 11:50am on 16 December 2000, we motored out of the Mana Marina. Jim Gibson's 34ft keeler *Jane Rhodes* was sailing just ahead of us and Chris Richmond's trailer yacht *Geisha* was near Mana Island. They had both waited for the clouds to lift before departing. Our line of sight was impeded by a slight drizzle, which left only two or three miles of visibility. The winds were light and although the genoa and mainsail were fully extended *Starlight* glided at a mere three knots. When we got down to one knot, Norm started the 15hp Honda outboard and we steered a 270-degree course towards Cape Jackson at the northern entrance to Queen Charlotte Sound. We were on our way across Cook Strait.

Low cloud obscured the landmarks but it started to clear about 1:30 pm. After a quick lunch I took a GPS reading and marked it as Cook-1 on the GPS waypoint record and with a pencil cross on Chart NZ 46, Wellington to Patea including Cook Strait. We were close to Fisherman's Rock and noticed craypot floats nearby. An hour later, the low cloud engulfed us like a fog and visibility was reduced to 50 metres. The fog also cut off the other vessels from us, so Norm had his foghorn ready.

I remembered an experience we had some years ago, while we were exploring Golden Bay and Tasman Bay. Soon after we left Puponga, at the base of Farewell Spit, to head for d'Urville Island, we were surrounded by a thick fog. It was an awesome feeling to be engulfed all day – no landmarks, only the compass and a transistor radio to guide us. We had no GPS in those days and we thought we were lost. We sailed on, not knowing where or when we would find land. That evening the wind dropped and we carried on motoring. Norm used our transistor radio to get a fix on the Nelson and Wellington radio stations. He held the transistor upright and turned it around until the transmission from

Nelson was very faint, then took a compass reading and marked it on Chart NZ 61. He did the same with the Wellington station, marking it at Titahi bay where the radio mast is placed. His rough estimate put us about five miles off Greville harbour on d'Urville Island. But we were not sure. We just kept going in a southeasterly direction, hoping to recognize some landmarks. While I was resting in the cabin, I prayed that we would pass over or miss the Beef Barrels, a dangerous group of rocks at the south end of d'Urville Island that are just covered at high tide.

An hour later I was still resting in the cabin when Norm called out, "Land ahead!" He had to quickly change course to avoid a rocky headland. I came on deck just in time to see *Starlight* passing the point. We found a sandy beach and anchored for the night, still unsure of where we had landed after twelve hours sailing and motoring in the fog. The next morning we headed out of the bay to find the fog had given way to low cloud and we were just north of Croisilles Harbour and south of French Pass. We had come right across Golden and Tasman Bays, passed south of d'Urville, avoided the Beef Barrels and had ended up at Pahakorea Point and Taipore Bay. Our charts showed us that we had travelled over 50 miles in a thick fog.

Now we were halfway across Cook Strait in the same conditions, but thankfully the thick fog lasted only an hour and a half. Then the sea freshened to moderate with enough northerly wind to sail again. We added ten degrees to the Autohelm course to compensate for the southerly drift in the outgoing tide. Although the cloud was low, we could see The Brothers to port and the northern entrance to Queen Charlotte Sound just ahead, flanked by Cape Koamaru and Cape Jackson. The wind died away and the sea calmed, so we dropped the sails and started the outboard motor just before we entered the sound. Norm checked our speed – six knots – and started the 10hp outboard as well, and with both motors going we made eight knots. This reassured us that we could tackle a tidal rip of seven or eight knots if we needed to. Once we had passed White Rocks and we were in the sounds we carried on using the 15hp outboard only.

We checked our yacht's speed with the GPS as the speedo was not working. We thought it might be a faulty connection – another repair job for Mr Fixit. However the fog thickened and low cloud engulfed us again. Our course was 210 degrees. The rocks and islands appearing to port were unfamiliar to us. Where are we, I wondered? Are we lost? Then we recognised the eastern side of Long Island. Motuara Island was completely covered by fog and even Long Island looked different with tops cut off by low cloud.

The Cook Strait crossing from Mana Marina to Resolution Bay had taken just over six and a half hours. We were a little too far east but we soon motored around the south end of Long Island and headed west towards Resolution Bay. This was to be our starting and finishing point for the circumnavigation of the South Island. We felt as though we were really on our way.

Pat and Graheme Sowman greeted us warmly as we berthed at 6:30pm. A cup of tea and a chat with them, in the dining room overlooking this beautiful calm bay, brought us up to date with their news. Several years ago we had taken Pat for a tour of the Pelorus Sound, visiting places that used water power to generate electricity. We had invited Graheme to do a leg with us as far as Nelson, but he was unable to leave the camp so near to the busy Christmas season.

Since *Starlight* was launched in 1981 we had called many times at Resolution Bay. Between 1981 and 1983 we did thirteen trips from Mana to the Resolution Bay Cabins, a Christian holiday camp. We brought supplies of wood, pipes, three hand-basins, a washing machine, a stove, a P-class yacht (and its trailer on the next trip), a sewing machine, clothes and lots of other goods for the camp. It had been an interesting mission and given us good excuses to do weekend trips across Cook Strait.

Norm recalled the time we were off Mana Island heading home in strong northwesterly winds and 40-ft waves. We only had the jib up but *Starlight* broached, staying upright as she slid sideways down a steep wave. Then the wave broke over us both as we sat tight in the cockpit, pouring water up to our waists. The yacht made a loud popping noise as the water emptied down the outboard well. Norm was able to correct the steering on to a course at right angles to the long close swells and bring us safely around the south end of Mana Island into the lee shelter.

We had a good evening reminiscing with Pat and Graheme, but eventually said goodnight and went off to anchor in the sheltered northwest corner of Schoolhouse Bay. The sky was still cloudy and only one solitary star peeped through the mist. The birds, mainly tui, sang us a lullaby and during the night I heard the owls' 'more-pork' calls.

The sun shone brightly the next morning and warmed up the yacht. The repaired dinghy expanded in the heat and popped the zip open, so after lunch we motored to the jetty, let out some air and used all four hands to pull it closed. We filled up our water containers with clean, soft spring water.

We were on a tour of the camp, admiring the new cabin and the garden, when news came through that a tramper had had a heart attack and died on the Queen Charlotte Walkway. He was the grandfather in a family group walking the track, and some of the group came back to Resolution Cabins to call for help. Police? Ambulance? Helicopter? Who would come? Coping with the tragedy would obviously take Pat and Graheme the rest of the day and the jetty would be needed, so we shifted back to our spot in Schoolhouse Bay.

Starlight sails in a turbulent sea between the headland and Cape Jackson lighthouse, at the end of a reef. The mv *Mikhail Lermontov* struck a rock here in 1986 and sank in nearby Gore Bay.

We were well sheltered there from the stiff southerly wind and choppy sea that had sprung up.

We could see part of the Queen Charlotte Walkway. It had become popular in recent times, with over 18,000 trampers a year walking through. They came mainly from Ship Cove where they were dropped off by mail boat from Picton to start walking. They passed through Resolution Bay and Endeavour Inlet, walked along the ridges to Kenepuru Sound, and finished at Anakiwa. Accommodation was available along the way and there was a good launch service that picked up their packs from one overnight stop and delivered them to the next.

We filled our petrol tank from the reserves and pumped the dinghy up from the compressed air in the dive bottles - but not as tight as before. The early morning birdcalls greeted us as we woke on Monday 18 December. We saw that several other yachts had found shelter there overnight and were anchored nearby. The sea was calm, the sky cloudy and the weather forecast favourable for our next leg, so we prepared to move on. We were at the start of our circumnavigation of the South Island. How long would it be before we came back to this spot? We did not know.

We left at 7am and were soon motoring north with Motuara Island to starboard and Ship Cove to port. The 15hp outboard purred smoothly at the stern. When we were opposite the Baker family's old house, I telephoned Raewyn to 'log us in' as we had mobile phone coverage. I recalled the splendid VHF radio service the Baker family provided when the mv *Mikhail Lermontov* struck rocks near Cape Jackson in 1986 and sank in Port Gore.

"We're going towards Cape Jackson, Pelorus Sound and French Pass," I told our daughter

"All written down. Love and best wishes for a safe trip," Raewyn replied.

The sea in the pass at Cape Jackson, was calm – no rips, runs or whirls. The new light on top of the cliff was to port and the old lighthouse structure, which marks the end of a rocky reef extending northwards, was on our starboard side. On many previous occasions *Starlight* had faced turbulent, steep and choppy seas here, but today the sea was calm enough to take photographs of both the old and new lights before we turned west.

A spectacular vista of capes, headlands and islands opened up ahead as we faced into the northern corner of the South Island. Even Stephens Island, to the north of d'Urville Island, appeared through the mist. Soon the sun shone brightly and dispelled most of the cloud. We put on our sunhats, sunglasses and sun block, and ate a late breakfast while the Autohelm steered a steady course. We noted the characteristic shapes of Cape Lambert and Alligator Head looming ahead of us, and it wasn't long before we were passing Titi (Motungarara) Island, a wildlife sanctuary, then the north end of Forsyth Island at the entrance of Pelorus Sound. We had previously explored this sound, with its many arms, reaches, bays and sheltered nooks ideal for yachts, launches and powerboats, in some detail in our powerboat and then in the yacht. We chose to bypass it this time, as we were attempting a much longer journey.

The 15hp outboard kept us moving at a steady pace. I took a GPS reading near Ninepin Rock on the southern tip of the Chetwode Islands. The yacht's speed was 6.5 knots and I marked this, with our latitude and longitude, on Chart NZ 46. However we had nearly sailed off the edge of this chart so I unrolled BA 1096, a British Admiralty chart that had details of French Pass, Catherine Cove and Current Basin. We also carried Chart NZ 615, Marlborough Sounds. Because the sails were down we were able to fit a cover over the boom to shade us.

We saw a flock of stormy petrels and several blue penguins on the surface of the oily blue sea as we passed Clay Point and entered Admiralty Bay. A southwesterly course put us in a direct line towards French Pass. The tide was on the make and going with us, with high tide not due until 2pm. We steered close to the French Pass settlement and noted that the petrol station still had pumps outside it, but we did not call in. We went through the pass with the tide, Norm carefully steering *Starlight* through the eddies and safely out into the other side. A large aluminium fishing boat followed us through.

I thought of the time in 1988, while we were on our way to Greville Harbour, when we had tried to go against the tide here. Both motors were going at full speed but we stopped moving ahead, the power of water against us was so great. It was not until we inched towards the centre of the torrent that we made forward progress and then it took us twenty minutes to clear the massive flow. A short time later a sturdy fishing boat came thundering by but it was also stopped as it hit the out-going tide. That fishing boat also took twenty minutes to clear the pass and resume normal speed, and I felt that our trailer yacht had done well. All this had happened on a clear calm day and I wondered what it would be like in a storm. We would certainly not tackle it then.

Soon after we had cleared French Pass a westerly breeze sprang up, so it was off with the boom tent and up with the sails. We only sailed at one to two knots, but it steadied the yacht. Norm started the 15hp outboard again but kept it at half speed. Opposite Croisilles Harbour I took a GPS reading and marked it on Chart NZ 614, Tasman Bay. Here we saw a pod of dark grey dolphins leaping out of the water and doing somersaults but they were too far away to capture the display on camera.

All afternoon *Starlight* travelled alongside the coast of Tasman Bay. I marvelled at the scrub, native bush and pine trees growing on the steep slopes that were once bare rock. The sea became moderate as we approached the boulder bank near the Nelson Harbour entrance. I called the marina on the VHF but raised the Harbour Board operator instead and got instructions to berth in the marina on the south side of D jetty. We found it easily and tied up at 7pm after twelve hours at sea.

We appreciated the friendly welcome from other yacht owners who gave us a hand with mooring ropes and passed on the security number needed for the use of the toilet and shower facilities. A hot meal and a warm shower restored some of our energies, as we were both suffering from sunburn and heat exhaustion, but it was not until we had a good ten hours of sleep that we felt fully recovered.

Our shopping list included 45 litres of petrol, some fresh food, a trip to the bank and paying the $10 a-day fee to the marina office. The petrol station was close by so we filled up first. The marina was over a kilometre from the town so we decided to walk there and take a taxi back. We had thought of bringing our collapsible bicycle to use for getting supplies, but even though it could fold up it took valuable space and we had to leave it behind. The brightly decorated town of Nelson was crowded with pre-Christmas shoppers. It was rush, rush, rush at every counter. We were not used to being away from home at this time of year but we managed to buy all that we needed – fresh fruit, vegetables, meat and a pre-cooked Christmas pudding.

The marina had hundreds of berths for small and large boats. We were invited to have tea with Harley and Diane Watts from Waitara who had a 15.8 metre (52ft) motor-sailer, *The Return*, moored nearby. It had been built on a slipway near their house on an estuary of the Waitara River in Taranaki. They told us that it could be hauled out onto a cradle. Some trailer yacht, we thought – this we would have to see for ourselves some day.

Norm finished making a small table to fit over the centre plate while it was down. While he was doing that, Diane took me to the nearby laundromat in her daughter's car. It cost $3 for the automatic washing machine and $3 for an hour in the spin-drier. That evening Norm's cousin Marilyn, with her husband Des Fielding and their sons James and Stephen, came aboard for a visit. They helped run the nearby Bridge Valley Christian Ranch for families and young people. "One group of 45 went out today and another group of 110 comes tomorrow," they told us. They enjoyed working with children and it certainly kept them busy.

In the evening I photographed the brilliant red clouds in the sky with yacht masts silhouetted in the foreground. The weather was fine and very hot but with strong gusty southwesterly winds and rough seas. We slept well, secure in the marina.

The next day we contacted Bill and Noeline Black, Norm's friends from his younger days. They were very fit, keen trampers and travellers who had even been climbing in Nepal. Their adventures made our tramps in New Zealand seem very insignificant by comparison. Bill was interested in Norm's brass band training scheme so we arranged to get him a copy of the manual book. Bill wanted to teach his grandson.

Norm purchased a small 12-volt TV at the nearby marine shop, but it had no reception despite extended aerials and checks on power strength in the yacht's batteries. It just would not work for us so Norm took it back. He walked to the shops in the city to buy another TV, but was unsuccessful. This delayed our departure until 12 noon on Friday 22 December. Gary and Carolyn from the yacht in the next berth, as well as Harley and Diane, bade us farewell with their best wishes and a piece of Diane's Christmas cake.

The southwest wind was gentle out in the Tasman Bay. We hoisted both sails and soon we were sailing at two knots heading 330 degrees. Then the afternoon sea breezes took over. They were northwesterlies and gusty. The calm sea became moderate and choppy. *Starlight* bounced and banged over one-metre swells as we headed into the wind at 270 degrees. This course took us towards Motueka until 4pm when the wind had veered to north-northeast and we were able to steer 300 degrees.

Although we were making three to four knots and going with the tide we sailed too close to the shoals near the shore. Bump, bump! Did we touch the bottom? I went onto the foredeck in very bouncy conditions to drop the genoa sail and secure it. Norm changed direction to avoid more shallows, and with only the mainsail filled by the wind we were able to sail at 330 degrees for a short time. Did the rough seas and those brown patches ahead of us indicate more shallows? It was time to start the motor and change direction to 60 degrees towards the centre of Tasman Bay and into deeper water.

It wasn't long before we were able to steer 330 degrees again with the mainsail filled and quarter speed on the outboard. We passed Pitt Head and cleared some green marker-posts that guarded a reef and some rocks. We had considered going into Torrent Bay for shelter, but as the wind had died away and the sea became calm we carried on. The mainsail was dropped and we increased the speed of the motor. Soon we were passing Bark Bay, Tonga Island, Cottage Loaf Rock, Abel Head and Awaroa Head. We noted that the area from Bark Bay to Awaroa Head was a marine reserve (no fishing or anchoring), so we were not surprised to see dozens of shags resting on the rocks and trees nearby. It was full tide as we entered Awaroa Inlet at sunset.

We anchored behind the sand spit at 8:30pm with the main anchor dropped into a deeper eddy and a stern anchor on the spit. The flock of oyster-catchers resting on the sand were undisturbed by our arrival. Powerboats were whizzing about the full inlet and trampers were walking along the shore heading towards the hut. Lights in one of the few houses nearby twinkled as the daylight faded. A few bright stars appeared and we settled in to one of our favourite isolated anchorages. We lifted the centre-plate, outboard motors and rudder as the tide was dropping. During the night the hull settled on the sand, and the lap, lap, lap of water against the yacht heralded the tide coming in again at 5am.

It was not full tide till 9:30am, so after a late breakfast we positioned *Starlight* on a flat part of the sand using another stern anchor at an angle to the first one. A slight easterly breeze and an outgoing tide made the yacht move around a little on the fore and aft anchors, but by 1pm *Starlight* was settled in the sand. We walked along the pristine sand spit and beach (no seaweed, debris or footprints) to look for Awaroa Lodge. We found a wide track that led to the lodge nestled in the bush, some 300 metres from the shore.

White manuka blossoms were falling on the path like snowflakes in a breeze. Brightly-coloured flower gardens, a sauna hut, umbrellas shading large wooden outdoor tables and chairs, and a heavily-built stone wall sheltered this secluded cosy oasis. The main building housed the dining room while several cabins were dotted around, all hiding among the trees. Trampers and lodgers were enjoying lunch and drinks in very pleasant surroundings. It was hard to believe that this luxurious retreat was so isolated. We knew that access was only by light aircraft, walking the tramping tracks or by sea. At several places along the coast, visitors could hire kayaks and canoes. We had seen them paddling north and then using kites to tow them south in the frequent north or northwest winds. What a way to travel.

By the time we started our return walk, a stiff northwesterly wind had come up making the sea choppy. We saw three aqua-taxis bounce in the rough surf as they unloaded and loaded passengers, luggage and supplies. We watched them take off and splash their way north through the turbulence towards Totaranui. As we walked along the sand spit, the strong wind lifted the coarse golden sand and it hit us head-on. It was like being sandblasted. We found the deck of our yacht covered in gritty sand, some penetrating the cabin. The tide came in and *Starlight* floated but the anchors were strained so much that all three moved a little. In the evening, the wind slackened and we were able to re-position the anchors so the yacht could head into the wind in the shallow water behind the sand spit.

The morning breezes were light. We enjoyed a refreshing swim in the clear waters just after high tide, then repositioned the two stern anchors, selecting a flat spot for the yacht to rest on as the tide went out. However the predicted strong northwesterly winds came at 1pm and blew noisily. The weather forecast for the Abel marine sea area, on VHF channels 16 and 67, was for westerly winds rising to 25 knots then a 15-knot northerly turning to 10-knot southwesterly. The outlook was for winds rising to 25-knot westerlies and rough seas in the north. We decided to stay where we were for a day or two.

An afternoon stroll along part of the Abel Tasman track, from the sand spit to the DOC hut, brought us in contact with many trampers. Some had booked bunks in the hut at $14 for the night and others, who carried small tents, paid $6 per night for the use of the camping sites. The tide was well out and many trampers were able to walk across the mud flats. This was only possible two hours either side of low water. I felt sad for the trampers moving on because they would miss the beauty of the clear blue-green waters filling the inlet at high tide. Although the weather was windy and cloudy, it was very warm. During the night the westerly winds were noisy and I slept intermittently in the double berth while Norm stretched out on a centre berth.

The next day was Christmas Day – Monday 25 December 2000. After breakfast we read two chapters of the Bible from Isaiah and then a chapter from Luke about Joseph, Mary and the birth of Jesus, refreshing our souls from these readings. We felt privileged to be in these unspoilt, pristine surroundings. Those in less fortunate circumstances around the world, as well as those living in or visiting the Tasman Bay area, were included in our prayers on that special day.

As the tide came in, the repositioned stern anchors were useless in the 35-knot westerly winds that blew big waves towards us. The yacht rocked as if a large powerboat's wake had passed by. Norm started the outboard motor, put it in reverse and dragged *Starlight* across to another sand spit. He swam ashore and buried a large log in the sand – called a 'deadman' – to hold down the admiralty anchor. The yacht now pointed into the waves generated by the wind and tide, and this new heading reduced the sideways movement.

After the tide went out, *Starlight* rested comfortably on the sand. We walked along the sand spit and beach to telephone our family from the land line at Awaroa Lodge as we were outside the coverage areas for mobile phones. Christmas greetings were exchanged with our daughter Raewyn and her family and also with our grandson Karl and his wife Noel who were visiting Wellington from Boston, U S A. We were sorry to have missed them.

We spoke with some of the 40 visitors from many parts of the world – Japan, Wales, England, Sweden, France, Germany and Australia – while we waited for Christmas dinner at the Lodge. Our meal was served at 5:40pm, and it cost us $25 each. This was a delicious treat for me as I usually cooked for twenty people on Christmas Day. We enjoyed a meal of ham, turkey, stuffing, salad and freshly cooked vegetables in generous servings, more than we could eat. We had no room left for Christmas pudding. The attentive waitress kindly clicked our camera to capture the moment for us.

A leisurely walk back to our yacht was timed just as the tide began to surround it. The wind and sea had died down and the sky had cleared to reveal a beautiful calm evening, quite a contrast to the gusty weather earlier that day.

The next day *Starlight* floated at 11am. We hauled in the anchors and motored out of the inlet as a smaller yacht came in. We had seen it stuck high and dry on the beach of Awaroa Bay, the other side of the sand spit, the previous day. The crew of two had managed to float it off as the tide came in. The sea was choppy as the northwesterly wind was against the tide. It took us an hour to motor north to Totaranui, a popular place with a golden beach, a motor camp and the DOC headquarters for the Abel Tasman Park. We joined four yachts anchored in the lee of the headland. We had a meal, then a very gusty northwest wind came funnelling down the gully in an otherwise calm sea. The tide was dropping and exposed the nearby rugged rocks, and we enjoyed watching several family groups exploring them. After listening to the 5:33pm weather forecast on the VHF radio, which told us the wind was easing, we decided to move on.

The north-northwest wind was still gusting and the sea became short and choppy as we motored north towards Separation Point. The tide was going against us but we made good time – three-quarters of an hour from Totaranui to Separation Point. I unrolled the next chart NZ 61, covering a large area from Stephens Island at the north of d'Urville to Karamea on the West Coast. After rounding the point the sea became rough but *Starlight* rode over each wave, some very steep, and the motor churned on at half speed. A large 'seventh wave' crashed over the bow and impeded our progress as we headed west into Golden Bay. Norm was steering the yacht and keeping us well out from the shore. I persuaded him to head towards the shore as I could faintly see the old quarry that the cement company had used many years ago (it closed down in 1988), but we couldn't see the tall chimney and found out afterwards it had

Mavis and Norm enjoy Christmas dinner at Awaroa Lodge, 25th December 2000

been demolished. The tall white Abel Tasman memorial was an identifiable landmark, however, and soon we could see the breakwater of Tarakohe Harbour. The leading lights guided us in at 8:30pm.

The wind was whistling straight in and churning up waves inside the harbour and the mooring buoys in the centre were leaping up and down.

"No way are we going to hook onto one of those buoys," Norm declared emphatically. So we found a sheltered calm spot at the end of the private moorings and dropped our main anchor. The rough rocks protruding along the shoreline were too close for comfort and I took a sounding using a fishing line and a heavy sinker. There were four and a half metres of water below us. The tide timetables showed that low water would be in eight hours time and that a rise and fall of the tide could be up to four metres here. We put out two stern anchors to avoid swinging, as well as two fenders on the port side in case we bumped into the launch next to us. We changed our damp clothes, had a hot meal and crawled into the bunk at 11:30pm, very tired but relieved to have found shelter after such a short bouncy trip.

I woke at 5am to listen to the marine forecast and had a peep outside. I was surprised to see that the wind had dropped and that the low tide had exposed very rugged rocks covered with sharp pacific rock oysters. However *Starlight* was floating in two metres of water and the anchors were still in position. Later we rowed ashore to put a rope from the bow to rocks on the starboard side and adjusted the stern anchors. We left the dinghy firmly tied high and dry on the shore and disposed of our rubbish, then walked the three kilometres to the Pohara Motor Camp carrying two empty petrol cans and a bag of laundry. Here we showered, used the laundry machines and rang our friends Brian and Margaret Sharland.

"Where are you?" Brian asked.

"*Starlight* is tied up at the Tarakohe Marina. We're ringing from the Pohara Camp," I replied.

"I'm coming to get you," he said and he was there within minutes to pick us up.

"I know the harbourmaster," he told us and took us to see him.

"I saw you this morning," the alert harbourmaster Colin Pettit told us. "You'll be all right where you are anchored." We were surprised that he had spotted *Starlight* and grateful that we were allowed to stay where we were rather than have to move onto a bouncy mooring.

Brian drove us to their house, where we chatted and had tea. They told us that their grandson had had an accident in Margaret's car. She had bought another car but the damaged one was in the backyard. Norm soon repaired the damaged door and side panel with a sledgehammer and a piece of four-by-two wood.

"It's got a warrant of fitness and it's registered," Brian told him. "You might as well use it while you're here."

We listened to the forecast – heavy rain overnight and 25-knot north-westerly winds, turning to strong south-westerlies later. It looked as if we would be here for a few days so we accepted the offer of the car.

While we were launching the dinghy, Norm had knelt and put pressure on the front hatch while it was propped up. Crack went the thick Perspex, right from top to bottom. Would it leak? Would it last the trip? I thought it needed replacing. I took exact measurements and we took the car and went shopping in Takaka. There was no replacement hatch available, not even in Nelson. The advice from a shipbroker was to ask Waitapu Engineering to cut a strong aluminium sheet to fit over it. We did this and it cost us $56.67. Back at the yacht, Norm unscrewed the hinges on the cracked hatch, filed the corners of the new sheet to fit, and used glue and longer screws to fasten it to the damaged hatch. It did not close properly on the old rubber sealing hose because the pivot point had been altered. After visiting lots of places we found a firm servicing milking machines and they sold us two metres of hose which had a smaller diameter and was very pliable.

"It's expensive," we were warned. "It's made in Wisconsin, USA."

"How much?" Norm enquired.

"That will be $10.16."

We thought this was pretty cheap compared to the cost of the original rubber tube. Our problem was now solved, and hopefully the hatch would be waterproof. I decided to use some pliable plaited rope to make a downhaul for the forestay. I tied the rope to the top of the jib and threaded it through the hanks on the forestay, over the roller on the toe-rail at the bow and through the guide back to the cockpit. This would allow us to drop the foresail from the cockpit without going to the bow, and also to tighten the downhaul rope as well as the sheet attached to the clew. Hopefully the sail would not flap too much in the wind and the hanks would not ride up and down the forestay if we had to drop the jib in a stormy sea.

On Sunday 31 December we went with Brian and Margaret to the 9:30am service at the Anglican church. We met the minister, Reverend Andy Thomas, who preached a sincere sermon. "Life doesn't come in cellophane-wrapped packages," he told the congregation. "King David and his family had problems and tragedies too."

We heard that Andy was a keen powerboat owner and we arranged for him to sail with us on Tuesday, weather permitting. That evening was New Year's Eve. We listened to the 2YA radio programme, *Sounds Historical,* and went to bed reflecting on the year 2000 and the many events that had passed so quickly.

We had a surprise visit the next day from Goldwing riders Maureen and Michael Dew of Christchurch, who were camping with friends at Pohara. We visited them later and were amazed at how comfortable they could make their tents with blow-up furniture, all carried on the motorcycles. Maureen mentioned how much she enjoyed my articles in the Goldwing magazine about our 1995 Australian motorcycle tour. This was very encouraging for a novice writer.

On Monday, the weather report was good for the Abel and Stephens areas but there were still three-metre southwesterly swells forecast for the Grey area on the West Coast. I studied the charts and books for our next leg and estimated that it would take 20 hours at six knots or 40 hours at three knots to travel from Tarakohe to Westport. The West Whanganui Inlet (also known as Westhaven) south of the Cape Farewell Light, was investigated as a possible stopover. The charts showed lots of shallows and mud banks. An old 1977 Pilot book, lent to us by Peter Foster, recorded some notes on Westhaven. "Vessels of 8-10 feet draft have crossed the bar – but only enter there at high tide in moderate weather and in daylight." Some locals told us that the tide rips out of there like French Pass – it was neither a promising shelter nor an easy entrance.

In the evening, two trailer yachts came into the marina and moored beside us. They were *Blue Inn,* a Noelex 25 owned by Keith Maydon and *Ceol Mara,* a Farr 6000 owned by Murray Watson. Both were from the Otago Trailer Yacht Squadron. They had towed their yachts all the way from Dunedin, launched them at Nelson and were exploring the Abel Tasman Park coastline. They only stayed one night but we were to catch up with them later on.

After Andy arrived on Tuesday morning we pulled up the four anchors and coiled in the shore rope. As we left, we saw Peter Foster coming into the harbour on *Reliance.* We waved and called out to him, "We're going into the bay for a sail." The northwest wind filled the two sails and took us towards the middle of Golden Bay at five knots. It was a pleasant sail. We passed a large area with many floats, indicating mussel farms. The wind eased at lunchtime as we drifted off Collingwood, and this meant we had to motor back, so we chose to go closer to the shore.

The car was useful for obtaining supplies of fresh food, water and petrol but once we were stocked up again the weather reports were for strong northwesterly winds. The four keelers moored on the buoys were bouncing as the northwest swells were coming directly into the harbour. Gusty afternoon breezes made boating in the bay uncomfortable. We noted that the numerous cars with boat trailers that had been parked by the ramp earlier in the morning had all gone home.

It was not until Thursday 4 January that we were ready to leave. The 5am forecasts for Abel, Stephens and Grey coastal areas were for fine weather, light breezes and no swell, but we would have westerly and southwesterly 15-knot winds in slight seas later on. Norm returned the car to the Sharlands with our grateful thanks. Our Bible readings and prayers for the people of Golden Bay reflected our thanks for their kindnesses, and concern for their economy as well as asking a blessing on their land. We also prayed for God's guidance during our next leg.

We left at 6:30am. The blue-green sea was oily calm and no wind. We motored north heading towards the end of Farewell Spit. I felt as though we were going off into the unknown, towards the vast empty horizon surrounded only by the sea.

Propelled by the 15hp motor, *Starlight* glided northwards and Fred, the Autohelm, steered for us while we had breakfast. Soon the trees at Bush End Point crept over the horizon, then we could see the white tower of the Farewell Spit lighthouse peeping over the top. We knew that the sand spit extended some distance eastwards beyond the land, and at two hours before low water we could see the waves breaking gently over the sand. We headed further east until there were no waves breaking before crossing over the shallow water to enter the deep blue Tasman Sea.

The sea was slight as we turned west. At 10:18am I took a GPS reading and marked it on chart NZ 61. I telephoned Raewyn and later the VHF radio operator with the message that we were heading west, then southwest towards Westport. Our ETA was sometime Friday.

We were about to travel down the dreaded West Coast.

10

The West Coast

All thy works with joy surround thee,
Earth and heaven reflect thy rays,
Stars and angels sing around thee,
Centre of unbroken praise;
Field and forest, vale and mountain,
Blossoming meadow, flashing sea,
Chanting bird and flowing fountain
Call us to rejoice in thee.

Henry van Dyke

A *westerly wind* sprang up and the sea became moderate. We travelled parallel to the shores of the Cape Farewell sand spit and motored just outside the breakers. We could see six four-wheel drive tourist vehicles moving along the sand at low tide and as we watched, some of them stopped near a high sand hill to let the people climb up to the top.

After we changed our course to 285 degrees, the westerly wind grew stronger until it was almost right on the nose. We had left the areas we knew behind now, and we were facing the unknown. My knees were knocking and my heart was thumping as my thoughts raced ahead. What lay ahead of us? Could we cope? We were certainly going to give it our best shot, but all our careful preparations and all the skills we had gained from our previous experiences would be tested along this long and rugged coastline.

We passed the Cape Farewell lighthouse, standing on higher ground (166 metres) at Pillar Point near the base of the spit, and steered 240 then 210 degrees. The wind was now coming from the southwest and it grew stronger with gusts up to 30 knots. The waves were breaking at the tops and the sea became rough - so much for the predicted 'slight sea'.

Norm was at the tiller steering, as the Autohelm was unable to cope with the turbulence. Large waves crashed over the yacht and drenched him despite our spray-dodger. I took over the steering while he topped up the five-gallon tank with petrol, and I found that the waves pushed the yacht around so much I was only just able to hold the course. I needed all my concentration to slice through the bigger waves at a slight angle as they hit the bow.

We listened to the 5:33pm VHF weather forecast, but it carried the same wrong information. We decided to abandon our overnight trip to Westport. Should we go back, or should we go into West Whanganui Inlet? Norm was uncertain. His grey, sober face showed signs of weariness, or perhaps he was on the verge of seasickness? The high tide was due at 7pm, so the inlet was a possibility.

"Let's give it a go," I said. We carefully watched the breaking waves near the entrance and crept closer inshore, reading the deeper water. We made our way slowly, cautiously keeping to the channel, and followed the flow of the incoming tide into the calm inlet.

It was difficult to find deep water even at high tide, but eventually we found a spot south of the entrance. All around us was beautiful bush right down to the high tide level. I sounded the depth at four metres – it would be just enough to keep us floating at low tide. We changed into dry clothes and enjoyed a warm meal before retiring to our bunk at 9pm, very tired and weary but glad of this secure calm haven.

During the night I saw a galaxy of stars and constellations shining brightly. One star setting in the west shone a pathway of light over the water directly towards the yacht. I recalled reading David Lewis's book, *We, the Navigators* where he told stories about the Polynesian sailors who knew how to steer at night by the stars.

A refreshing sleep restored our energies. The 7:33am VHF weather report was still the same but the outlook for the Grey area was for northeasterly winds the next day. The wind had calmed down overnight but by 10am the southwest wind was howling again, much more than the fifteen knots forecast. The sea, just visible through the entrance, was rough outside the breakers and breaking heavily over the bar. The extensive mud flats around us appeared out of the water at low tide. A seldom-used road skirted part of the shore and a small cottage close by had no sign of occupancy. Two farmhouses on the hilltop facing west were a long way off, and only faintly discernible. There was not a soul around all that day.

I used a fishing line to measure the depth of water under the hull, and found it was 1.75 metres at low tide. The hull displacement with the centre plate down needed 1.12 metres, so if it had been a full moon or new moon with bigger tides, which rose and fell 3.2 metres in that area, we would have had to lift up the centre plate.

While we were having a late breakfast the next morning we were surprised to see a fast inflatable powerboat come speeding around the headland from the south. There were five people on board, all dressed in wetsuits. They whizzed past us without a glance at our yacht and took the path to the open sea where we had come in. Through the binoculars we could see that the sea had calmed down considerably, with only a few breakers at the bar. It was full tide so we decided to give it a go, reasoning that if the sea was too rough we could come back to this sheltered spot.

We left at 9:30am and, using the 15hp outboard, followed the path that the powerboat had taken. We were soon out in a much calmer, slighter sea than we had experienced coming in to the inlet two days before. The southwest wind was light, only five knots, so we continued motoring and at 10am radioed the Farewell Maritime Radio on VHF 68 with our intentions to go as far as Karamea, ETA about 7pm. The plan was to go there and see if the lagoon and river mouth was navigable.

As we journeyed along the coast, it appeared as though we could sail 210 degrees on the light westerly wind, but in fact there was not enough 'puff'. Norm thought he could see a faint outline of a mountain on the northern horizon to the northeast. Was it Mount Taranaki? It had the correct bearing. Later he looked south as the sun was setting to see a brownish shape on the horizon. Was it another mountain? Then the shape changed – it was only a coloured cloud. We both had a good laugh.

We saw the powerboat that had passed us earlier fishing off the Paturau Shoals, and at 1pm we were off Kahurangi Point where there was a large lighthouse. A one-metre southwest swell, a five-knot headwind and a choppy sea faced us as we steered 200 degrees, and after we had passed Wekakura Point we altered course to 160 degrees. The rugged mountains were heavily wooded and fell steeply to the sea. We could see the lofty Tasman mountain range clearly, and as we motored closer to the shore we saw rata trees with their bright red flowers high up on the slopes. At 4:30pm we identified the bluff at the Heaphy River mouth. We knew this shape as we had seen it before when we walked the Heaphy Track.

The sea calmed down a little. The motor churned on at five knots with the Autohelm steering but the one-metre southwest swell still prevailed. At 7:30 that evening, we consulted the chart and looked for the mast that marked the entrance to the Karamea River. What happened next, Norm will never forget so he can tell it in his words.

"A large group of about 20 small grey Hector dolphins had been accompanying us for some time, swimming and diving effortlessly alongside the yacht. As we approached the entrance to Karamea, we turned as though to go in. We could see the small waves crashing right across the bar without a break; no channel even at high water. At this point we were travelling between the unbreaking waves close to the shore. Then the dolphins around us turned on their sides and using their tails splashed the water with tremendous gusto.

Water was all over the yacht. The sight amazed us. It was as if the dolphins were telling us, 'No, don't go in – we've measured the yacht's draft and you won't be able to get over the bar'. As soon as we turned out towards the open sea they stopped splashing and resumed their normal swimming beside the yacht. They probably realised that we got their message. How wonderful they are."

At 8pm I reported our change of plan to the maritime radio, and estimated our ETA at Westport at about 5am. It would take us seven or eight hours at a steady four knots to get there. I unrolled the next chart; NZ 71, Greymouth to Kahurangi Point. The sea became calm with only a small southwesterly swell, and at 9:15pm the sun set in a brilliant, golden ball. I slept from 10pm until midnight, and then I took over the watch while Norm slept. Fred the Autohelm steered the yacht about three miles off shore. The three-quarter moon shone clearly until 1:45 am when it set in a golden-coloured crescent, and after that there were only a few intermittent lights along the shore. The Cape Foulwind Lighthouse was flashing every twelve seconds, guiding us for some time. We were getting closer to Westport.

At 3pm I called for Norm to help me identify our position as I could see dim, shadowy shapes ahead of us in the water.

"They're like ships at anchor," I told him, but he pointed out they were not. We both knew that anchored ships would have lights on them. A brilliantly-lit settlement was to port of us and another bright light was ahead. Norm slowed the motor down while I took a GPS reading, checked it on the chart and found that we had gone right past the Westport Harbour entrance. The bright light I had been steering towards was on the big chimney of the cement works closer to Cape Foulwind. *Starlight* was heading straight for the Three Steeples Islands and some rocks off the cape, about two miles away.

We quickly turned *Starlight* around and headed back until we could distinguish the red and green flashing lights, at the entrance to the Westport harbour, from the multi-coloured town lights. We hove to and waited for daylight. As we sat there with the motor idling, the strong current was taking us swiftly south towards the rocks and we realised that our early arrival was due to the calm sea and the southerly tide set. We must have done much more than five knots during the night.

At dawn we could see the breakwater and the navigation lights, still flashing, as *Starlight* approached the harbour. The half tide highlighted the channel and by 6am we were tied up at an empty fishermen's berth. It was Sunday 7th January 2001.

We climbed up the ladders to the almost-deserted wharf and went ashore. We met a fisherman who told us to tie up against *Serene*, owned by Johnny

Wilson, as this boat was not going out for a while. After a large cooked breakfast we slept soundly for two hours – and we needed to.

The friendly fishermen took a great interest in our trailer-yacht and the trip we were attempting. David Arthur off *Crystal Voyager* saw us unloading our empty petrol cans onto the jetty.

"Take my car. The keys are in it," he called out. We were astonished at his trusting generosity. Norm drove the car to the nearest service station and we bought 72 litres of petrol, the amount we had used to travel 140 miles in 33 hours of running. We also replenished our fresh water and hooked up to the 240-volt power on the wharf to charge a flat battery. At low tide it was difficult to board the yacht, as we had to go down narrow slippery ladders at three levels onto the jetty and climb over many mooring ropes.

I visited the Harbourmaster and told him where we were berthed. "That's okay", he said, and told us that the river silt sometimes blocked up the entrance and it would take a big flood to clear it. Thankfully it was navigable now.

Later on Norm talked for hours with David Arthur – on health, fishing, religion and shelter spots in the Fiords. Fishermen Wayne Mangu, Denis Sisson (off *Dolphin)*, Doug and others came aboard. They were impressed with the details recorded in the Mana Cruising Club's guides to Fiordland and Stewart Island.

"You can get in here …good shelter there … lovely spot in there … good fishing around there … you can tie up here," they told us as they pored over the diagrams and charts, marking on them their own valuable local information.

"Where can we get copies of these books?" they wanted to know. Ours were too useful to part with, so we told them to write to the club. We were very grateful for their tips and encouragement even though some wondered at our chances.

"You're brave … Go for it … Good on ya!" And, most reassuringly, "You'll get in anywhere we can go."

We contacted Salvation Army Lieutenants Murray and Wendy Sansom and their family, including Wendy's parents Jim and Bernice More from Dunedin, and enjoyed a good sing along at a rest home. The next day we had a barbeque tea with them and they all came to visit us on *Starlight.* Norm even adjusted the tappets on Murray's Morris Minor van, because it had been running on only three cylinders, and got it running sweetly again.

On Tuesday Norm bought some more vodka for the compass, made a lock-down bar for the 15hp outboard bracket and sealed off the outboard well because water was coming into the transom. I did the laundry at the nearby fishermen's facilities, which also had showers and toilets, and walked to the shops for provisions. Jim Fern, president of the Westport Yacht Club, paid us a visit. He owned a Noelex-22 and sailed it at Lake Brunner. He told us that not many yachts came in to Westport, so we were a novelty.

The weather report for Wednesday was good, with a light northeasterly breeze and calm seas in the Grey area, so we left at 7:30am hoping to sail south. However we ended up motoring on a calm, oily sea with no wind. The journey was very pleasant with Fred steering the yacht. We decided to go towards Punakaiki Point to get a close view of the Pancake Rocks. The widely-spaced two-metre southwest swell and high tide created the best possible conditions for waterspouts to erupt between the layered rocks, but although we went within one wave of the rocks, I found it hard to capture the spouts on camera even with a telephoto lens.

Starlight continued south, motoring along about two miles out from the coast. We had a clear view of the steep Paparoa mountain range behind the lower-lying coastal hills. Several river systems broke the pattern and at one spot we saw a light rain shower in the gorge, but we had no rain out at sea.

We arrived outside Greymouth Harbour entrance at 4:45pm. I called the Greymouth Harbour Board on VHF channel 63, then 16, but the reception was poor and broken. The Coastguard contacted us and relayed the message that the bar was too shallow, because of big tides, and low water was at 5:30pm. As we were not locals, we were advised to heave to until 9:30pm.

"The quick-flashing blue light at the entrance is against you," they said. "It means do not enter."

"That's all right, I'll cook tea while we're waiting," I told them. We had caught a kahawai on a lure, and since the sea was flat calm it was easy to get a meal ready.

Very soon a fast tourist boat came by with about twelve people aboard and several kayaks strapped to the canopy.

"Do you want to abandon ship?" the skipper asked.

"Thanks, but not yet," I replied politely.

We watched them take off and noted their path as they negotiated the channel to the Grey River entrance some way off. We had just finished our fish and chip meal at 7:15pm when the fishing boat *Kutere* came by. The Coastguard operator called us on the VHF to say we could follow it in and we were delighted, as the harbour was totally new to us and we wanted to get in and find a berth before dark.

Our 15hp outboard motor kept up with the speed of the fishing boat as it lined up the channel and led us into deeper water. The swell lifted *Starlight* slightly as we followed it in. The *Kutere* swung from side to side as it traversed the waves but Norm, handling our tiller, steered the yacht straight, not letting the waves buffet us. I managed to take some photographs of this exciting approach. The ocean swells become high, forceful surf as they travel over shoals near the shore. I had heard of the tragedies of boats being tossed and wrecked in the shallow, unpredictable entrance to Greymouth and was pleased we had an escort.

"These fishing boats should have hydraulic tillers at the stern instead of wheels to steer with, then they could line up the bow and keep a straight course," Norm commented as he watched the vessel in front of us. "The tiller would give their boats instant correction. Wheel steering is too slow when you're riding the big, rolling surf." But I was not sure how this would work.

We could see about twelve cars parked on the breakwater at the entrance, and there were a number of people lined up watching us. We didn't think anything of it at the time but we heard afterwards that many local houses had VHF radios and these people had heard my unfamiliar voice on the VHF so they had come out with their cameras hoping to record our capsize. But we made it safely into a berth on the eastern fishermen's wharf between two fishing boats.

Some cars raced around the lagoon and stopped beside us, and we were greeted warmly by members of the Coastguard. It was their weekly meeting night and they had been hoping to get a ride out to rescue us, for practice. They chatted for some time while we attached long springs from the wharf to the yacht – very necessary in those four-metre tides. The assistant harbour manager David Stapleton came too, and offered to call the next day to take us to get petrol at the service station on the other side of the town. Two other cars stopped, and two boys on bicycles turned up. The boys were very knowledgeable about boats, as their fathers were fishermen. We must have been the talk of the town.

Our family contacted us that night by cell phone.

"All's well. We're at Greymouth. The coverage along this coast is patchy but thankfully it's good here," I told them.

An easterly wind, coming through the Grey River gorge, blew strongly all night. In the early morning we had to watch the mooring ropes because of the very low tide. Then, true to his promise, David Stapleton took Norm to buy 22.5 litres (five gallons) of petrol to replace what we had used in our ten hours of motoring since Westport. Norm topped-up the 3kg LPG gas bottle too. So far we had used only 2kg and it cost $3.30.

The weather was hot and clear but the forecast was for southwesterly 25-knot winds. Lots of people came to see the yacht and they talked and talked. We shared drinks, biscuits and sweets. Talley's facilities for shower, toilet and laundry were made available to us and we chatted to a dozen or more fishermen in their lunch room adjacent to the laundry. They were preparing for the albacore tuna season. They caught the tuna with long lines and lures on heavy rubber loops attached to two poles, one on each side of the boat, with six lures on each. We bought two rubber loops in preparation for the next leg. Perhaps we too would hook a tuna as we went south.

John Brady was on the fishing boat *Victory* berthed behind us. He recognised our yacht from meeting us in 1981 at Picton, when he had a trimaran.

"Have you had *Starlight* all this time?" he asked.

"That's right," we replied, "We had it built especially so we could sail around New Zealand, and now we're doing it." And so we chatted on about boating, fishing and life at sea.

Every time we walked to the town we carried our shopping back in standard supermarket plastic bags using handgrips made from one inch wooden dowelling, six inches long, with grooves for the bag handles. These simple bits of wood saved our hands from being cut into by the plastic bag handles and made carrying our groceries much easier. We knew that supplies would be scarce further south, particularly in the fiords. Our grocery list included freeze-dried vegetables, potatoes and meat, mung beans, muesli, tinned meat and vegetables, fizzy drinks, extra flour and dried yeast, milk powder, cheese segments and lots of biscuits. We topped up our supply of sweets, which included barley sugars, paper-wrapped lollies, jaffas, oddfellows, chocolate bars, peanut slabs, nuts and dried fruit.

We contacted Lieutenant Brett Harris and found that the Salvation Army services started at 10:30am that Sunday, so Norm took his cornet along and played with the five-piece band. We met Shirley Curtis and her son Tim, Jim Rankin and others whom we had not seen for many years. That afternoon Jim took us sightseeing. We visited the old Brunner coal mine where dripping water broke a ghostly silence in the tunnels that had been abandoned and closed in 1906. This was the site of the worst mining disaster in New Zealand's history – 67 men were killed in 1896 by a blast explosion and choking gas. It certainly made me ponder on the risks of working underground.

Jim also took us to Woods Creek where we walked through a forest filled with large trees, insects and native birds. The loop track took us past old tunnels, caves and trenches excavated by Chinese miners in 1898, when picks, shovels and blasting powder were used to drive through sandstone to reach the gold-bearing gravel. This was washed through a sluice-box to extract the gold – what a lot of effort went into getting the gold, I thought. The walk took about an hour and when we returned to the car park Jim made us a refreshing cup of tea.

While we had transport we bought two new 10-litre cans and filled them with petrol at the service station located two kilometres from the wharf, as I thought we would need to store and carry more. We now had 135 litres (30 gallons) on board. Would this get us to Milford? We anticipated sailing some of the way, but knew we would need to do some overnight hauls. Was there any shelter between here and Milford? Could we get petrol at Jackson Bay or anywhere along this long coast? These were just some of the questions we tried to find answers to.

We were waiting for favourable northerly winds but kept getting southwest fronts, which brought cold, showery weather. The fishermen were also waiting for a break in the weather. One night a storm blew at 50 knots and a fishing boat could not get in. We heard that they waited out at sea for three days and eventually went elsewhere to unload their catch. We found ourselves lashed by the strong winds even though *Starlight* was securely tied up at the wharf. The southwest winds built up a choppy sea across the small lagoon, pushing and bouncing the yacht against the wharf and we had to reposition our fenders frequently. The winds shook our boom tent and the rain drove into the cabin so much that we waited for a lull and turned the yacht around 180 degrees so that the bow faced into the wind. Then the wind changed to westerly, and the squally showers kept up all day.

Several fishermen and one woman stayed in the tearoom discussing the swells of three metres or more on the bar, sometimes coming from the southwest and at other times from northwest, that made getting in and out far too risky. "It is easier to come in than to go out against the surf," they told me, but I was not convinced. Weather fax maps showed a southwest front clipping the South Island and another forming in the Tasman Sea, so we were prepared to wait. Shirley sent some rice risotto for our tea, and later cooked us a chocolate cake. We felt very privileged.

One fisherman told us in some detail how to tackle the entrance to the Riverton River.

"Go in on the incoming tide, just before high tide, when there's six feet of water over the sandy bar," he said. "But it dries at low water and then you can walk across it."

He told us that the channel was marked by beacons, and we should keep to port. "There's plenty of places at the wharf for boats," he added. We thanked him and privately wondered if we would need to use his helpful information.

We visited the Greymouth Museum, which had displays of boats, coal, gold mining and sports. Then we made the mistake of watching a frighteningly-vivid video of boats crossing the bar in big seas, one capsizing in heavy surf with a helicopter rescuing the crew. It made me fearful but resolute – we had to wait until the sea and surf subsided before attempting to leave.

We paid David $49 for seven days berthage. He showed us the maps and charts of the area we were heading for, and then he gave us a depth chart of the Greymouth bar, just outside the breakwater heads. We had really needed this to come in to Greymouth but it was still valuable information for us to use going out. We made inquiries about the places further south.

Okarito had a sandbar at the entrance to the lagoon. At Hokitika, the pilot book recorded a railway bridge spanning the river half a mile from the entrance. The harbour was no longer used and all the navigational aids had been removed. Bruce Bay had shelter from southwest winds, and so did Jackson Bay, but the heavy swells made it uncomfortable to moor there. We found out that petrol was available at Haast, some five kilometres from the Jackson Bay wharf.

We realised it could be a long leg from Greymouth to Milford with not much shelter in between, nor were there any suitable places to call into and buy petrol.

We were still in Greymouth when we heard reports of storms and strong winds lashing Wellington, Christchurch and Hokitika, damaging some houses. My brother Kelvin Clark and his wife Rachel were campervanning in Southland and had hoped to meet up with us at Milford. He telephoned us to say that we were not to risk going to Milford on their account, nor anyone else's. They had experienced 140-kmph winds at Invercargill that blew the awning and rocked their van all night, but they were now inland at Manapouri in calmer weather and enjoying the excellent scenery. Another call came from our daughter-in-law Barbara and her son Morgan, who were walking the tracks in Southland. They were due to be in Milford on 22 January. We told them to keep in touch, but explained that the weather was holding us up. It was Tuesday, 16 January 2001.

We had several more visitors including Doug Sail, a reporter from the *Greymouth Star* newspaper. He interviewed us about the trailer yacht and our plans to encompass the South Island, fulfilling our dream. The resulting article, with a coloured photograph, made the Wednesday evening paper and – lo and behold – we had more visitors. Some fellow Goldwingers had seen it. Richard Crawley, who owned a GL1500, and Freeman Rhodes, who owned a GL1100, were both from Christchurch and they came the next morning with Kelly Briggs, who owned a 48ft yacht in Nelson. These three were on holiday together, travelling by car along the West Coast roads, and had been surprised to see us in the newspaper. They had to climb down the ladder as the tide was out and

David Sail, reporter for the *Greymouth Evening Star*, interviewing Mavis on board

Starlight was a long way below the wharf. Our conversation was about boats, motorcycles, touring Australia, campervans and overseas trips.

After lunch we walked around the Erua Moana Lagoon, passing the Coastguard boatshed, ramp and slipway. Then we went past the many fishing boats berthed on the western side of the lagoon. We followed the road to the harbour entrance so that we could see the swells, shoals and sandbar just outside. It was low tide and the one-metre waves were breaking in the shallows, but we could clearly see the deeper channel where there were no waves breaking. I was extremely moved when I read the many memorial plaques to those who had lost their lives on the bar.

Some of the fishermen were planning to leave on the evening high tide, but they advised us to wait till the next morning. By now we had been in Greymouth for nine days. Norm paid David the extra two days berthage fees and we checked and stowed all our provisions as we prepared to leave.

We woke early and listened to the marine weather forecast – calmer seas, lighter winds and generally much more suitable weather for the voyage south along the West Coast and towards Milford. We had a quick breakfast and filled the Thermos flasks. We found that there were lots of muddy ropes and fenders to bring in, wash, coil and stow away.

The sea was slight and the waves in the channel were not breaking at all as we motored out at 6:30am. There was not a soul on the breakwater at that early hour. We set the foresail jib in a slight offshore breeze but kept using the

15hp outboard to keep our speed up. We passed the Hokitika River entrance at 10:25am, and I took a GPS reading and marked it on chart NZ 72, Waiho River to Cape Foulwind. I noted the deep water of the Hokitika Canyon, where the fishermen catch hoki and orange roughie. It was here that the first friendly albatross glided around our yacht.

We enjoyed our lunch of filled rolls in sunshine and calm seas. Later we passed Wanganui Bluff and Abut Head, noting our progress on the chart. We were steering a course of 210 degrees. There were lots of Hector dolphins swimming beside *Starlight* as we motored along in a slight sea with a one-metre southwesterly swell.

We came to the entrance of the Okarito River at 6:30 that evening, exactly twelve hours after leaving Greymouth, and I checked the GPS carefully to make sure we were at the right place this time. The Okarito River drains a shallow lagoon and part of it is a sanctuary where the rare white herons nest. We went close inshore at high tide to look for the entrance. There were houses to the south of the entrance, some built up on a hill, and we saw a limp windsock but although we searched the shore we could not find a navigable entrance. We had to assume that it had silted up with sand and mud. According to the *New Zealand Pilot,* "…the Okarito River entrance can be used by small craft with local knowledge and there is a wharf on the eastern side of the sandy peninsula, but it is subject to frequent changes and is sometimes entirely closed."

Our next plan was to carry on overnight towards Jackson Bay where we could find shelter from the southwest winds. We contacted Fox Maritime Radio on VHF but although they could hear us, the reception on our VHF radio was broken-up and noisy. Still, they had heard our change of plan and that was the important thing.

By this time the southwest wind had freshened up and the sea became moderate. I dropped the foresail by using the downhaul rope. This fastened the top of the sail down to the deck level, and the sheet tightened the clew end. We carried on motoring into a turbulent sea with a two-metre southwest swell which we met head on. The wind was gusting at 20-25 knots and the yacht banged down into the troughs after each big wave. I tried to get some sleep, but it wasn't for long, and then I went back on watch.

Only a few stars were shining and there was no moon but the Heretaniwha light was flashing a long way off. The darker hills and shoreline were just visible. We passed a few headlands but they were hard to see or identify. I checked our position with the GPS at 1am, then had another short sleep. Norm continued on watch.

"It seems as though the dark clouds over the land are coming towards us and I need to steer further out to sea," he told me. At 2am the half-moon rose and by 4am the sea was calm with little wind as we came abreast of the lighthouse. We headed southwest for over an hour and then heard the forecast at 5:33am on VHF channel 67, predicting rain coming from the south, stronger southwest winds and rough seas. In the dim early morning light we could see large banks of clouds billowing in the south.

Reluctantly, we decided to go into Bruce Bay for shelter. I reported our decision to the Fox VHF radio. Norm had been seasick and was getting very tired, so I took over the tiller and steered towards the light. There was a light shower as we reached the shelter of Bruce Bay and by 6:30am we were anchored by a big rock in the lee of Heretaniwha Point.

The calm water was a deep blue colour and the friendly Hector dolphins swam around *Starlight* in a royal welcome. A cup of hot Milo and four hours sleep was greatly appreciated. The weather forecast at 1:33pm predicted more southwest winds, a change to moderate northerly winds, then rain. There was a gale warning – southwest winds for both Grey and Milford areas. It was quite a mixed bag of stormy weather. What should we do?

Norm suggested that we put the yacht on the nearby sandy beach until the stormy weather passed. We needed more rest after our tiring overnight trip and we thought that we would not have enough time to get to Jackson Bay before the arrival of more strong southwesterly winds. So we hauled in the anchor and lifted up the centre plate and rudder, then motored around to find a flat sandy spot to rest *Starlight* at low water. I put out the main anchor in deeper water and we eased *Starlight* across the breakers into the shallows by the beach.

Norm was scrubbing the muddy hull when a man and his two sons came along the beach. They introduced themselves as Bruce, Jacob (11) and Gareth (9). Bruce recommended the river lagoon so we followed them across the sand spit to inspect the river and its entrance.

Despite its shallows and some half-buried logs, we felt it would be suitable as we thought the sand spit would give us protection from the storm and give us a calm night. We lifted the anchor, repositioned it near the river mouth and tried to get into the lagoon at half tide. The river ran parallel to the beach so we backed across the shallow water over the small sandbar by using the outboard and easing the anchor rope. The ground was soft sand and the anchor slipped slowly, but the waves and the incoming tide pushed the yacht onto the riverbank. *Starlight's* starboard side was grounded on a stony bank, and more waves pushed her from the port side, jamming the yacht into a stuck position. I was busy on the foredeck coiling in anchor ropes and Norm, at the stern, had difficulty with steering the yacht. The motor couldn't pull us off sideways so Norm quickly donned shorts and aqua shoes, jumped over the side and tried to push the stern out into the flow by putting his back to the hull. He was not strong enough to move the yacht against the tide and wind. I thought of launching the dinghy and rowing across with a very long rope to pull the stern free with a winch.

I was anxious. Was this where we abandoned ship? Did we get out the tent and camp on the bank? Would our insurance cover us?

Then I looked up and saw two men coming along the beach towards the river bank. They had been fishing near the mouth of the river and saw our predicament. One of them added his strength to Norm's, then the yacht moved a little. I couldn't see Norm at all.

"What's going on?" I called from the bow where I was still coiling up mountains of rope.

"He's on board again," was the reply. They had managed to get *Starlight* floating again and as soon as Norm started the motor he was able to steer the yacht into mid-stream. We called out our grateful thanks to these men who had come to our aid at just the right moment.

We motored into the lagoon and noted the many half-submerged logs. Where could we find an anchorage? But it wasn't very long before we decided on a spot and the main anchor was dropped near a sandy bank.

"Looks pretty flat here," Norm said, so we positioned two more anchors on the sandy sheltering bank. Finally *Starlight* was safely anchored in the Mahitahi River. I realised it was 9pm. Where had all those hours gone? We heated up the damp cabin by using the gas stove, cooked tea and filled a hot-water bottle before turning in.

During the night the yacht settled on the sand at low water, with the bow up and the stern down in a hole created by the river. But *Starlight* was still upright. Norm woke up and noticed the 45-degree incline so he got up, repositioned two anchors and took a photograph. He disturbed my deep sleep so that I could turn around and lie across the double forepeak bunk without having my feet up in the air, and he spent the rest of the night on the centre bunk.

After a calm night, I woke to find *Starlight* resting on the sandbank in the lagoon among the high mountains of the Southern Alps. I counted seven peaks, all over 3,000 metres high. The highest, Mount Cook at 3,752 metres, had been visible the previous day but was now obscured by cloud. The massive forest of native trees grew right down to the riverbank. The main highway was close by but traffic was light, only a few buses, campervans and cars speeding past our secluded spot. The oystercatchers squawked noisily on the sandbank. The rain we expected came early in the morning, the sea roared and the mountains disappeared in the mist, but we felt hardly any wind.

We were outside the coverage area for our mobile phone, and when we searched for a clear station to get the news and weather forecasts, National Radio was right at the other end of the dial. Hordes of small sandflies invaded our cabin so we used citronella and fly-spray to get rid of them. We topped up our supply of fresh water by putting containers out to catch the drips from our boom tent as the river was mainly saltwater at high tide. (We found out later that we could use fresh water from the river at low tide.) We had heard that the river often flooded with melting snow and ice from the glaciers in spring, but thankfully it now had a steady, low flow.

We had used 45 litres of petrol in our 24 hours of motoring, and hoped that we might be able buy some from a local resident. We walked across a shallow part of the river at low tide, carrying our dinghy with our empty cans in it, then rowed across the river channels to a rough landing. There we met Carole Condon, who took us to her house in a farm truck and gave us a hot cup of tea and some banana cake.

We also met her husband, Daryl, and their three children. Daryl's family had farmed beef cattle, deer and sheep on their land for over 150 years. Carole took Norm to a relative's place nearby to buy 18 litres of petrol, while I used their landline and our calling card to telephone Raewyn at Porirua, Barbara at Christchurch, and Kelvin at Queenstown. Kelvin had left Milford that morning after experiencing atrocious stormy weather. Martin Condon, who sold us the petrol, had seen the article about us in the Greymouth paper and recognised Norm from the photograph – how news travels.

We rowed back across the river to the yacht with the tide coming in. Norm noticed that the propeller blade on the 15hp outboard was bent. He sharpened and re-pitched it, then put splints on and taped up the broken VHF aerial which had been the cause of our poor reception, and put out another anchor. We hoped that *Starlight* would settle nicely on the flat sand again, and looked forward to a good night's sleep in calm conditions. High tide was due at 11:20pm and we listened to the 9:33pm weather forecast which came through loud and clear. The prediction was still for rough seas and strong southwesterly winds, but the rain was clearing.

In the morning *Starlight* was stable on the sand with four anchors spread out, but the tide was coming in. The forecasts for Grey and Milford areas were for strong southwest winds, three-metre southwest swells and rough seas with poor visibility in rain. Even though a high pressure trough was over the central and northern parts of New Zealand, frequent fronts came across the Tasman Sea towards the south of the South Island bringing storms, high seas and strong southwest winds, with only a few lulls between the fronts.

We visited Brian and Eleanor Titheridge who lived near the riverbank. Brian was a retired crayfisherman and Eleanor kept a beautiful flower garden and grew lush vegetables in a large hothouse. They were able to sell us six gallons of petrol from their tank. Yes, the pump was still in gallons – most New Zealand petrol pumps had been in litres since 1967.

Eleanor took us to Bay Takeaways, a small restaurant selling food, drinks and snacks (but no ice creams) from a long caravan run by Bruce and Julie Lougesen. It was parked by the main road near the beach, where tourists could stop to buy snacks and take in the view of Bruce Bay. We supported this local enterprise by buying fish, sausages and chips, an unexpected treat in so isolated a place. After we had rowed back to the yacht, we collected a few smooth, pure-white quartz stones from among the many coloured stones scattered over the sandbank. We stowed our petrol away and settled for the night.

After dark the tide came in with a roar and the waves threw the yacht around violently, straining on the anchor ropes. What's happening, I wondered? The waves got bigger and the surge got stronger and there seemed nothing we could do but hope that the anchors would hold. From 11pm until 2am *Starlight* swung from side to side with the ropes tugging as each one took up the slack. We could hear the stones on the sand rattling against the hull – rattle, rattle, rattle – as we were tossed from side to side. It was pitch black outside, not a hint of light anywhere and we were thrown about helplessly inside the cabin. What's causing all this, I wondered?

We found out later that there had been a larger southwest swell, a rough sea and a bigger tide rise. How we ever endured those hours I will never know, but at 2am the yacht settled on the sand and we went back to sleep, not knowing what damage had been done but unable to do anything else in the darkness.

At first light we inspected the scene. Three anchors had let go and their ropes were well tangled, some around the outboard motor which had dropped down from the high-tilt position. Its propeller was buried in the sand. *Starlight* had twisted around to lie alongside the riverbank at a 90-degree angle to her previous position but she was still upright. Just before the tide came in we managed to untangle and retrieve the three anchors and their ropes, but the fourth anchor and most of its chain was buried deep in the sand. This sturdy admiralty anchor had held the yacht firmly through the turbulence of the night and now all our efforts to dig it out were futile. Norm took off the long rope and tied an empty water can with a short rope to the top of the anchor chain to to serve as a float.

We had to find a more secure place to anchor – but where? We motored up-river to find a deeper hole. The surges and tidal bores of the tide pushed the yacht around and the swift current going out made anchoring in the river difficult. My throat was tight, my mouth dry and my stomach aching with anxiety as we both worked hard to secure two long mooring ropes and buffers to a grassy but stable riverbank. The north wind coming straight into the bay grew stronger and the waves at the bar roared loudly. Some of the locals came to check on us – they had noticed our mast had gone from their view and they were anxious.

After breakfast another visitor, Paul, came along and advised us to go around the corner into an eddy with a little pool, sheltered from the northerlies, with a sandy bottom and very little current flow. We heeded his advice and took off, dropping the anchor near the entrance. We backed *Starlight* into the eddy and Norm waded out to secure a long rope to a strong log on the other side of the pool. Paul helped us secure two more ropes to logs and posts on the bank. The yacht was now floating in a metre of calm water about three metres from the bank. We knew that we were secure in this sheltered haven. Paul's local knowledge and his timely arrival before the rain descended was much appreciated.

That afternoon Norm borrowed a large spade from Eleanor so he could dig out the abandoned anchor while the tide was out. He dressed warmly in a Swanndri jacket and large raincoat, rowed back to the sandbar, walked to the spot, found the float and dug a large hole, getting half a metre down in the sand before he located the top of the anchor. He estimated that the whole sandbar had shifted a considerable amount overnight and had deposited all this sand to cover the anchor. I had a hot drink and tea ready when he arrived back, and later we took the spade back to Brian and Eleanor with our grateful thanks. It was raining steadily as we walked back and used the dinghy to board *Starlight*. Everything was wet, damp and cold. It was early to bed for us in that 'no movement' inlet, a luxurious berth where the tide coming in or out was barely noticeable.

On Wednesday 24 January the weather report was for a fine day but strong winds and more rain were forecast. I took the opportunity to do the laundry using fresh river water. At 6pm we walked to the river mouth to see the entrance and sandbars at low tide. That evening Brian and Eleanor came aboard and we enjoyed a cuppa, a piece of Christmas cake and a chat. Our yacht was a novelty for the area.

"Never had a yacht in the Mahitahi before," some of our visitors told us. We took some photos, little knowing that one would become precious to a local family as the man we photographed died soon afterwards.

Another front from the south was expected to pass the next day – light rain and poor visibility with a not-so-good forecast. Eleanor offered to buy bread for us as she had a friend who worked at Fox and lived nearby. It was a rest day, and that night we felt the strong northwesterly wind buffet the bow even in our sheltered pool.

The forecasts on the following day were for strong southwest winds and gales at Milford and rough seas in the Grey areas, so we spent yet another day in our haven. We were much more relaxed and refreshed after nearly a week at Bruce Bay, just waiting for a chance to travel south. We could go to Okura – could we get into the river by the motor camp there? Or should we go to Jackson Bay, to the wharf or onto a fisherman's mooring? Maybe even to Milford?

We visited Eleanor in the evening and paid for the two loaves of bread. Much to my surprise, she gave us a freshly-baked fruitcake and some fresh vegetables grown in her glasshouse. I was very grateful. We now had fresh provisions for a few more days.

On Saturday 27 January the weather forecast was for light northeasterly winds in the Grey area – just what we had been waiting for – and the outlook was 25-knot northeast winds for Milford. We decided to leave just before the high tide that afternoon. I walked to the houses to telephone our family by landline but everyone was either away at work – Eleanor worked at the local salmon farm – or had gone to a gala at Hokitika. I left a jar of my homemade raspberry jam and a letter for Eleanor, explaining our intention to leave and apologising for not being able to thank her personally and say goodbye. It would be some time before she heard of our progress.

We could hear the weather forecasts on VHF 71 but there was no answer when we tried a TR. Eleanor, when she read my note, would be the only person who knew we were going.

After retrieving our ropes and anchor, we motored out of the river carefully avoiding the logs and stumps. We looked for a break in the surf and headed towards it. Bump…! The centre-plate, with only a fraction down, had touched the sand under the waves. So we turned back a short way up river, spun *Starlight* around and had another go. This time Norm steered towards the deeper water. The 15hp outboard motor pushed the yacht up and down the bigger waves as we went through the surf and out into the bay. Whew!

As we approached Heretaniwha Point we passed two fishing boats anchored in the calm sea. We were not surprised, as we knew that these boats often used the bay for shelter, especially in southwesterly conditions. A crewman was sunbathing in the late afternoon sun. They had been tuna fishing. "Got a few," he told us. We anchored near the rock about halfway along the point, had tea and tidied up the yacht before retiring. The sky was blue, every mountain was clear and the sun, setting in the west, gave the snow-caped peaks of Mount

Cook and Mount Tasman a glowing pink colour. I took three photographs of this beautiful scene.

I had a refreshing shower, using the one-litre plastic bottle filled with warm water, and went to sleep at 11pm expecting to get away at 5am the next morning. But two hours later a violent rocking of the yacht woke us up and made further sleep impossible. It was like being in an agitator washing machine. We wondered what was causing the movement, so I looked out. There was no wind, but a light northerly swell had come straight into the bay. We had been told that a northerly wind made anchoring uncomfortable and often untenable there. It certainly bounced *Starlight* around.

"What do we do?" we asked each other.

"Get going," was the obvious answer.

Using the outboard motor, we carefully steered a westerly course straight out from the bay to avoid the rocks below the lighthouse on the point. Then we changed direction to the southwest. It was a starry, moonless night. I slept from 3am to 6am and it was daylight when I took over the watch duty. The sun rose at 7am over the high coastal mountains. We travelled about three miles off the coast and had a clear view of the land. Fred, our Autohelm, was doing a good job of steering the yacht accurately. The wind was light and variable all night but the northerly swell kept pushing *Starlight* along, giving us an extra one and a half knots. I checked our position every two hours, recording it on chart NZ 73, Abut Head to Milford Sound. Norm caught up on three hours of sleep in the morning, and by 10am I could see the lighthouse high up on Jackson Head on the south side of Jackson Bay. The yacht had been going at a good speed for eight hours, so we pressed on. How far would we get that day, I wondered?

The northerly swell increased to two metres and the sea became moderate. The yacht slid down the big waves as if surfing. Fred was not handling the backs of the swells very well, taking a long time to correct the course setting, so we used the tiller to hand-steer the boat. The pressure of water against the centre-plate caused some slop to come over the casing into the cabin, but no water broke over the bow and we were dry in the cockpit. The northeasterly wind freshened in the afternoon to ten knots and I unfurled the jib. The breeze almost filled the sail, steadying the yacht, lifting the bow and adding another knot to our speed. The GPS showed our phenomenal speed of 7.1 knots, due to a combination of sail, swell and motor. We were making good progress.

Norm pointed out the magnificent waterfalls that tumbled from the cliff-top into the sea at Cascade Point. We saw a cruise ship steaming north about five miles off the coast, and we enjoyed a quick lunch of sandwiches and a hot cuppa from the Thermos flask as the coastline sped past. Longridge Point, Awarua Point, Big Bay, Long Reef, Hollyford River mouth and Martin Bay were identified from the chart. We saw some rocks that amused us – they looked like the faces of people wearing green hats. We were getting nearer to Milford. Would we get there before dark, I wondered?

The waves grew stronger and bounced *Starlight* all the more as she sped into the troughs, but we were able to steer comfortably using the tiller and the now-fully-filled jib steadied *Starlight* so that she went down the swells without swerving. Very little slop came into the cabin. I took a GPS reading at 5:30pm and consulted the chart. We made progress with caution because there were a lot of black clouds hovering around the high hills. We were very mindful of the narrow entrance to Milford Sound and did not wish to by-pass it. I took another GPS reading as we passed Yates Point at 6:15pm. This reassured us that we were getting near the entrance. We wanted to avoid the rocks between Brig Rock, an islet 3.1 metres high, and the shore. We saw a crayfish boat working close to the shore. Even though the light on the point had not started flashing, I turned on the navigation lights because the clouds were so dark. The visibility had been reduced to less than a mile.

We went through the narrow entrance at 7pm in a slight choppy sea. The huge mountains high above us were enveloped in dark clouds and the sheer, vertical cliffs impressed us with their magnitude. Just inside the entrance we turned a sharp bend in the sound, passing the dark clouds, and suddenly we could see blue sky and fluffy white clouds above us. The dark clouds were only at the entrance. No wonder Captain James Cook missed Milford when he was exploring and charting New Zealand.

"That same black cloud must have been there for him," Norm decided.

The tide was going out and made a ripple on an otherwise calm sea. Two large dolphins swam around the yacht in a friendly welcome as we motored up the sound. The cliffs and mountains loomed high above us and we wondered how the moss, scrub and trees hung onto the steep sides. We noted a snow-capped mountain – truly an amazing sight. Was it Mount Pembroke, at 1999 metres, that I saw? It took another two hours to get to the head of the sound.

I had been really anxious all day about this trip. Could we make it before the next southwesterly winds blew strong? Would we get there in daylight? But the predicted 25-knot northeasterly winds never happened. It had been a long day but a fast trip, with an average speed of about six knots.

Even though we had been given details of the channel to Deep Water Basin, it was a new experience for us. As we approached the head of the sound (really a fiord) we noticed a fishing boat ahead of us so we followed it in. Red markers to port and green markers to starboard all clearly indicated the deeper

An albatross taking off from a calm sea in Foveaux Strait

channel. Then we tied up to an empty jetty, only to find out that it was a private jetty belonging to the boat we had followed in. Garth Haggetty on *Equinox* had gone ahead to unload his catch of crayfish at the main wharf, but when he came back to claim his berth he told us we could use the jetty next to his as that boat was out of the water on a trailer for repairs. Garth gave us a loaf of frozen bread and six frozen meat pies as he was cleaning out his refrigerator before taking off by car to his house at Invercargill. I heated up two pies – Norm's favourite – for tea. We were over-tired but grateful to have arrived safely, and in daylight, after 19 hours at sea. It was a miracle.

Our prayers that night were full of gratitude for the people along the coast who had given us so much information and hospitality, for the weather that had enabled *Starlight* to carry us so sturdily along, and to God who had guided us safely into the haven at Milford. We were soon sound asleep.

11

Milford

The purple-headed mountain,
The river running by,
The sunset and the morning
That brightens up the sky:
He gave us eyes to see them,
And lips that we might tell
How great is God Almighty,
Who has made all things well.
Cecil Frances Alexander

***Starlight* was now** in Milford Sound, the most northern fiord of New Zealand's Fiordland region in the southwest corner of the South Island. Milford Sound is accessible by road from Queenstown or Invercargill via Te Anau and the Homer Tunnel, and tourists flock there in buses, campervans and cars. Trampers also arrive on foot after completing the four-day Milford Track. From the head of the sound, excursion boats take passengers to the entrance and back, enjoying the huge mountains and spectacular waterfalls on the way. We had walked the track and done the boat trip back in 1992. We consider it to be the best boat trip in New Zealand and always recommend it as a must for visitors.

Now we were tourists once more, but the boat was our own. Over the years since our last visit, the fishermen's jetties had been moved to Deep Water Basin and the tourist fleet now berthed in a man-made secure harbour with lots of parking nearby. The ample facilities had access for people in wheelchairs and included a walkway to view the nearby Bowen Falls.

We arrived on Sunday evening, 28 January 2001 and I soon contacted Raewyn, using a calling card on a landline to let her know where we were. Then I left a message for Barbara Millar and her son Morgan Slykerman on their mobile phone.

I was in the Department of Conservation facilities the next day doing the laundry when Barbara and Morgan bounced in – a joyful surprise. They got my message in Invercargill and had left there at 8:30am, stopping only briefly at Te Anau for lots of fresh food; bread, rump steak, vegetables and fruit. They told us that light snow had fallen while they walked the Kepler Track a few days earlier. It made me realize how unpredictable the weather could be in that region, even in summer. "Would we be able to do a leg with you on *Starlight*, perhaps to Deep Cove?" they begged. From there they would be able to bus and launch out. Deep Cove was the only other place with public transport to the fiords. Elsewhere, people had to get in and out by private boat or helicopter.

The summer season was in full swing with over 90 buses coming into Milford each day. On a fine day, tourists could fly back to Queenstown in small planes utilising a special bus, boat and plane package. The aeroplanes were buzzing on this sunny day, which was a rarity as the fiords are well known for heavy rainfalls and poor visibility. Helicopters were busy delivering goods to huts and equipment to DOC track workers as well as operating sightseeing tours. Morgan, now 23 years old, was learning to fly small aircraft and I knew he would enjoy a scenic ride, so I took the chance to book a half-hour helicopter flight for the two of us.

With a whizz of its rotors the helicopter took off, flew us over the Arthur River, passed Lake Ada, and went close to some trees on a high cliff face. Then it landed on a spot at the top of the Sutherland Falls near the outlet of Lake Quill, a lake much larger than I had imagined. A huge volume of water fell vertically 580-metres down a sheer rock precipice into the head of the Arthur Valley below, an awesome sight with a thundering sound. The multitude of high mountains dwarfed Mitre Peak. Next we flew over the McKinnon Pass, looked down on the Clinton Valley and saw the Milford Track winding its way up towards the pass, a saddle that reached 1154 metres at its highest point. The time went very quickly. It was an expensive ride, but well worth every cent.

Later on, I was drying out the yacht's wet carpet when the *Milford Haven,* a large tourist boat, came close to our jetty. "Ahoy *Starlight*!" skipper Davy Bourne called out. "When did you arrive?"

"Sunday night," I answered. He said he had been told by his friend Peter Foster to look out for us.

"Is Peter here?" I asked.

"Had to turn back."

"Last time we saw Peter, he was at Tarakohe," I told him. I was not surprised that Peter had turned back as the weather had been consistently-strong southwest head winds and Peter, on his keeler *Reliance*, would not have gone into Greymouth or Westport for shelter. Keeler yachts rarely enter these harbours because the changing sandbars do not have enough water over them, even at high tide, for their two to three metre drafts. Most Mana Cruising Club yachts sail or motor straight from Nelson or Tarakohe to Milford, taking several days. It was good to get news about Peter.

There was a glorious blaze of colour at sunset that evening, high-lighting the nearby steep cliffs and mountain peaks. Then the light faded at 10:30pm to reveal a starry night sky. New Zealand daylight saving time meant long evenings and late sunsets (9.30pm that evening) in this part of the world.

The next day we decided to go fishing. Where to? We pored over the charts, noting the limits of the marine reserve. As we motored out, a stiff southwest wind came up the sound; choppy waves and dark clouds appeared. We motored as far as Harrison Cove where we passed a group of people in kayaks paddling furiously. Here we saw a furry seal basking on a rock. It wasn't long before strong winds and a moderate sea made us turn back into the calm of Deep Water Basin.

More steady rain and low cloud prevented the smaller aeroplanes from landing so it was much quieter, but the buses still came with their numerous tourists. Barbara took us in her car to buy 54 litres of petrol. We drove along the access road to view The Chasm, a tumbling waterfall and a swift-flowing cascading stream etching out huge caverns in the rocks, and then we travelled on through the Homer Tunnel to admire the surrounding valleys and large mountains on the other side. We were back at the yacht by mid-afternoon when the rain lifted. We all went in *Starlight* to nearby Sandfly Point, at the end of the Milford Track, and Norm kept watch on board while Barbara, Morgan and I walked back along the track. The Arthur River was cascading noisily over big rocks. We walked along the muddy track, enjoying the smell of damp moss and the sound of rainwater dripping off the leaves. There was evidence of the DOC workers who had been repairing the track using mini diggers. It took us an hour to walk to Lake Ada and a bit longer to walk back. In the meantime, Norm was entertained at Sandfly Point by some Japanese trampers who thought he had brought the launch to take them back to Milford. "Not in my small boat," he explained.

Thursday started out calm with few clouds so we headed west for our day's fishing, using the 10hp outboard motor as it needed a run. We passed several seals and dolphins and eight cruise boats, then went out into the Tasman Sea in a one-metre southwest swell and a slight sea. We surveyed the coastline, which was engulfed in a murky haze, and came back into the sound to anchor at Anita Bay just inside the entrance. We had given up the idea of taking Barbara and Morgan to Deep Cove in Doubtful Sound, as they would need more time and better weather to be sure of the trip. Morgan was surprised at how easy it was to catch fish. The showers came and went but did not dampen our enthusiasm. We started catching small fish, which we threw back, and then hauled up bigger tarakihi, blue cod and lots of dogfish which are really small sharks. A tourist boat came by and we heard their patter on a loudspeaker.

"Show us a big fish," they called out to us. Morgan held up the largest.

"Only a dogfish," he told them.

"That will do. It's still a fish," they said, and went on their way well satisfied. At 3pm the low cloud and steady rain made us decide to head back along the magnificent waterway – still beautiful in its shroud of mist and rain, with its many waterfalls and high cliffs – to our berth at Deep Water Basin. Of course it was fish and chips for tea that night.

Friday was clean-up day. Norm and Morgan repaired the navigation lights and pumped up the dinghy. Then Morgan enjoyed rowing and testing it in the calm water of the basin. Barbara and I went to the Milford Lodge, where the freedom walkers stay, to do the laundry and buy a few supplies but they only stocked small quantities of groceries and frozen bread. Back at Deep Water Basin we gave the on-shore shower and toilet facilities a good spring clean as a token of our appreciation. The fishermen usually left this chore for Valmay, who lived permanently in a caravan nearby, but as she worked full-time in the fly-back company office she had very little time to do it. Our efforts did not go unnoticed.

Barbara and I walked to the famous Bowen Falls, which were certainly beautiful with their cascades of water. Afterwards we spoke to the Fiordland Travel desk attendant at the nearby tourist terminal. I asked after Davy and the attendant called him up on the ship-to-shore radio.

"The lady skipper off *Starlight* is asking for you," she said. Davy was in charge of the *Milford Monarch* that day and we were invited to come aboard after the tourists had disembarked. Davy told us the working channels for the local area were VHF 8, 9 or 10. No wonder we had not been able to find forecasts or chat sessions on channels 67, 68 or 71. We also found out that the reception was very poor inside the fiords, with barely a crackling sound for VHF and national radio. Had we made a mistake here? Should we have splashed out on an expensive SSB radio? We wondered if our Venturer radio would receive news and weather in other parts of Fiordland.

Davy arranged to call us on the VHF later that night and at 7:15pm our radio crackled into life with Davy calling *Starlight* on channel 16, the emergency listening channel. He told me to go to channel 67 and his voice was loud and clear as he relayed the latest weather forecast. (It was still north to northwest 20-30 knot winds with poor visibility and rain.) I thanked him, much relieved that our VHF radio worked well at close range. We were told that once we were offshore we should be able to pick-up relay stations and the fishermen tending their nets or craypots, we just needed to tune into their listening channels.

We said goodbye to Barbara and Morgan on Saturday after they had been with us for five days. We had enjoyed their company and the things we had done together in this unique place, but now it was time to make plans for the next leg. We talked about how many fiords we would visit and how far we would need to travel each day. We had to consider whether we would need more petrol and more stores, whether we had enough charts and information and whether we should wait for better weather. I estimated the distances between the various fiords to the south – there were fourteen of them – then added the length of each fiord. If we had to motor most of the way from Milford to Riverton, my guesstimate was that would need 252 litres of petrol. Could we get petrol at Deep Cove in Doubtful Sound or at Preservation Inlet? I was not certain about either place.

Even though we only carried 67.5 litres of fresh water, that was not a problem because the frequent heavy rainfall meant we could catch rainwater off the boom tent.

During the week, Norm had made friends with Ray Speden, the manager of the Fiordland Lobster Company. Ray had grown up in Gore and knew our friend, Fred Collett of Christchurch, a fellow motorcyclist. He had been expecting us because Kelvin had telephoned him twice before we got there to see if we had arrived. Norm's years as a mechanic and garage owner came in useful yet again as he showed Ray how to sharpen his drills and advised him to use a 'borrow' book to record the tools he lent out.

Each time we walked along the wharf to our berth we picked up the small pieces of wire left behind by people repairing their craypots. The rain kept exposing new ones to the light.

"Do you ever get punctures along here?" Norm asked Ray.

"About 20 a month," he replied. "Why?"

"Should be a lot less now," Norm commented.

Trevor and Debbie Willetts, off the fishing boat *Solitaire* berthed next to us, visited us that evening and marked places of interest on our charts. They showed us the safe anchorages and good fishing spots as well as the rocks and hazards throughout the fiords.

"You must go to Dusky Sound. Don't miss it out, it's a beautiful place," they insisted. Although they had been crayfishing, they were now preparing for the tuna season. Trevor had 30 years of experience and Debbie had been on the boats for fifteen. It was still quite unusual for women to live and work full-time on a fishing boat so I asked her, "Do you keep a diary?"

"Yes, all the time," she told me.

"Why don't you write a book about your experiences?" I suggested.

"I will some day," Debbie said. I hope so, as it would be very interesting to have a woman's slant on life in a fishing boat.

The Willetts told us that fishing was very good in Doubtful and Dusky Sounds but that fishermen found it expensive to work there as the transport costs and isolation problems outweighed the benefits. Because Trevor replaced

Milford Haven on her mooring at Milford, with Mitre Peak in the background

the ropes on his the pots each year, he gave us some old ones. Norm soon had them spliced together and coiled in a high pile on the cockpit seat. The Willetts took their boat out every day, even though it was often raining and the sea was rough, to tend their pots, and they came back to tie up beside us each night.

Sunday was a day of rest. We read two chapters from Isaiah and prayed for the people along this coast that God would bless them. I read through all the information in *A Boatie's Guide to Fiordland* and *The Stewart Island Cruising Guide*. I checked the diagrams for possible safe all-weather anchorages, marking those ones with a bright pink highlighter. I also marked the charts with bright pink blobs so we could see them quickly and make wise choices about the nearest and best safe anchorages at any time. There were so many coves, fiords, waterways and anchorages in Fiordland, but some would be comfortable only in certain winds.

A large yacht came into Deep Water Basin and anchored by the cliff face. It was called *Southern Bear*. Later on we spoke with Chris, the skipper, when he brought his yacht over to the wharf to refuel. He had left Nelson in company with Peter Foster on *Reliance*. Both yachts had fought against strong southerly head winds and big seas. Peter gave up when they were off Greymouth and went back, but *Southern Bear* had more power and could make headway.

Chris had gone further south into Jackson Bay for shelter and had stayed there for three days in uncomfortable stormy conditions. He had motored all the way, and when he got to Milford he had to take on 355 litres of diesel. We were pleased to find out what had happened to Peter as we had been concerned when he hadn't arrived. I was also greatly surprised and relieved to know that other yachts sometimes needed to motor all the way. It made our own trip down the West Coast, when we had used 198 litres of petrol, more acceptable in these atrocious weather conditions. We are definitely not pure sailors.

The next day I rang the bank's 24-hour number to get our account balances, transfer money from our savings account to our cheque account and pay the Visa. I did all this by punching in numbers into a telephone, thanks to the amazing technology we enjoy these days. I also used our calling card to contact Sam Medland at Napier. He and his wife were planning to visit their son at Christchurch and then holiday with his family until March.

"Could I join you on *Starlight* again?" he asked. "Perhaps at Riverton or Bluff?" This gave us about four weeks to cover the fiords.

Trevor declared a day off fishing, and invited us to go with him and Debbie to the Hollyford Valley in their 4WD ute. Norm had cut his finger when he was making a draining tray, Debbie had cut her hand while preparing bait and Trevor had strained his back, so it was time we all had a rest day. It was also a New Zealand public holiday, Waitangi Day, 6 February 2001.

The day got warmer as we drove along a road lined with beech trees. We could hear and occasionally catch glimpses of the fast flowing river rattling over the rocks. At the end of the gravel road we noticed a swing bridge across the river. This led to the start of the Hollyford Valley track that follows the river to Lake McKerrow, where a wilderness experience house has been built by the lake. It is a place where visitors can use kayaks and revel in the feeling of being away from civilisation, but can still be 'fed and watered' in comfort. A very small aeroplane runway, like a gravel road, prompted Trevor to reminisce about his piloting days. I looked up to the high mountains and could faintly see the Routeburn Track winding its way along the ridge. I shared some of our experiences of walking the track, and our memories of when we looked down on this very spot from the lofty heights of the mountain ridge.

A stop at Gunn's well-known store and museum was a must. Murray Gunn's easy-going manner soon put us at ease as we yarned about the past and learned about the present. Murray was Trevor's second cousin, so he invited us to have a cup of tea with him. I told him about buying a pendant incorporating a slide of Mitre Peak, made by Fiordland Souvenirs at Riverton, from his store nearly 30 years earlier. Murray had been there all that time.

In the afternoon we went back to Deep Water Basin and Norm decided to repair the cracked outboard motor bracket on the stern. He put on his shorts and gumboots then launched the dinghy so that he could work on the bracket from below. Then I heard a loud splash – Norm had tripped over the ropes for the boom tent and flipped head over heels into the sea.

"Man overboard!" I yelled. Then, as I watched, he slowly came to the surface. Fortunately he was able to hold onto the dinghy for support as he carefully took off his gumboots and handed then to me. Amazingly, he still had his glasses and his hat on.

He started working on the bracket from the dinghy anyway, but soon gave up and climbed back on board to change his clothes and have a hot drink. "That bracket really needs replacing," he declared.

On Wednesday, Norm contacted Garth Haggetty off *Equinox*, who put us on to an Invercargill company called Pleasure Boats Ltd. They had a stainless steel replacement bracket and it arrived at mid-day on Friday. Even though it was raining we beached the yacht just after high tide on a shallow gravel spot near the launching ramp. As the tide went out, the yacht settled on the bottom. We held *Starlight* in place with three ropes and the anchor, and Norm put on his waders to work at the stern. He was standing in water half-way up to his knees, but I had the arduous job of lying on my back inside the quarter berth, tightening up the inside nuts of the repositioned bolts. To do the job Norm had to borrow a large drill bit from Ray at the Fiordland Lobster Company and this became the first entry in Ray's new borrowing notebook.

There was quite a bit of activity nearby and on the ramp. Kayaks were going out and coming back, and small powerboats were being launched and retrieved. Two large powerboats came in laden with fishing gear, and we spoke with the owners while they were waiting for their trailers to arrive. The five men had been away for five days fishing and camping in the rain at Bligh Sound.

"How did you get petrol?" I inquired.

"We had drums of it delivered by a fishing boat." Quite an effort, I thought. They were curious about our keel as the yacht was sitting upright on the hard, so we explained that *Starlight* was a trailer-yacht with a retractable centre-plate. Our type of yacht was not common in the deep fiords.

Norm had the bracket installed, and the outboard motor fastened to it, in plenty of time before the tide slowly started to rise around the hull. We had tea and waited. At 9:15pm there was enough water around us to make *Starlight* float so that we could let go the three ropes. Then we both pulled hard on the rope attached to the anchor, by now embedded in a deep hole, until we retrieved it. We cautiously steered *Starlight,* using the 10hp motor, back to the jetty in the dark. The high mountains and dark clouds hid the moon but the jetty lights guided us, and I used a big torch to locate and hook on to the mooring ropes as we slipped into our berth beside *Solitaire*. The day had been well spent and it was time for a well-earned rest.

We needed to arrange more petrol supplies. Ray told us to use some of his empty 20-litre plastic containers, which had held diesel lubricating oil, if we needed then for petrol storage. "The fishermen leave them behind and I usually have to burn them," he said. This was a real bonus. Norm cleaned out six containers and then Ray lent us his ute to drive to the petrol pumps and fill them up. We now had 262 litres of petrol, but where could we put them? I lashed four of them together, placed them on top of the flat front hatch, covered them with a spare waterproof boom cover and tied them down securely to the toe-rail. The other two were tied onto the seat in the cockpit. We now had all the petrol on board that I thought we would need.

The weather had been cloudy, misty or raining most of the week. One evening we noticed a small floatplane trying to fly out, and we watched with great interest as the pilot taxied off the water and flew along Milford Sound towards the sea, then came back again at a height of about 200 metres, just under the mist. He flew along the Arthur Valley but came back again. He was looking for a gap in the cloud so that he could rise above the high mountains and fly back to Te Anau, but he could not find one. He landed back in Deep Water Basin and had to tie up for the night at a jetty, but early the next morning he had gone. He must have found that elusive gap.

During our stay at Milford we saw several cyclists laden with camping gear. They were allowed to camp at the Milford Sound Lodge area, but campervans and tents were definitely discouraged alongside the jetty. Two German cyclists visited the Deep Water Basin, looking at all the fishing boats and the lobster pots stacked up on the wharf

"How did you manage to ride through the Homer Tunnel?" I asked them. "It must have been so dark in there."

"We just followed a car through and used their lights," they replied. Going downhill would have been relatively easy but I wondered about the return uphill journey. Perhaps they had some very low gears.

All week the marine weather forecast had been for rain on and off, rough seas, gale warnings for Puysegur and Milford areas with strong southwest winds and poor visibility. One day an unusually high tide made it very difficult for *Solitaire* to get back into the berth beside us. The water was swirling in all directions and the jetties were almost covered.

Our fresh food was running low, despite Trevor and Debbie's generous gifts of a freshly cooked crayfish and some frozen tuna. The leftover package lunches from the various tours were dropped off at the DOC facilities for the fishermen (and us) to help ourselves. They included filled rolls, chicken legs, apple turnovers, cheese and crackers, and these tasty delights kept us going for several days. I noticed a fishing boat with a large box of fresh fruit and vegetables on the deck, so I asked Ray Speden how we could get supplies from the supermarket at Te Anau.

"Is there a bus I could catch? Or is there a service for the fishermen?"

"The buses come in the morning and go out in the afternoon, but I'm going home to Te Anau this afternoon," he told me. "I'll do your shopping."

I was surprised and delighted. I quickly wrote out a long list of items and gave him $100, and a few hours later he was back with all the stores and the change.

"You can do my shopping any day," I told him gratefully. Later on we met his wife, Raye Speden, when she visited the lobster depot. We found that we shared many interests and we talked for hours.

Valmay Coker, Ray and Raye Speden at Deep Water Basin, Milford.

The weather was settling down and the sea was much calmer. We used the shore power to charge up all the batteries and we stored more water. We had a good supply of food, including some frozen bread, ready for the next leg. Norm connected the Venturer radio to the backstay using speaker wire. The backstay had two insulators, one at each end, and this greatly improved our radio reception. We could now hear the National Radio station and get the 5am marine forecast and the 12:30pm five-day forecasts.

It was time for us to move on. I had enjoyed our time in Milford Sound, the most northern fiord in New Zealand's largest park. (Fiordland is a 1.2 million hectare world heritage park.) Now I was looking forward to exploring the rest of the fourteen great glacier-carved fiords with their rugged, steep-sided mountains, often tree-clad, in pristine condition and unchanged by human intrusion. I wondered how many fiords and inlets we would enter, where we would anchor and what the weather would be like inside the fiords or along the wind-swept west coast with its high sea swells beating onto the rugged shoreline.

On Sunday 11 February the weather report was promising, with a good outlook, but we were uncertain until Trevor contacted us on the VHF. He was crayfishing outside the sound in clear, calm weather with just a low cloud hovering above.

"You'll be okay in this," he told us. We donned our wet-weather gear, said goodbye to Ray, gave him a cheque for the DOC facility fees and thanked him for all his help, then motored along Milford Sound in damp drizzly conditions. Soon the mist lifted and we were out in the calm open sea. We had spent fourteen memorable days in Milford Sound but now we were back on our journey, encompassing New Zealand on *Starlight*. We wondered how long it would be before we went ashore again. What was in store for us this time?

12

Fiordland

When through the woods and forest glades
I wander and hear the birds sing sweetly
in the trees,
When I look down from lofty mountain grandeur
and hear the brook and feel the gentle breeze:
Then sings my soul, my Saviour God, to thee:
How great thou art! How great thou art!
Carl Boberg

We motored out of Milford Sound to face the open sea, wondering what lay ahead. The waves were moderate with three-metre high, widely spaced southwest swells. There was very little wind, and although there was low cloud coverage we had clear visibility at sea level. We headed southwest, noting the headlands and keeping about two miles off the coast. *Starlight* climbed up the swells, slid down the backs of the waves and glided along the troughs effortlessly. The 15hp outboard easily propelled the yacht along at five knots. The big swells crashed against the rugged shoreline making huge pounding splashes on the protruding rocks. Using chart NZ 7413, George, Bligh and Milford sounds, we identified and passed Poison Bay, Sutherland Sound and Bligh Sound, then at 5pm we entered George Sound.

Once inside the fiord, the sea swell soon diminished to only a slight push. We noted the dark coloured water caused by the tannin in the fresh water flowing from the bush and floating on top of the seawater. Blue-nosed dolphins and seals greeted us as we travelled south in this beautiful sound, surrounded by high bush-clad hills. I consulted the detailed and helpful sketch of George Sound in *A Boatie's Guide to Fiordland.* As we passed Anchorage Cove and headed further into the fiord, the swell disappeared and the water surface became like a shiny-black mirror.

Everything was perfectly reflected. The clouds obscured the sun and the diffused light made no shadows. The shore had a one-metre band of green moss and another one-metre band of yellow moss below it. Each band was reflected – green, yellow, yellow, green – and it was difficult to tell where the sea ended and the land began. After we passed the South West Arm, I went to the bow to keep a lookout for a submerged rock marked on the chart. It was impossible to see anything below the surface in such a shiny-black sea, with no breaking or moving water to indicate a rock. The hills were perfectly reflected in the completely still water. I was awed by the scene, which continued for about fifteen minutes as one small headland after another came into view.

Where was that rock? We kept close to the shore and missed it. Soon we were rounding the last knob and there in front of us was the Alice Falls with water cascading down huge boulders like a big staircase. Wow – what a picture. A large wide path of tumbling white water fell from a height of 56 metres, bouncing over rocks and between tall trees and bushes to flow into the sound.

Just beyond the falls was a sheltered cove with a mooring float and ropes in perfectly calm water. This was our spot for the night. But in all the excitement and allure of the splendid scene I had forgotten to take a photograph. "We'll get one in the morning," Norm reassured me.

Sandflies in their thousands greeted us. Norm waged war on them with a can of fly spray and soon *Starlight* was covered with black blobs. Our Venturer radio, now hooked up to the backstay aerial, produced a variety of stations in the evening; an Australia station sending out Pacific News from Melbourne, the BBC, a German station, the Voice of America. Eventually we found our own New Zealand National Programme. Before we went to bed we were pleased to see the three-quarter moon and a few stars shining in the night sky.

The 5am weather forecast was good, with favourable 15-knot southeast winds and moderate sea, but there was still a two-metre southwest swell. We decided to untie the ropes and be off again. The morning breeze had ruffled up the water, which put paid to my early morning reflection photograph, but the imprint will always stay with me in my memory.

At last we had enough wind to sail. Both sails were unfurled as we headed north along George Sound. The wind was fickle – light, then strong, from this direction and that. Halfway down the sound we had a knockdown. I quickly dropped the jib, using the downhaul rope, while Norm steered the yacht around a full circle into the wind which soon subsided to almost nothing.

We kept the mainsail up to steady *Starlight* as we motored out of the sound and turned south again. We came across several craypot floats and many large patches of thick foamy salt-drifts. We had to avoid several acres of the stuff. The big swells that pounded the rocks produced this phenomenon – we were later told that the foam could be meerschaum clay. We identified headlands and bays from our chart NZ 76, Western Approaches to Foveaux Strait, which covered a wide area from Caswell Sound to the west coast of Stewart Island. We also used the more detailed chart NZ 7522, Caswell Sound to Dagg Sound and we noted many rocks and some small islands near the shore. There were steep mountains, mostly covered with wind and sea-beaten vegetation, and small reefs jutting out into the sea. The two-metre swells became three and then four-metre swells but were still far apart and we had a comfortable ride over them with the mainsail aloft. The sun was shining and it warmed our backs as we travelled south. We identified the narrow entrance to Caswell Sound but passed it by.

Shortly after this, the sea became rough and bouncy so we decided to motor into Charles Sound and find a calm spot to have lunch. We lowered the mainsail, turned off the outboard and drifted with the tide as we enjoyed our meal in this magnificent peaceful fiord.

We headed out into the Tasman Sea again and at 4pm we passed Nancy Sound, noting its small rocky entrance. We motored on. Colonial Headland, on the northern tip of Secretary Island, was a clearly identifiable landmark and indicated the entrance to Thompson Sound, but we had to dodge numerous craypot floats. The four-metre swells became closer together and we had to watch out carefully for the reef near the entrance – waves were crashing over it at half tide. *Starlight* handled this confused sea very well. We travelled along the sound in calm water until we came abreast with Deas Cove, and kept well clear of a reef protruding from the headland before entering the calm sanctuary.

An immaculate fibreglass fishing boat named *Exporta*, owned by Jerry Exell, was tied up to the mooring, so we hooked on to a very heavy stern rope that went some distance to a tree on the shore. *Exporta*'s skipper was using a dinghy to wash the dirty waterline on his boat.

"Those four-metre swells out there were a bit too much for me, so I finished checking the craypots early," he told us. He had an SSB radio so we asked him to contact Carol Brown of Fiordland Radio and let her know that we had arrived there safely after two days out from Milford.

Early the next morning he motored out but we didn't hear a sound. The weather report was for clear skies but northerlies up to 40 knots in the Milford coastal area. Heavy dew left everything on the deck very wet, so after a late breakfast we tidied up the yacht with the sun shining and blue-sky overhead. At 11am misty cloud and a light wind stirred the peaceful scene.

"Is that just a breeze or can I see gusty wind and rain clouds?" I wondered as we stared towards the north. "Let's cast off and sail," Norm agreed. Yes, there was enough wind to hoist the jib and head south along Thompson Sound. *Starlight* took one and a half hours with only the jib unfurled and the tide pushing it to reach Common Head on the southeast corner of Separation Island. *Starlight* sped along at four knots. We passed Bradshaw Sound and headed towards Doubtful Sound.The wind eased but the tide rip, between the headland and Seymour Island, pushed the yacht gently south instead of going southwest. Without any way on, steering was difficult and we had to take action to avoid the rocky shore. Norm reluctantly started the motor and steered *Starlight* into the Malaspina Reach. From here we could see the steep-sided and rugged First Arm ahead of us.

We turned southeast and waved to the sightseers as they passed us on a fast catamaran and a multi-coloured powerboat. These fast boats usually covered the vast and varied Doubtful Sound with its three deep arms in a few hours, as well as taking a look at the open sea. The passengers hoped for a glimpse of dolphins or whales.

Next we passed Crooked Arm, noting the bush-clad entrance. The wind gusted to 30 knots as we came close to Fergusson Island on our port side. We were astonished when Browne Falls came into view high up on the hills to starboard. It was like a huge river of white water tumbling down the steep mountainsides – an incredible sight.

We soon passed Elizabeth Island to port and then the entrance to Hall Arm opened up to starboard. At 2:40pm the tourist catamaran passed us again, heading for Deep Cove. It quickly disembarked its passengers, embarked more visitors and at 3pm was heading out for another tour of Doubtful Sound, passing our much slower yacht for the third time.

At last we arrived at the fuel wharf hoping to get petrol but only bulk diesel was available for cardholders. I went ashore and walked along the deserted wharf and the dusty road in warm sunshine until I came to the hostel manager's house. I asked him about buying petrol.

"There's some coming soon," he explained. "It comes in from Te Anau across Lake Manapouri on a barge, then it's freighted to Deep Cove." He arranged for us to get petrol on Friday. He also mentioned that the skipper of *Southern Bear*, which had left only that morning, had told him to look out for us in our trailer yacht.

The operator on the multi-coloured powerboat came in, unloaded his passengers by the ramp and took his boat to a mooring. He returned in a dingy, loaded up his van with gear and people, then headed off over the Wilmot Pass road to Lake Manapouri. From there a launch service would take them across the lake to the Manapouri settlement and the road links.

Eventually I found someone who could give us permission to tie up alongside *Alert II*, a 60-ft carvel-built wooden launch on a mooring. I walked back to *Starlight* and we motored the short distance across to the mooring and tied up. From the number of fenders and ropes dangling on the starboard side of *Alert II,* we worked out this was a common event. We had tea and settled for the night in this cosy spot along the tree-lined shore, shared with the usual thousand sandflies. Norm heard the weather forecast on the radio, which had a surprisingly good clear reception. "Heavy rain in Fiordland, heading north," the forecaster told us cheerfully, so we erected the boom-tent in anticipation of a downpour.

The next morning, Wednesday 14 January, the crew of *Alert II* came back and said we could use their mooring until Sunday. While they untied their ropes, we let go and motored out into the cove, then we came back to pick up their strong bow and stern buoys and tie up to them. The heavy rain falling on our boom tent soon filled all our water containers. We noticed the Helena Falls and other waterfalls around us tumbling and roaring. The small creek nearby became a rushing river and water splashed over its rocks at low tide, then into the fiord.

I sewed up a green fine-meshed net to fit the rear hatch, hoping that the sandflies would stay outside. We mixed up a concoction of half Dettol, half baby oil and a teaspoon of kerosene in a small bottle to use on our bare skins. This seemed to keep them off us, but Norm sprayed them again and again until our yacht was polka-dotted with black spots on the yellow deck and cockpit.

The VHF radio was not receiving or sending, so Norm joined a piece of extension wire from the radio to its aerial and hoisted the aerial up the mast using the spinnaker ropes. After 7pm we called the hostel manager on channel 10 and he came through loud and clear, not surprising as the hostel was only a few metres away. Hopefully we could get other listeners on the VHF while we were out at sea. During the night I looked out and saw the clouds parting with a small moon shining, but most of the light was coming from the tailrace area hidden behind some trees. What was going on there? I knew that a tunnel had been completed in 1969 to take water from Lake Manapouri through a hydro-electric generation plant built deep in the mountains, with the outflow spilling into Deep Cove. Now a second tunnel was being drilled to utilise the same water for more electricity. Were they working on the second tunnel during the night, I wondered.

Heavy rain again, but the tour boats ran despite the rain. Our mooring was secure and the surface water only joggled us a little, probably due to the tide turbulence and from the stream or tailrace spilling water into Deep Cove. The temperature was a mild 15 to 18 degree Celsius and there was no wind. The birds, mainly tui, sang us lovely songs even in the rain. We could peep out and see a large seal sitting on the nearby jetty. I prepared a meal of ham and pineapple casserole with carrots and onions, cooked in the fry pan with the lid on, with potatoes and pumpkin in a saucepan and cabbage in a steamer on top. All this was cooked on the two-burner gas stove. We finished our evening meal with a cup of tea and a piece of fruitcake. Yes, my Christmas cake had lasted over two months and still tasted yummy. Norm often remarks when I serve a meal in *Starlight* that, "It's a great place to have a picnic." Our Venturer radio had six channels and Norm soon found a variety of stations from Australia, Germany, Holland, Voice of America and Serbia giving out international news. But the New Zealand National Programme was faint at midday and we only just heard the five-day weather forecast. The rain was clearing on Friday for the West Coast and Fiordland areas, there would be showers on Saturday with westerly winds, but a ridge of high pressure was expected over New Zealand from Sunday to Tuesday, bringing fine settled weather and light winds to most areas.

The next day, the sun was shining between the clouds, there was very little wind and only a few showers forecast. At last we launched our dinghy, loaded it up with empty petrol cans, a bag of laundry, toilet gear and the rubbish, and rowed ashore.

Paul, the friendly, easy-going but busy hostel manager, was trimming some branches growing over the petrol tanks. He kindly allowed me to use the laundry at his house so I put our clothes into the automatic washing machine, set it going and then wandered around the area. I spoke with a group of twelve kayakers preparing and packing their gear into six kayaks for a three day and two-night excursion around Doubtful Sound. The trip was advertised as a "Wilderness Adventure" and the tour guide told me that it was getting more and more popular, with trips running from September to May. Everything they carried, including tents, sleeping bags, food and clothing, was packed in double layers of waterproof material and fitted into small spaces in the kayaks. It was a sunny day, but I wondered how they would have managed if it had been raining. They were soon off, paddling down the sound towards their first stop.

There was information about several walks nearby, some with very steep tracks, but as we were curious about the tunnel construction we decided to walk to Helena Falls.

Back at the laundry I put our clothes in the dryer, set it for 90 minutes and then Norm and I set off to find the track. We walked along the road, turned left and crossed a bridge where a friendly woman in a ute stopped and called out, "Follow the path and the signs, you'll go and come back the same way." She worked at the construction site and had only been there a week, but she told us that the drilling was going on 24 hours a day in shifts. There were only offices where we were. The workers' accommodation was at West Arm, about half an hour away by road, and the office staff commuted from Manapouri each day.

We soon found the path. It wound through exquisite lush ferns and bushes until we came to the steep track over the portal. We climbed up the steep incline over slippery rock and damp moss, with water trickling down the path. There was a safety fence made of heavy metal mesh attached to strong metal posts over the portal and soon we were up there looking over the site. We watched the conveyor belt take crushed rock from out of the mountain, then over the bridge spanning the tailrace of the original tunnel. The engineers were building a second parallel tunnel that would use surplus water to generate more electricity. We were told that the tunnel was nearly through. It had been started in 1997 and should have been finished in September 2000 but the rock was too hard for their drilling machines and this had delayed progress. However, the engineers were close to a tunnel breakthrough. The long bridge, mounted on tall thick concrete posts, took the spoil, gravel and rock to a dumping area. Graders, dump trucks, diggers and bulldozers were shifting the spoil and compacting the soft spots. Piles of graded gravel sat ready for use. Where, I wondered, as there were few roads in the area.

The track wound downhill and we rested in a shady spot and ate our nibbles. The path led past some of the earlier fill, which had been landscaped with grasses, shrubs and bushes. More tracks led us through bush and trees towards the falls. We saw a chirpy robin, a kea, a woodpigeon and a fantail, and a tui sang us a tuneful song. The track ended at a small stream near the falls, the view obscured by bushes, so Norm waded into the stream to photograph the falls.

We arrived back at the hostel after three hours of walking. Our laundry was dry. The petrol had arrived and Norm bought 47 litres at $1.80 per litre. It was the most expensive rate we had to pay, because of the isolation of the place and the difficulty of transporting fuel in, but we were very glad to be able to top up our supplies. We also bought two litres of oil for the four-stroke outboard, and the all-up cost was $95.80.

There was no telephone at the hostel or the manager's house, so Paul took me to the construction site office where I was able to use my calling card and contact our daughter Raewyn. She was surprised to hear from me but interested in the places we had visited and she passed on family news. I told her that we could be out of touch for a few weeks as we would be outside of both the mobile phone and the VHF radio coverage areas. We were extremely fortunate to have the use of this landline as it was the only one in the place and would be disconnected when the tunnel was completed.

We had the luxury of a shower at the hostel, and I gave Paul a donation for this and the use of the laundry. There was nowhere to dispose of our rubbish as we were in a National Park. Everyone had to take out their own rubbish or pay for others to do it. As we only had a small amount we took it back to the yacht, intending to dump it at the next port. Going back to *Starlight* meant two trips in the dinghy as the petrol and oil weighed heavily.

Our day had been full of activity and we were tired but well pleased with it. We were ready to move on, but the weather turned to showers and then heavy rain, with not much wind. We caught up with our Bible readings by sharing the last four chapters of Isaiah, truly a great prophet to whom God spoke about events yet to come.

We cleaned out the chilly bins and did a stock-take of our provisions. The bread would hold out for a few more days, and we had one more meal left of cabbage and lettuce (both kept well-wrapped in newspaper) but we had eaten all the tomatoes. We did not have a refrigerator and I did not expect such food to keep for long, but I wondered which non-perishables would be the first to run out. People often ask what we do when we are cooped up inside our yacht on wet days. I was kept busy reading the charts and books about Fiordland, writing a diary and planning the next leg. This took time as all these places were new to us. Norm carried out essential repairs, collected the rainwater and battled with the sandflies that seemed much larger here at Deep Cove. And of course we listened to the forecasts.

The five-day predictions sounded good for all of New Zealand. The next day, Sunday, the marine forecast was for showers in Fiordland but four metre swells, strong winds and rough seas outside. The outlook was for 30-knot northwest winds, but fine weather was forecast Monday through to Wednesday. The *Alert II* was due back on the mooring we were using, so by 9:30am we had packed up and left. We planned to explore Hall Arm, Crooked Arm and Doubtful Sound as far as Blanket Bay, where we would stay overnight as it would be sheltered from the southwest and northwest winds. We passed Paul in an inflatable runabout, and stopped to thank him and ask him to pass on our thanks to the owner of the mooring.

The weather was cold, misty and damp as we motored out of Deep Cove and into Hall Arm. We had heard it was very beautiful and we were not disappointed. The valleys were full of big trees, bush, ferns and moss which grew right down to the waterline. We motored to the head of the inlet, then turned back to the main reach and headed north. We came across kayaks beached on one of the very few gravel strips in the fiords, their paddlers resting and having lunch.

Next we entered Crooked Arm where we spoke with the skipper and crew of *Time Lord*, a 52ft steel motor-sailer from the Marlborough Sounds. He had not sailed yet, due to strong head winds, but in these calm waters motoring was very pleasant.

After rounding a sharp bend the strong southwest wind blew head-on, and at the head of the arm we found the charter launch *Takaroa* anchored there. Some of the ten guests were boarding an inflatable, planning to go ashore and walk the short 30-minute track, between Crooked Arm head and Dagg Sound. But the rain was torrential.

"They must be crazy!" Norm called out.

"They're mad!" the skipper replied.

But they were well prepared, with waterproof clothing and strong footwear.

The high 1300-metre mountain peaks ranging along the edge of Crooked Arm gave way to a low valley connecting the two fiords. The charts were not clear and I was interested to trace the contours of the surrounding high hills and see them drop down to expose the connecting valley, now enveloped in mist. We thought it likely the launch would wait for the trampers to return rather than go around and pick them up in Dagg Sound.

We had a late lunch in the calm waters at the head of Crooked Arm, then the southwest breeze stirred and we hoisted the mainsail. It was very pleasant sailing with the wind from behind. *Starlight* did two knots for the hour and a half it took to sail down the silent black waterway, with reflections all around us. There was an enormous crack, like a rifle shot. Norm saw a huge hunk of rock, as big as a house, break off the top of the mountain and start a long, noisy avalanche careering down to the valley below. I came on deck in time to see the dust and steam rising high as the rocks crashed through the trees, taking several minutes to roar down the hill. We were thankful that we were only onlookers and were not underneath the landslide.

We met *Time Lord* again, the crew fishing for cod. They were going to anchor for the night somewhere nearby in Crooked Arm. We told them our plan to cross the main reach to an island near Blanket Bay. We got to the island at 6pm. A private Bluff Fishing Company used the jetty and sheds on the island but the sign, 'Blanket Bay Hotel', was still there. No hotel services at all – fishermen used to use the fuel tank and freezer facilities here, and often met to have a chat, a coffee and the occasional beer, hence the name. The area was now used extensively for landing live crayfish, whereas it used to be all frozen tails. The island is thought to have got its name from the original purchase from a tribe of Maori for the price of a blanket, but this may be a 'fishy' tale. The cruising guide, which relates the history of Blanket Bay, advises against tying up to the jetty as there is a ledge of rocks close by, so we found the mooring opposite, anchored and hooked onto it.

It was a reasonably calm spot. The sky was clear blue and the sun shone warmly as I prepared our tea. Norm topped up the petrol tank and changed the oil on the outboard, which had done many miles since we left home. The sun highlighted the tops of the birch trees as it set around 9pm, and I noticed a few rata trees scattered around the hillsides still displaying red blooms. The forecast for Fiordland said, "Fine tomorrow".

We had a broken sleep due to the mooring float bumping the hull and a slight rocking motion caused by surges and tide flows. However we rose refreshed, had breakfast and left before nine for the next leg at sea. It was a cool 10 degrees Celsius so we wore our Swanndri jackets, woolly hats and gloves.

Chart NZ 7522 showed two channels out of Doubtful Sound, each side of Bauza Island. We decided to go through The Gut, a narrow but deep passage between the north of Bauza Island and the south of Separation Island. This area is a marine reserve and we could see the blue triangles on the shore marking its limits. The Gut is popular with divers but has very little shelter and only a few places suitable for anchoring.

A small westerly swell of only one metre ruffled the otherwise calm water as we motored northwest towards the open sea, but we could see waves breaking regularly and splashing high on the Shelter Islands and over the many rocks at the entrance so we knew there was a bigger swell out in the open sea. It was amazing how this calm deep sound was so protected by the islands at the entrance.

We steered around the north of Bauza Island, cleared the small islands and rocks, passed the headland to the south of Doubtful Sound and headed into open sea. The southwest wind was light but the swell increased to three metres from the south. *Starlight* rode over each swell and slid down the troughs easily, propelled by the 15hp motor. The ride was bouncy and a few waves broke over the bow. We could see the coast clearly from two miles off as we headed 210 degrees once more. We passed the entrance to Dagg Sound at 11:30am and decided to punch on as the weather was clear and the sea not too rough. It seemed to ease a little as we passed Coal Bay, but gained strength to give us some more rough seas further south.

I unrolled chart NZ 7612, Dusky and Breaksea Sounds, and studied the entrance to Breaksea Sound. The southwest wind increased to 15 knots and the swells to four metres, so we were anxious to be inside as soon as possible. We soon identified Breaksea Island ahead by its pyramid shape. As we came between this island and the headland to the sound, the sea eased and became moderate. We turned southeast and soon we were in sheltered waters.

After motoring east and going north of Entry Island, we located Sunday Cove, a sheltered bay just inside Breaksea Sound on its southern shoreline. Here, much to our surprise, was a large rusty ship permanently anchored. It was about 37 metres (120ft) long, with UNI painted on its port hull. It had a newish accommodation block near the stern, complete with a TV aerial, and a helicopter pad on the top of it. A runabout was hooked onto davits at the stern but there was nobody on board. At 3pm we tied up to the large tyres hanging down the side and had lunch. There were a lot of craypots in the cove, so obviously the ship was a base for some fishing company.

This was not an all-weather sheltered cove, and as strong northwesterlies were predicted we took off to find somewhere more suitable. I had marked Stick Cove with my bright pink blob and thought this would be ideal. We travelled south along the Acheron Passage in clear weather. The steep hills on either side were covered in blue-green bush and trees, the sea was a calm deep blue and the sky overhead was clear light blue. I could only marvel at the beauty of the scene, the most awe-inspiring so far. I thought about the sailors who had sounded this passage back in 1851, serving under Captain J L Stokes in HMS *Acheron*. Their vessel was a barque-rigged steam-driven paddle steamer built in 1838. Our chart, with soundings still in fathoms, had been updated in 1985 but it was essentially their original work. It was mind-boggling to be there a hundred and fifty years later and see it exactly the way they must have seen it.

After travelling south for about an hour, we turned east into Wet Jacket Arm. We consulted the sketch in the guide and soon found Stick Island. The narrow channel between the island and the shore was deep enough for our centre-plate to stay down, so we dropped the anchor mid-channel and caught the stern lines which floated in a jumbled mess of branches, moss and mussels. These secured us to the shore. It was an ideal all-weather mooring, but there were lots and lots of large sandflies again.

While we were in the rough seas we had noticed water spilling over the centre-plate casing. The last time this had occurred was when we took a heavy load of wood across Cook Strait to Resolution Bay. The yacht had to be at least two inches deeper in the water for this to happen. This time we didn't have a heavy load, but after we had mopped up a half a bucket of water from the cabin we noticed minute cracks in the floor with small amounts of water seeping through. We guessed that the air compartment between the floor and the hull had been gradually filling up with seawater and making the yacht heavier. We wondered if the hull had been damaged.

"Is the yacht water-ballasted?" I asked. But I knew it wasn't designed to be. We glued patches on the cracks but a tiny amount of water seeped through. I slept peacefully that night but Norm stayed awake for some time trying to figure a way to stop the seepage.

It was misty in the morning and while I was sitting in the cockpit writing, I heard voices and then the rumble of a big engine. Was I imagining it? The noise grew louder and, much to my surprise, around the bend cruised *Takaroa*. The trees on the island had hidden the boat's approach. What a surprise they must have had to see us moored there. I was amazed that their launch could fit in the narrow channel but they must have been there before.

The two owners and their ten visitors were on a seven-day cruise from Deep Cove southwards to Bluff. The conversation was an exchange of where, how and what next? Since we had last seen them at Crooked Arm, they had spent a night in Breaksea Sound and were now exploring Wet Jacket Arm. They were amazed at our small boat travelling around these parts.

"How do you get on in the open sea?" they asked.

"A bit bouncy there, but well sheltered here," Norm replied.

"Did you enjoy your walk to Dagg Sound?" I asked.

"Yes. Even though it rained."

They had been fishing off-shore and had caught several big groper.

"We've got a good cook," they told us.

"I've got one too," Norm said, and they all laughed.

"Would you like some fish?"

"That would be nice," I replied. Lyn put five thick groper steaks, a newspaper and a lemon in a plastic bag and handed it to Norm. Her husband Bill Ayto was at the helm looking through the windows and their guests were on deck, delighted at the encounter. They glided on and were soon around the bend. We were overwhelmed by our unexpected and generous visitors. Some time later our friends Colin and Mark went cruising on the *Takaroa* and heard the story of the little yellow yacht hiding behind Stick Island.

"We know that yacht," they grinned.

I cooked two of the groper steaks for lunch that day and they were delicious. After the 12:30pm forecast we decided to move on and explore Dusky

Motoring southwards in Acheron Passage, between Breaksea Sound and Wet Jacket Arm

Sound. We motored out of our sheltered spot, went north around Stick Island and into the calm waters of Wet Jacket Arm, then turned into Acheron Passage, travelling south in mist and low cloud.

It wasn't long before we rounded Passage Point, noting the many small caves and rivulets entering the sea there. We turned into Dusky Sound and travelled east for some distance in calm seas and clearing skies, admiring the lush foliage on Cooper Island. It had every shade from dark green to mid-brown, all intermingled in the bushes and trees which stood against a black sea – a truly pretty picture. At the head of Dusky Sound we found that Supper Cove's wide entrance was ruffled by the wind and exposed to the south. It was not a good overnight spot, so we went in and out again then carried on to nearby Shark Cove. This was reported as an all-weather anchorage but the tiny protruding reef was ineffective in sheltering us from the southwest wind beating into the cove. We turned out and headed west into a 15-knot southwest wind, aiming for a narrow rocky gap called Nine Fathoms Passage. The chart showed that it had only two and a half fathoms (about 4.6 metres), but that was plenty of depth for our yacht. It was half tide at 5pm when *Starlight* cleared the passage without a hitch.

We saw a large vertical waterfall pouring straight down into the water. It took another half an hour to reach the entrance to Fanny Bay, the next all-weather cove. It backed away to the south, turned east and hooked south again. The sea was calm there and we were well sheltered from the wind. We dropped the main anchor in very deep water using most of our anchor rope, and then eased back to hook onto a mooring rope attached to some big trees on the shore. The yacht swung out about twenty metres into the bay, away from the trees and too far for the sandflies. It was an ideal anchorage.

The next morning the sun rose slowly over the high hills and shone down on our small bay, a picture of serene tranquillity. At 10:30am we were ready to leave. We motored closer to the shore and let go the taut stern-line, then headed out into the bay until we were over the anchor. We both pulled in the rope and tried to lift the very heavy anchor but it wouldn't budge. We wondered if it had snagged onto a rock or a sunken tree. We pulled and heaved, then rested, pulled, heaved, rested. This went on for half-an-hour until very slowly the rope, followed by the chain and then the anchor, came on board. There were no snags, just a heavier-than-usual anchor in a very deep hole. We knew that many of the fiords were very deep close to the shore, but this was the first time we had a problem with it.

I was interested to read that the Maori name for Dusky Sound was Tamatea (captain of the *Takitimu* canoe) or Tataki. *A Boatie's Guide to Fiordland* describes its history as follows: "Captain (James) Cook sighted and named

Norm looks down on the Hollyford Valley 5000ft (1523 metres) below while walking the Routeburn Track

Dusky Bay on his first voyage with the *Endeavour* on 13 March 1770, but could not make the entrance before dark so sailed on. He was back again in 1773, this time on *Resolution*. After spending a night anchored in 50 fathoms off Anchor Point, Anchor Island, he sailed to a new anchorage in Pickersgill Harbour, entering through the narrow channel to the east of Crayfish island. He set up an observatory on Astronomers Point, and brewed spruce beer for his crew. Captain Cook and his crew explored and chartered nearly all of Dusky Bay."

The cruising guide also mentions a boardwalk erected by DOC around Astronomer Point and a commemorative bronze plaque placed by Charles and Neil Begg about five feet above the water near the spot where the *Resolution* was moored. There is a rough track up Cook Stream to Lake Forster.

There was much more information about Dusky Sound with its various inlets and anchorages, but time constraints stopped us exploring them all. We did take the opportunity to have a quick look at Cascade Cove and we passed Pickersgill Harbour, noting the narrow passage between Crayfish Island and the shoreline. I imagined Captain Cook's *Resolution* slowly gliding through, probably towed by a longboat.

We could see *Takaroa* a long way off, heading north on the other side of Long Island. A large ketch called *Thistle* and a runabout were seen in the distant Cook's Channel, heading towards the Two Sisters passage. No other boats were about – in fact we saw very few boats anywhere in these fiords.

While we had fine weather, our plan was to go 'outside' and see if sea conditions were suitable for the three-hour trip south to Chalky Inlet. If not, we would go back to Cascade Cove for the night. The ten-knot westerly wind and the three-metre southwest swells soon created a moderate to rough sea, but a fifteen-knot northwest wind was predicted. At 2pm we motored out of Dusky Sound, giving the numerous rocks at South Point a wide clearance. We turned south and steered 210 degrees. The sky was clear and we could see West Point ahead with big rocks jutting out from it. I changed to Chart NZ 7614, Preservation and Chalky Inlets.

The southwest wind diminished and a light northwest wind with a northwest swell developed, giving *Starlight* a good push. I activated my hand-held Garmin GPS and it read seven knots as the yacht slid down a wave. This most westerly point of our trip deserved to be recorded. We were off West Cape where the latitude was 45 degrees 55 minutes south and the longitude was 166 degrees 25 minutes east (Lat. 45° 55' S, Log. 166° 25' E). It was Saturday 24 February, 2001.

Since we were travelling in rough seas, we kept on motoring, changing course to 180 degrees then 170. Another headland came into view. It was Cape Providence with its distinctive flattened top. At 4pm we were abreast of the white tower of the lighthouse, 60 metres above sea level on top of the cliffs just north of the cape. Then the white cliffs of aptly-named Chalky Island appeared. The swell from the north was crashing over rocks and reefs along the shore. The sea became very rough and the northwest wind increased to 25 knots. It was so strong I had to push my sunhat firmly down on my head as the wind tried to lift it off. Soon we were approaching the western entrance to Chalky Inlet. We gave the many rocks and reefs a wide berth. I watched to port and Norm steered, keeping an eye out for rocks to starboard. It was very tricky, as the sea was very rough and the swell and tide were pushing the yacht around. Norm's steady hand on the tiller guided *Starlight* through several difficult patches, then I noticed a large area of green water swirling around a submerged rock to port.

"Watch out for that rock," I called out, pointing to it.

"Look at my side!" he replied. To my utter amazement, he was steering very close to some huge rocks. My heart was in my mouth as I saw two large pointed rocks loom up, so close that I could almost touch them.

"The swell will push us off," Norm reassured me. And it did. We passed well clear of the green swirls and were soon inside the Western Passage and in the lee of the cape where the sea became moderate. But it did not calm down until we passed through Return Passage, the gap between Great Island and Passage Island to the north of Chalky Island. We motored northwest and turned west into Ship Entrance, between Little Island and Great Island, to look for anchorages in North Port. The chart had a detailed sketch showing the depths and small rocks. I am truly grateful to the New Zealand chart makers and to the Mana Cruising Club for *A Boaties' Guide to Fiordland.* Without their sketches and instructions we would not have found any of these anchorages in Fiordland.

There was a small and picturesque island inside North Port. We motored around it and found the rusting hull of a ship, the ss *Stella.* How long it had been there we couldn't guess. We found a sheltered spot to the east of the island and dropped the anchor. We wanted to attach a stern rope to a tree to give us more stability in case the predicted 35-knot northwesterlies gusted right in. While I was on the bow letting out the anchor rope, Norm tried to get close to the shore by using reverse gear. No matter how hard he tried, something was stopping the progress. We had the centre-plate and rudder up and there was plenty of deep water under us, but *Starlight* would simply not go any closer to the shore.

Then I heard a crashing sound and some small, brown branches fell onto the deck. We looked up. *Starlight's* rigging was caught in some overhanging branches. We quickly rectified this by moving away from the shore and made a note – "Look UP near trees". We decided that swinging on the anchor would have to do, unless one of us found enough energy to launch the dinghy and row ashore.

We had muesli and pancakes with raspberry jam for breakfast as the bread had run out two days earlier. The cloud lifted and the occasional gust of wind hardly moved the yacht in this delightful sheltered spot.

We needed a rest day. We needed to tidy up, clean up, re-stock our provisions from the bulk supplies and dry out the carpet. The slop coming over the centre-plate casing had made the floor awash during our turbulent sea voyage but the seepage from below had almost stopped. Norm had drilled tiny holes in the floor cracks and screwed tap washers down firmly over them to block the seepage. Chores kept us busy until the afternoon, then we lifted the anchor and went searching for fresh water. The guide indicated a supply south of our mooring but the yellow and black striped markers on two rimu trees were hard to find. Once we were in the right place there they were, with a black polythene pipe between them. I dropped the anchor as close as possible, then Norm launched the dinghy and rowed ashore with the cans. He filled three of them with brown, brackish water, not ideal, but it would have to do until we got more rain.

Back at our sheltered spot we anchored again and heated up some water in the kettle. I filled our one-litre plastic bottle with warm water and enjoyed the luxury of a shower and a shampoo in the cockpit. By early evening the breeze had dropped and the sun warmed us. After tea I made some bread rolls in the frying pan, but by the time I had finished Norm was asleep.

On Friday 23 February we left Little Island Cove through the same Ship Entrance that we had entered, as the wind was blowing over the shallow northern small-boat entrance. By 9:35am we were heading north along Edwardson Sound in a slight sea, and from the head of the sound we motored through a narrow passage into Lake Cove which had trees and bush all around it. There were many logs that had come down from the Lumaluma River. The high tide had covered some of them but others were still protruding or floating. The guide showed an anchorage at a depth of twenty metres in the middle of the cove but we were unsure of anchoring there, fearful of snagging the anchor on a sunken log. We went close to the estuary and peeped at the bottom of the Cora Lyn Falls. "A rough track leads up to Lake Cadman which feeds the falls" the cruising guide told us. Did we want to go there?

"Big deal," Norm said. "We've seen plenty of those." We agreed to give the track a miss – mainly because of the risk of snagging the anchor – and went back down the sound. The grey slate mountain tops to the north impressed us so much that we took a photograph. Dense bush grew below the grey domes, and I thought they would make a splendid sight covered with snow in wintertime.

We passed Cunaris Sound, after a brief look in at the entrance, and carried on. We passed South Port at lunchtime, noting the weathered bushes on the low-lying isthmus. As we approached the Eastern Passage to the east of Chalky Island, the swell increased and the sea became rough.

We wondered if we could get round Gulches Head and into Preservation Inlet. Since it was a fine day with little wind, we thought we would give it a go. We kept a sharp lookout for Table Rock to the south and Balleny Reef to the southwest, where the swells broke heavily, and motored through Broke-adrift Passage. "There has to be a story here with a name like this," I told Norm. But we could only guess at it. There were tall, rugged rocks off Gulches Head and with the rough sea and the tide pushing the yacht this way and that, it made tough riding for about an hour. I tried to photograph the rocks but it was difficult as the yacht tossed me up and down. A very large, fast pleasure boat came from the north, also heading for Preservation Inlet. Later we saw a helicopter land on its deck then fly off again, and wondered if they were deer hunters. At 3pm we were around the headland, still in rough seas but with a swell pushing the yacht from astern. After consulting the chart we were able to negotiate around the many islands and enter Isthmus Sound. We motored to the head of the sound then turned back south to enter the all-weather cove behind Big Island and Little Island. Here we found a heavy mooring with several sturdy ropes attached to the shore. When we tied up, we could see the ropes going down through about twelve metres of unusually clear water, but we couldn't see the bottom. The calm cove would be an ideal spot for the night – or so we thought.

After tea I saw some small fish swimming around the yacht and was enticed to put down a fishing line. I caught three sizeable cod, enough for two or three meals, and cooked some for tea. Then we felt that we needed a good sleep after our bouncy ride.

During the night a slight northeast wind blew and the mooring buoy banged against the hull and woke us up. Then we heard the centre-plate grind and start to lift. It was 4am.

"What's happening?" I asked. Norm got up and shone a torch. He couldn't believe his eyes.

"We are close to the shore," he told me, bewildered. "The bow is right on top of a big rock." Hastily he put out a small anchor from the stern to hold us from going further ashore. Then he tried to start the outboard motor, but a mooring rope was caught around the propeller. I went to the bow to untie our rope from the mooring buoy, but when I pulled it in I found only a sash weight and a thin piece of pipe. That was all we had been attached to. We realised we had tied up to three stern ropes and not to a mooring at all. We felt deflated. It was a 'Millars' mistake', though certainly not the first of our boating bloopers.

"It's a dinghy job," I announced. "Take the dinghy out into the middle of the cove and put down another anchor. The tide is going out further." Fortunately the wind had dropped and the sea was calm as Norm rowed out into the darkness. I needed a torch to see as I paid out the long thin rope into the jet-black night. Norm dropped the anchor, rowed back and came aboard. The first anchor, by the stern, was holding well and we hauled hard on the rope attached to this second one, but to no avail. We could not pull *Starlight* off the rocks. The tide had gone out too far and the centre-plate was almost right up, with our bow resting on a sloping rock.

By 5.30am, we had done everything we could. Norm said, "It's time for a cup of tea." We sipped the hot brew and prayed an earnest prayer for guidance, a calm sea and little wind. The sunrise was not until 7:08am, so I tried to get some rest. How much further would the tide drop, I wondered?

At 6:30am, *Starlight* gently toppled over to rest on the rocks at a 20-degree tilt. It was now almost impossible to stand or sit up straight inside the yacht. The dawn was only just beginning to light up the sky on what promised to be a cloudy Saturday.

Norm climbed over the starboard side to view the situation. "An unplanned beaching," Norm called it. Our beachings were usually planned, and on a sandy beach – certainly not on rocks.

Norm saw that most of the rocks on the shore were covered with weed, moss or soft mush. He removed a few protruding rocks, examined the hull and took a couple of photographs. "Any noticeable holes?" I asked. We hoped not. There was nothing he could see, anyway.

At 7:45am we noticed the tide had turned and gradually the rocks were being covered. While we waited, we heard the morning calls of the tui, fantails and other birds in the bush around us. Unwelcome sandflies in their thousands bothered us and kept us busy.

The yacht gradually came back to a ten-degree tilt and then to a normal position. Norm climbed back on board as the tide began covering the nearby rocks he was standing on. At 9:45am *Starlight* was floating again. She gently slid off the rock and floated over the ropes. We cleared the ropes around the outboard propeller and pulled in the first and nearest anchor. Then we pulled on the long rope, towing the 'mooring' ropes with us out from shore until they were back in their original position in the middle of the cove. Finally, after a lot more hauling on the ropes, *Starlight* was swinging on the small anchor.

It was 11am before we had breakfast and a grateful prayer. "Thank you, Lord." It was a miracle that in all those hours since the beaching there had been no wind, and our yacht had suffered no damage.

We hauled in the dinghy onto the foredeck and fastened it down. Buckets of seawater were sloshed over the deck to wash away the dead sandflies, and we were tidy and ship-shape again. I then found the amended notes for the unnamed cove in Isthmus Sound, and read, "There is a double-buoyed stern line to serve the western anchorage." No mention of a mooring buoy – we had assumed wrongly that the Mana Cruising Club had installed a heavy mooring since the guide was written in 1992.

We were discussing whether to stay there or go on to nearby Long Sound, when a gust of wind caught the yacht. We felt that the small anchor was inadequate to hold us.

"We've got to go now!" Norm said. We motored out in a light drizzle, coiling and stowing the small anchor and its ropes as we went. The sea was calm and the visibility cleared as we motored around Colt Head and into Long Sound. The name was logical. It was over 30 kilometres long and narrow, with high hills either side, although I found that Dusky Sound was in fact the longest sound in Fiordland. We passed Useless Bay to port and Revolver Bay to starboard, then turned northeast into Narrow Bend, which was much wider than I had expected. We watched out for rocks and reefs, but were appalled to see a cliff with a large overhanging block of rock literally hung in space, just waiting to fall. The portion underneath it had broken off some time ago. Since our experience in Crooked Arm, where we heard and saw a huge rock break off and come crashing down, we were wary – and made sure we avoided the area and did not motor under the overhang.

At the mouth of a small river near Sandy Point we saw a flock of seagulls and another flock of oystercatchers resting on the sand with at least five metres segregating them. We turned north and then northeast towards the head of the sound, but the view was obscured by rain, so we made for Last Cove, a nearby all-weather bay. This time we followed the instructions in the guide to the letter. It was almost high tide and the water was darkly stained again. We dropped our trusty main anchor in the middle of the stream, where the water was not too deep but where there were no sandflies. What a relief we felt. It was time for a much-needed rest.

Later in the afternoon, Norm checked for leaks in all the compartments but found none. However the leaks in the floor around the centre-plate were oozing seawater and had to be constantly mopped up with sponge pads. It was useless having the carpet down so we lifted it up, dried it and stored it out of the way.

I gathered together the ingredients for a loaf of seawater bread and cooked it over a slow heat in the pressure cooker for 45 minutes. The crusty sides and bottom of the loaf came away easily from the cooker but the top was too moist. The instructions said to tip out the loaf, return it upside down and cook the bread for about 10 to 15 minutes longer on low heat. The smell tickled our noses and by the time the bread was done we had worked up good appetites.

The tide had dropped and we could see the reef at the southwest entrance and the rock off it, mid-way across the channel. Also the head of the cove had dried out a lot. We felt that our choice of anchorage was 'spot on' this time.

On Sunday 25 February we left Last Cove and motored northeast in Long Sound for over an hour in showery conditions, then we easily negotiated a narrow neck into Cascade Basin at the head of Long Sound. The sea was calm and there was no wind. We edged slowly into the sheltered estuary, noting the six fathoms (ten metres) of water marked on the chart. We motored on in much shallower depth until we had a close view of the waterfall at the head of the cove. Trees and bush grew right down to the rocky shore, and the waterfall dropped straight into the water of the cove making a tremendous dim.

We did not linger, but turned back and motored southwest in a joggly sea, ruffled by a slight sea breeze and a tide change. The mist lifted to reveal a blue sky and a few puffy white clouds. We carried on, retracing our route back down Long Sound, through Narrow Bend and into the main part of Preservation Inlet. Then we turned south and identified the well-wooded Woodhen or Weka Island, and found Cemetery Island off Kisbee Bay. It was half tide and the beach was covered in small rocks over some sand but there was no jetty. The cruising guide said there was a lodge there and we were curious.

"Preservation Lodge is nestled back from the beach in native bush. It is not a commercial operation, but may provide limited facilities (showers and laundry) IF the caretaker is in residence. The lodge keeps a listening watch on SSB 4417 and VHF 10, through Bluff Fishermen's radio and Riverton Fishermen's radio schedules. As it is situated a little further than 'the back of the beyond' and well past 'the black stump', potential visitors wishing to use its services should give as much warning as possible."

Well, we had not heard anything on our VHF for some time, so we tried contacting the lodge on channel 10 but there was no response. Would the caretaker be there? It would be great if we could contact someone who could pass on our whereabouts. We motored around until we saw a fishing boat tucked in behind Cemetery Island. It was tied to a mooring and had a long thick stern rope leading to the shore so we anchored and hooked on to the stern rope. Then we launched the dinghy and rowed ashore. We saw a black polythene water pipe draped along the shore. We changed our aqua shoes to our dry socks and tramping shoes, then easily found a rough track through native bush and ferns heading towards the centre of the bay. After about 30 minutes, we came to a stream and crossed over it on conveniently-placed stepping stones. We walked over a grassy patch, came across some notices and fishermen's gear, and then found a wide path lined with large stones.

We could not believe our eyes. Through the trees we could see a very large modern two-storey building with a long balcony. We knocked on the door. Yes, the caretaker and his assistant were in residence and were very much surprised to find us at their door.

"Do come in, take your shoes off, but don't let the sandflies in," Jeff greeted us. "How did you get here? I didn't hear or see you come."

"We're in a yellow trailer-yacht called *Starlight* and we have tied up near the fishing launch around the bend."

"That's my boat," he said. "You'll be all right there."

Jeff and his partner were minding the lodge for the two or three millionaires from Auckland who owned it. We found there were definitely no supplies or facilities for yachts there.

"Everything for the whole six months that I am here has to be flown in by helicopter," Jeff told us. "I am short of petrol for the runabout and I have to grow fresh vegetables to supplement our diet, but there is enough diesel to run the generators. They supply electricity for the heaters and the freezers. If the owners come in, they have to fly to Invercargill then hire a helicopter. It's very expensive."

The owners brought their own food and did their own cooking. But they rarely came. All Jeff had to do was look after the place. He was concerned that anyone reading the out-of-date information in the guide could be dependent on getting fuel at Preservation Lodge, and we agreed that it would always pay a boat-owner to check ahead.

Jeff and his partner took us on a tour of the 40-bed mansion. The big dining room had a huge wooden carved table and big chairs. The walls were decorated with guns and trophies. We were offered a cup of tea, which we gratefully accepted. As we had been out of contact with anyone for nine days, we gave them Raewyn's telephone number in case a message could be passed on to her. Jeff agreed to send a message to Bluff Fishermen's Radio that evening. We asked him to pass on the information that we would soon be heading towards Riverton or Bluff.

"There's a window in the weather. It may be short-lived but it's the best you can get around here. Go in the morning," Jeff said. We thanked him for his hospitality and his timely advice. He promised to contact us on VHF 10 later that evening, and we found out that the yacht *Southern Bear* had called in four days ago.

On the way back we passed over a grassed area where the helicopters could land, and heard about the large settlement of Cromarty which served the coal and gold miners in the late 1800s. There had been a school built on this very spot. We had read about some of the history of this area. It was very interesting to know about the Maori tribes and early settlers that had lived there.

The shadows of evening began to fall as we reluctantly said goodbye and made our way along the big stones along the beach at low tide, back to our dinghy. Norm took a photograph of me on the rocks beside the dinghy in the late evening stillness. That picture of the isolated bay is one of my favourite scenes.

Jeff contacted Meri on the Bluff radio at 9pm, using his SSB. She rang Raewyn by landline and relayed a message to her, then rang Jeff back to tell him that the message had been passed on, and Jeff gave me the news on VHF channel 10 after we had returned to the yacht. Norm and I agreed that this was a remarkable service.

We knew that it would be a long leg to the next shelter. Should we head for Riverton, a small river estuary, or go further on to Bluff which was a larger port. Both seemed a long way off. It all depended on the weather, the tides and our trusty outboard motor. The forecast was for a light 10-knot northwest wind, moderate sea, a one to two-metre southwest swell and good visibility in Foveaux Strait and around Stewart Island. Our Bible reading was short, but that night we said a long, sincere prayer of thanks to God for the two people who lived there and the unseen folk, on the radio and telephone, who cared for us. The beauty of the fiords had touched us too, in a timely reminder of God's wonderful creation.

We had an early breakfast and left at dawn. There was just enough light to navigate around the nearby reef and out of the bay into a calm sea. We heard a fishing boat reporting from Otago's Retreat, a shallow passage between Coal Island and the mainland, that the sea was calm with very little swell. The diagram in the guide showed that the channel had a sand and shingle bar across it with a shallow depth of one fathom (1.8 metres). We could handle it in calm weather, but a big swell from the sea would make the yacht bottom in the troughs. We decided to take the shorter route, as it would take an extra hour or more to go around Coal Island. We could see the fishing boat ahead of us as it passed through the channel and headed north. We were finally leaving Fiordland after four memorable weeks.

What kind of sea would we face at Puysegur Point? It was notorious for its very rough seas and enormous swells. Would there be a huge swell as we passed the lighthouse? These were the kinds of seas that Norm dreaded. If we had to anchor there in rough water, we could have the anchor cleat pull out of the foredeck. We would soon know the worst.

13

Foveaux Strait – Stewart Island

Will your anchor hold in the straits of fear,
When the breakers roar and the reef is near?
While the surges rave and the wild winds blow,
Shall the angry waves your bark o'erflow?
Priscilla Jane Owens

I dressed warmly in my woollen Cowichin jersey, hat and gloves for our trip out from Preservation Inlet. I thought that going around the dreaded Puysegur Point might be a bit rough and cold as the strong southwest winds could bring icy air from the Antarctic.

However the early morning air was no more than cool as we motored along, keeping close to the shore by Coal Island. We passed over the shingle bar in Otago's Retreat in a calm sea with no swell, although a one-metre southwest swell came soon after we had cleared the bar. On the opposite shore we could see a small cove enclosed by reefs and rocks

There was a swing anchorage there which, according to *A Boaties' Guide to Fiordland,* "should only be used while visiting the lighthouse, and then only in suitable conditions." Boaties were advised to ensure their anchors were well dug in and holding, and to take extreme care when approaching the dinghy entrance in the reef which might or might not be marked by stakes. "Once on the beach, pull your dinghy well above the high tide mark and tie it up. The old dinghy shed is now a DOC hut…"

There it was – the boat shed and the dinghy landing near the start of the track to the lighthouse. But we did not go into the cove. We would be satisfied if we could get around the point in clear weather.

To my surprise the sea near Puysegur Point was only slight with little wind. I sat on the cockpit seat in awe as I watched the sun rise slowly over the cliffs near the lighthouse just after 7am. The slight sea was deep blue with a one-metre southwest swell. The window in the weather had arrived for us.

The sky was cloudy as we motored along in an easterly direction towards Foveaux Strait. How long before the sea would be ruffled by a northwest or southwest wind? It was a long way by sea to Riverton and even longer to Bluff.

The sky cleared after the early morning cloud had lifted. The sun warmed me and my woolly clothes were replaced with lighter ones, my woolly hat with a sunhat. The southwest swell increased to two metre waves about twenty metres apart – easy riding as *Starlight* travelled east following the coast. We identified each headland from the chart. The first was Windsor Point, with a few rocks off it. Then Long Reef Point had a reef extending to about one mile off shore; the breaking swell made it easy to see. Green Islets had one island close inshore with a height of 42 metres. Price Point had a few high peaked rocks. At 12 noon we had just passed Long Point, with its lighthouse 23 metres above sea level. I marked GPS waypoints every hour and found that our latitude stayed much the same (around 46 degrees 17 minutes south) but our longitude was gradually increasing towards the east (from 169 deg 8 min then 169 deg 9 min east). When we looked to the south we could clearly see one of the Solander Islands, with a very steep side culminating at its highest point of 338 metres, sitting on a flat horizon about 20 miles away.

Lunch was a picnic meal on deck in bright sunlight and slight seas. At 1:20pm we were opposite Sandhill Point and Norm topped up the two outboard petrol tanks. Two more empty cans were tied to the rails. I was amazed to see that we were motoring at 6.5 knots. Was the tide assisting us? We could now see the high mountains of Stewart Island peeping out of the cloud to the southeast. I tried to contact Bluff Fishermen's radio on our VHF but both transmission and reception were spasmodic. I could hear fragments and wondered if they could hear my messages. Then Maureen, on Oban VHF radio, responded to our call. Norm turned the radio off and on again and our VHF sprang to life – it must have made a better contact with the switch. Now we could send and receive messages, and it was good to know that someone knew we were out there, in the vicinity of Foveaux Strait.

As the coastline dipped away into Te Waewae Bay, we steered east-southeast towards the next point in the distance which appeared as a light grey blur. At 3:55pm we had crossed this wide bay and were opposite Ruahine Hill. We saw Centre Island ahead but there were numerous rocks between it and the South Island shore. The fishermen had told us about a pass between the rocks and reefs but we felt unsure of it. I checked the GPS again at 4:30 pm because we were uncertain about our position relative to some of the submerged rocks. Yes! We had passed Fish Reef and were heading southeast, so we could go around Centre Island.

On this course we estimated it would take at least three hours to get to Riverton. This was not good timing. It would be well past high tide and the river level at the bar would be too low for us to attempt an entry. What were our options?

To our amazement an easterly wind sprung up. It grew stronger and the sea became rough. Light cloud obscured the sun. Norm took over the steering from Fred and headed southeast almost into the wind. We had a strong tidal current against us and we made little headway.

"Where did that wind come from?" I asked Norm. "It was not in the forecast." We could not understand the sudden change in the weather and it put us in a tricky situation. The tide was wrong for the Riverton River entrance but anchoring off that shore in an easterly wind with a very choppy sea would be dangerous. To push on to Bluff against a strong easterly head wind in a very rough sea would be impossible.

"We have to go to Stewart Island," Norm announced. "There's shelter there under those big mountains." I agreed, it was the only practical course. We steered south to avoid a very rough sea with big waves. The wind gusted up to 35 knots, and the clouds thickened and raced across the sky. At 6pm I took another GPS reading, then looked up the *Stewart Island Cruising Guide* published by the Mana Cruising Club. I found Waituna Bay, near Codfish Island on the west coast of Stewart Island.

"There's shelter from easterly winds there," I told Norm. We carried on motoring and steering south with waves crashing over the bow and the port side of the yacht. Even though we had some wind I did not unfurl the jib as it was too dangerous to go onto the foredeck to untie the sail. Instead I went below into the cabin to avoid the splashing water, and slept for two hours despite the yacht bouncing around. When I came back to the cockpit, I was surprised to see rocks and cliffs.

"Where are we?' I asked.

"Near Stewart Island," Norm replied, "Beside those high mountains." The GPS reading at 8:20pm confirmed our position with Codfish Island ahead and Red Head, with reddish rocks, off our port side. The two-metre swells and rough seas crashed on the rocks. There was no safe anchorage at Red Rocks, exposed to the north, nor at Sealers Bay on the north side of Codfish Island which was exposed to the northeast, so we carried on looking out for the sheltering reef off Waituna Bay.

The guide recorded that fishermen anchored behind the reef in easterly conditions, but it could be uncomfortable in a westerly roll.

I was hoping that the reef and the coastline would give us good shelter in these strong easterlies, but when we identified a small reef to the north of the bay we could see that it barely stopped any waves.

"Do you think we really are at Waituna Bay?" I queried.

"Let's drop the anchor in the middle of the bay anyway," Norm said. I crawled to the bow with waves and wind tossing the yacht like a cork. I had to hold on tightly as I undid the anchor-well cover and threw over the heavy anchor, the chain and as much anchor-rope as I could. I had great difficulty in holding the rope, and had to put my foot on it to stop excess rope from spilling out. It took me some time to fasten the rope to the cleat, then I watched the rocks and land to make sure that the anchor was holding fast before putting the loose ropes under the anchor-well cover. At last I was satisfied and crept back to the cockpit. The light was fading but the easterly wind was gusting over the saddle in the hill behind the bay, directly towards the yacht. I wondered if we really were in a safe place.

Norm changed into dry clothes and we had a hot drink of Milo. He was exhausted and climbed into the double bunk. "If the anchor doesn't hold we'll be blown out to sea," he said. "We'll be safe out there."

I was apprehensive. I put on a lifejacket-coat and prepared for the worst. Would the anchor hold? Did I let out enough rope? Would the rope chaff on the tow-rail? Were we too close to those rocks? The VHF radio came to life and it was Meri from Bluff calling *Starlight* on channel 65.

"Where are you?" she asked me.

"I think we are at Waituna Bay off the west coast of Stewart Island. We passed some red rocks on the way but the easterly wind is howling down from the saddle and hitting us."

"That sounds like Waituna Bay to me. You'll be all right," Meri told me, "You've done the right thing, Mavis. You'll be as good as gold." This reassured me a great deal. She also told me a fishing boat was sheltering by Red Rocks and would keep an eye on us. As soon as she had signed off, the fisherman on *Othello* called me up.

"I'm not far away and I'll keep a lookout for you," he told me.

"That's good news – much appreciated," I replied. I was most impressed by these calls but was determined to stay awake and watch what was happening anyway. I looked out and saw that the rocks were in the same places as before. The anchor must have been holding even though the wind was still gusting fiercely. A flickering light could be seen near Codfish Island. As there was no lighthouse or beacon recorded there, I assumed that it was another fishing boat sheltering there. The sounds of the yacht swinging on the anchor and the waves banging against the hull were steady and rhythmic as *Starlight* kept her

Brent Ballentyne, in the wheelhouse, and his crew on *Othello* visited *Starlight* at Waituna Bay, Stewart Island

position. At regular intervals I looked out into the dim surroundings and satisfied myself that we were still in the same place. Yes, those rocks looked the same, they were certainly not any closer, I thought, despite the wind and waves tossing the yacht tumultuously. I was anxious, not knowing if the anchor would hold or the rope would fray or the direction of the wind change. I prayed for guidance and gained a reassurance that calmed my fears.

I must have dozed a few times. Then at 2am the noise seemed to be less boisterous. I looked out again. The easterly wind had quietened but the sea still roared, mostly from the swell that was whipping up waves and crashing on the rocks. I sat up in the cabin and dozed again, with my lifejacket still on.

I listened to the 5:05am marine forecast for Foveaux Strait. It was not good. Northwest 35-knot winds, then southwest 30-knot winds and rough seas. Where could we go – south or north? We certainly would not want to go west, out to the open sea.

By daylight the sea had calmed with only a slight swell going towards the shore, and the wind was almost nothing. Norm woke up and I said, "The sea is calm now. Let's get going." At 7am we were preparing to leave when the fishing boat *Othello* came alongside. The skipper, a curly-headed young man, popped his head out of the wheelhouse and said, "Get going now while it's calm. It takes three hours for us to get to Oban from here, but you'll take much longer." He called Stewart Island Radio at Oban on Channel 65 to say that *Starlight* was heading there. The miracle was that the rough seas had abated and the sea was as calm and smooth as glass.

We motored north past Red Rocks and Rugged Point, then turned east following the coast. I had been using chart NZ 76, Western approaches to Foveaux Strait, since leaving Preservation Inlet. This chart was sufficient for travelling east along the South Island coast but the new chart NZ 69 covering the whole of Stewart Island had not yet been printed. I had to make do with portions of other charts, like NZ 68 and NZ 681, and diagrams from the *Stewart Island Cruising Guide* as we went towards Oban. We passed Cave Point, Bishop and Clerk Islands, Black Rock Point and Saddle Point, and then turned south. Some light showers and low cloud did not spoil the view of the coastline.

Our companion albatross circled us again. At each part of the open sea journeys, we had a large albatross following us, coming closer and swooping down near the yacht. There had been a large one at Preservation Inlet and a younger one with it; both had often rested on the water near *Starlight*. This bird had a young one too, and we wondered if the same pair had been with us at each leg. These magnificent birds, with black and white plumage and a yellow-grey hooked beak, have a large wingspan. Each time they came close to our yacht Norm called out a greeting and they seemed to know we were there. We wondered how they collected their food as we never saw them dive for fish.

There were large bundles of thick seaweed growing along the shoreline and we often saw them floating on the reefs. We were not keen to have it tangled around the outboard motor propeller, so we kept a careful lookout.

We were surprised that our appetites had dwindled. Neither of us had eaten since lunchtime the previous day, and all we could swallow was a muesli bar and a few nibbles. However our Thermos flask still had some hot water in it, enough for two mugs of Milo. The storm was over but our nervous stomachs were slow to revive.

We motored past Port William and Mamaku Bay, with Fish Rock on our port side. After passing Horseshoe Bay we went into Halfmoon Bay, noting the large red beacon in the middle. It had taken us six hours to get there. The numerous boats and dinghies moored there gave Halfmoon Bay and the town of Oban a picturesque look. The fast ferry was getting ready to leave for Bluff and we were directed to tie up at a place behind the wharf shed. At 3pm we had a good meal, the first for 26 hours. We had breakfast cereal and spaghetti with sausages, and it was great. We walked to the motor camp for a shower but there were no laundry facilities we could use. On the way back we stopped at the 'Ship to Shore' store for bread and supplies. Then we came back to the yacht for tea and I finally flopped into a bunk, clothes and all.

Fortunately Norm was awake enough to realise that the yacht was banging too hard against the wharf. There was an easterly swell coming into the bay, and a strong surge at low tide made the mooring ropes take up violently. He was anxious in case the cleats and fittings were pulled out of the deck. He put out more fenders and tied four car tubes into the mooring lines and springs, so that the elasticity of the tubes would take up the shock and ease the strain. It worked well but he didn't get to sleep till much later, after the tide had risen to halfway up and he was satisfied the surging was much less.

The next morning we counted up the petrol cans – only 90 litres left. We had started with 262 litres at Milford Sound and had bought another 45 litres at Deep Cove, so we had used 216 litres, which was less than my estimated 252 litres. However if we had not been able to buy petrol at Deep Cove we would have been down to 45 litres, half the comfortable margin we would have needed to go further afield or weather another storm.

The 52ft ketch *Thistle* was berthed nearby so we walked around to it and perched on the wharf to talk with the crew of six men. They had seen us motoring out of Dusky Sound and we shared experiences. To our delight, the young cook gave us some delicious paua fritters to sample. Bill, the skipper, told us he was from Auckland and they were preparing to return via the East Coast, perhaps calling into Akaroa. They filled up their water tanks, took on diesel, hauled up the dinghy and secured it on the aft deck. Just before they cast off they told us that they had heard the yacht *Southern Bear* on the radio when it was at nearby Glory Bay. This was good news as we were hoping to catch-up with *Southern Bear* and her crew.

I asked Norm to take a good look at the anchor as I thought it had been damaged at Waituna Bay. I was right – one of the fluke supports had broken off and the anchor was bent. "It's an arc welding job," Norm said. He took it to the local garage and they kindly let him use their arc welder. He was able to do the repairs using two stainless steel arc-welding rods he had thoughtfully packed in the tool kit. While he did that, I carried our laundry to the hotel where I was allowed to use their coin-in-the-slot machines. Our tasks took us just over two hours.

While I was walking near the school fence not far from the shore, I found a spot that had coverage for our mobile phone so I was able to contact Raewyn and tell her we were safe at Oban after the storm in Foveaux Strait.

"We're having fine dry weather in Wellington," she told me, and reminded me about the census coming up in March. We bought colourful post cards of Stewart Island, wrote messages to friends and family, posted them and then walked up the hill to find Maureen and Ted Jones' house. We wanted to thank them in person for their VHF radio service and give them some chocolate biscuits. Norm took some of our empty cans up to the garage to buy more petrol, and was lucky enough to be offered a lift by a local man. We bought 45 litres at $1.41 per litre.

We had tea on the yacht, but it was low tide again with more surging and banging. We were not very comfortable so we untied the ropes and motored across Halfmoon Bay in the twilight to Braggs Bay, where we anchored beside a moored boat. This time we were well away from the easterly swell, but Norm kept watch again. It was an unfamiliar bay and there were clumps of seaweed floating nearby. Were there rocks underneath the seaweed? When the tide changed, he had to push *Starlight* off the neighbouring boat as they swung, almost touching. Finally he was able to go to sleep in peace.

Our Bible readings had been a bit irregular lately, but that night we read two chapters and had a grateful prayer for the generous guidance from the radio operators and the fishermen, the warm hospitality from the people at Oban and the safe haven we had found there.

The next morning we left Halfmoon Bay to explore Paterson Inlet. The sea was calm and there was no wind but the 5am forecast was for a change. A front was approaching the Foveaux marine area and by mid-day there would be a 25-knot southwesterly wind and high seas, with two-metre swells, rain and poor visibility. We motored between Ackers Point, which had a lighthouse on it, and Barclay Rock. We noted that the gap between Native Island and the shore was all sand and rocks so it was not a navigable passage. We easily found the entrance to Paterson Inlet between Native Island and the low-lying neck. As we motored around Ulva Island and reefs in the centre of the inlet, the cloud thickened and a dark blue bank of cloud appeared towards the south, an ominous sign of the front approaching. We did not stop to fish beside the reefs but went into Glory Cove, an all-weather sanctuary to the south. We anchored in the southwest part of the cove and I tried a bit of fishing there (and caught only spotties) while Norm had a well-earned rest.

By midday small drops of rain were falling and a couple of hours later heavy rain and strong winds buffeted us. I noticed that *Starlight* was drifting out into the centre of the bay, and realised the anchor was slipping, so Norm started the motor while I hauled it in. We soon found a spot with less turbulence, in the lee of a small headland with a higher contour. I dropped the anchor and fastened the rope and Norm rowed ashore to attach two stern lines to trees. But the anchor didn't hold for long. The wind was gusting around the knob, pushing the bow from side to side and *Starlight* was drifting towards the shore. We dropped another anchor from the bow at a 90-degree angle to the main one. Then I tied a very long rope to the bow and Norm rowed ashore to tie it to a tree on our starboard side. This rope took the thrust of the southwest winds. The rest of the bay was now a turbulent choppy sea with 'white horses' coming into the entrance and wind gusting over the nearby low hills to the east.

Our spot seemed calmer, however. We changed into dry clothes and had a cuppa, the gas stove warming up the cabin.

We called Maureen to report our situation and position, and then *Southern Bear* called us. They had been to Port Pegasus and were now at Lords River, both places off the west coast of Stewart Island. "It's beautiful," Chris told us. "Well worth a visit." We considered whether we had enough time and petrol. I had heard about the long, deep Lords River and wondered if we would have a chance to go there.

Friday 2 March was my 69th birthday. Since the weather was still unsettled we had a 'rest' day – tidying up, cleaning up and drying our wet weather gear and generally getting the yacht ready for the next leg south. We sorted out our petrol cans and found we had 117.5 litres left. Norm worked to stop various leaks and I mopped up the seepage on the floor. The mid-day forecast was for fine weather during the next three days. It sounded good.

The next morning we untied the two stern ropes and coiled them up, hauled in the second anchor, retrieved our shore line, lifted the dinghy on board and tied it down, hauled the main anchor aboard and finally motored off past the islands in Paterson Inlet. *Starlight* glided out through the entrance, then we turned south.

We had only done a few miles when I discovered that the mobile telephone had coverage, so I rang Raewyn.

"We all want to wish you a happy birthday for yesterday," she said excitedly, and I passed on my thanks in return. I told her we were off to Lords River and hoped to be back near Oban by 5 or 6 March. Norm had turned off the outboard motor so I could hear clearly, and when I had finished he said, "Look behind us." I was surprised to see three big albatross resting on calm water only a few feet away. I grabbed my camera and took a hurried shot as one of the birds lifted its wings for take-off. As we motored off, five of these magnificent birds circled the yacht, coming quite close at times.

Shortly afterwards we saw a fishing boat heading for Oban, the fishermen cleaning and sorting out their catch and throwing the gut and waste overboard. There were over 50 albatross circling. I found out later there were over twenty species, of which the Royal Albatross was the largest, but these were the black-browed albatross more commonly called mollymawks.

The coastline appeared to be a series of low headlands and rocky outcrops. Some reefs offshore could be clearly seen since the southwest swell and waves were breaking over them. We could identify most of them from chart NZ 68, Nugget Point to Centre Island including Foveaux Strait, and NZ 6842, Plans in Stewart Island. We passed between Weka Island and Weka Reef, marked on the chart as having a depth of two metres or less. It was always covered with broken and turbulent water. Further east we could see spectacular large splashes as the southerly swell crashed on Theresa Rock. The headlands to Port Adventure were on our starboard side but we did not go in, instead we passed east of Entrance Island and its rocks.

We cleared the Breaksea Islands group, which included many scattered reefs and rocks, then steered southwest looking for Owen Island and the entrance to Lords River. Somehow we could not find the island, only headlands. The southwest swell increased to two metres and *Starlight* pounded into a rough sea. It was unpleasant travelling. We steered into a bay and out again. I took several GPS readings and somehow one of the waypoints ended up on the land. At 3pm I looked south and could identify Black Rock.

"I think we have passed the entrance and gone too far south," I confessed to Norm, so we turned the yacht around. I was right – now when we looked to the northeast we could see and identify Owen Island and the narrow entrance to the river. With the big sea swell now pushing us from behind, the yacht sped along and soon we were in the dogleg entrance to the calmer river estuary. I sighed with relief.

We saw patches of big kelp, a few rocky reefs and several coves with small golden sandy beaches. We passed a hunters' camp and went into The Nook, where we used the diagram in the guide to find a hawser stretched across a narrow recess in deep water. It was just the place to tie up to for the night and it even had a fresh water pipe attached. The time was now 4:30pm and it had taken seven hours to travel the leg, much longer than I had anticipated. But I reminded myself that at sea there are no signposts to show us the way.

We were in a very remote area surrounded by low hills covered with bush and short, scrubby trees. That evening three hunters came in to The Nook in a dinghy and dropped one man who went off into the scrub. Soon we heard a loud gunshot. Did he get a deer? Just before dark, the dinghy came back to find the hunter with his prize, a young whitetail deer. As they passed us, they called out an invitation to visit their camp. "Later on, perhaps tomorrow," we said.

The sky clouded over a little and it was dark by 9pm. During the afternoon Norm had pointed out some high, thin silvery clouds and they reminded me to look out for the Aurora Australis or Southern Lights which were often seen in these southern latitudes in March and September. Lords River (latitude 47 deg 5 min) would be the furthest south we would go. That night I had a good look at the sky but saw only patchy cloud and a few stars.

Next morning we raised the centre-plate and rudder halfway, unhitched our rope from the hawser and motored into the main flow of the river. The cruising guide recommended exploring the river by dinghy, going up on the last of the flood tide and returning with the start of the ebb, and suggested keeping a sharp lookout for logs.

We motored into the main river flow just after high tide and headed inland. We had heard that it was navigable as far as a waterfall about three miles upstream. We wound around several bends, enjoying the beautiful lush vegetation, but about half way to the waterfall we could see the sandy bottom in about a metre of water. Since we did not want to risk hitting anything or grounding, we decided we had seen enough and turned back. We motored to the cove where the hunters were camped, and anchored off near a lot of very thick bull kelp. There were seven men at the camp, dropped off the previous day by the chartered boat *Mana*. They would be there for ten days and had tents, camping gear, two dinghies and outboards, petrol, water, food, clothes, shooting gear and several dozen cans of beer. It was a well-used campsite, built and improved over the years by successive hunters, and had a stove, toilet and bathtub. Their main bivouac was a structure made by heavy canvas ex-railway wagon-covers stretched over a rough frame of irregular manuka branches. When we went inside it was dark but dry. It was furnished with old tables, easy chairs, a gas stove on a table and a sink, and we sat down to a welcome cup of tea. It was interesting to exchange experiences. They told us of the times that they been lost in the bush as each hill, valley or ridge looked the same, but now that GPS was available it was a great help. "A good compass could be handy too," we commented.

In the afternoon we moved to another cove with heaps of floating heavy kelp. The cloud lifted and the sun shone brightly, warming us a little, but a light easterly wind blew across the inlet. I had heard stories of huge seaweed 'like pillars that hold up the town hall' growing around Stewart Island, and wanted to have a look. I put on my wetsuit and flippers, fastened a snorkel and goggles, then swam around the inlet among the seaweed. The underwater plants were huge. Thick columns of a variety of plants in the sea were like a colourful garden, some with bright yellow pods and others with vivid green fringes. It made a pretty picture. I swam among and around this tangled tightly packed growth for over an hour. Small fish swam among the plants; perch, butterfish and shoals of tiny fish which seemed undisturbed by my presence. Although the air temperature was a cool 18 degrees Celsius, the water was comfortable and fresh. I was not disappointed, it was a truly great experience. But Norm was not a starter – he would rather have a chance to spear a big fish.

We weighed anchor and travelled back to The Nook for tea and a good night's sleep in calm surroundings.

That evening we discovered that the VHF radio had water in it from a leak in some screws in the toe-rail on the deck above. We took it off the shelf and replaced it with the reserve VHF, then glued up the leak. With this reserve radio hooked to the rear aerial we were able to call Maureen at Oban and get an incredibly clear reception. Our conclusion was that the number one radio had been malfunctioning for a while due to dampness, and that the aerial we had previously attached to the back-up radio was ineffective. Hopefully we would now have more dependable reception. We asked ourselves why we hadn't tried these options before.

It was just daylight as we left The Nook and motored out of Lords River into a slight sea with little wind. We had decided not to go further south to Port Pegasus, nor to go round the South Cape. Heading into the rough seas and strong southerly swells that were expected would take more time and petrol than we could spare, so we turned north and motored back to Oban with a following sea and an incoming tide.

By 10:40am we were berthed at the wharf in Halfmoon Bay. We went shopping for petrol and stores, then treated ourselves to lunch at the hotel to celebrate my recent birthday. We finished just in time to catch 'Billy the Bus', an old yellow Toyota wagon that seated 10 people and ran a one and a half-hour tour of the island. Sam the driver took us over all thirteen kilometres of local roads, gave us a lively commentary on the island's history and stopped at the bays with scenic views. The best lookout point was at Golden Bay overlooking Paterson Inlet.

The islanders told us they were relishing the fine weather. "Summer has come in March," they said, meaning that the weather had been unsettled and wintry up until then.

The land and sea forecasts for the area around Stewart Island were difficult for the weather experts to predict because of the lay of the land and the tunnel effect of Fouveaux Strait. We found that it was a case of keeping a good lookout for changes in the weather. However the climate is usually very mild with very little snow in winter. Stewart Island seemed like a potential tourist mecca, but we were puzzled by the low population (only 500) and the small school roll (which had dropped from around 80 children to 27). Was the isolation a deterrent for young families? Perhaps the fast ferry and the light aeroplane services from Bluff or Invercargill to Oban might put Stewart Island on the tourist map one day.

At 4:30pm I walked to the Post Office to buy some stamps and also picked up the census forms, one for a household and two for the occupants, which were due to be filled in the next day. We chatted with a maintenance worker at the hotel who had been questioning us about our life on board. He told us he had given notice and was catching the ferry to Bluff and then was off to Picton to buy a boat he had seen advertised.

"You've inspired me," he explained. "If you two can do it, so can I. I'm a bit younger than you and I have always wanted to have a boat to live on." We gave him our best wishes and hoped that we had not given him a false idea of what boating could be.

We left Oban and motored to Paterson Inlet. We anchored in the almost fully-enclosed Kaipipi estuary, putting a stern line on to a large log near the shore. The sea was calm and there was no wind, making it a very comfortable mooring. We reported our position to Ted at Oban, then Meri from Bluff Radio called us with great news.

"Your friend Sam is in Invercargill and is wondering when you will be at Bluff."

We told her to pass on the message that we would cross Foveaux Strait between Wednesday and Friday, timing it to arrive just before high tide. The moon was almost full so the tides were big, and we knew that the tidal flow at the entrance to Bluff Harbour could be very strong. Our next VHF call was from *Southern Bear.* Yes, it was them that we had followed into Paterson Inlet. They had gone on to Prices Inlet and we arranged a visit for the morning.

It was 6 March, 2001, census day, and we had a good laugh as we filled in our forms. How many rooms? Only one. Did we have TV, microwave, computer, Internet? No. We duly reported that we cooked with gas and had a cell-phone but no hot-water system. Somehow the questions seemed rather irrelevant. However there was a place for our usual address, so we would not be part of the 1.5 percent of the population that got missed out. At last we caught up with Chris on his spacious well-built 43-ft Roberts GRP yacht. *Southern Bear* was a welcome sight as it glided into the inlet at 11am. Chris had been away two months and had another month to go, and his new crew of three had just joined him at Oban. He was going back to Auckland by travelling north along the east coast, perhaps stopping at Akaroa.

He told us a bit about his trip. He had struck a 60-knot storm at Jackson Bay. He had often sailed or motored overnight between the fiords, entering at daylight and motoring inside during the day, so he didn't get much sleep at times. They had been in to Deep Cove too, and had done the bus trip to Manapouri Power Station, while we had walked to the Helena Falls. Like us, Chris had difficulty finding the entrance to Lords River and like us, he had used the Mana Cruising Club's books as his 'bibles' and guides. We spent a great two hours looking over each other's yachts and then Chris took off to Oban in his yacht to get census papers.

That afternoon Norm repaired the leaky compass. I realised that we had promised Pat and Graheme Sowman of Resolution Bay that we would visit their son Mark who managed a salmon farm in Big Glory Bay. We contacted him through Maureen on Oban VHF and the reply was, "Call tomorrow and I will show you around."

We motored in a calm sea and a light easterly breeze. It wasn't easy to find the Kiwa Salmon Farm rig with so many mussel and salmon farms in Big Glory Bay, but we were soon berthed at the loading bay. Mark took us on extensive tour of the complex. There were twenty on the staff, working seven days on and seven off, and Mark flew in from Invercargill each Monday morning then flew back on Thursday evening so he could be with his family for the weekend. The feed for the fish came all the way from South America and was processed into dry pellets in Australia. When we went into his office, I noticed a message on his white-board "Norm fish". Sure enough, he took us to a fish-pen and scooped an overgrown salmon into a net.

"Can you use it?"

"Of course I can. Anything we can't eat, I'll bottle in the preserving jars," I told him gratefully.

"I don't want you to waste it," he replied as he handed me the big fish. Then he told us that his father Graheme had recently had a heart attack. This news surprised and saddened us, and our heartfelt prayers that day were for Graheme in hospital and his wife Pat at Resolution Bay.

Next we motored over to Sailors Rest, a small shallow cove off Big Glory Bay, and had lunch. A stiff westerly wind had sprung up and we felt it was not safe to stay there so we headed back to Kaipipi, punching into a choppy rough sea all the way. It took us twice as long to do the return journey.

With two anchors out from the bow and a stern line back to the trees we felt secure as the southwest wind gusted to about 25 knots. I cooked a large piece of the delicious salmon for tea and bottled some in two jars in the pressure-cooker. We still had enough left over for two meals. It was a big fish.

Thursday's forecast was for rough seas, three metre swells and 25-knot southwest winds in Foveaux Strait – not a good time for us to cross. We made good use of the rest day by cleaning up and sorting out gear. I cleaned out the dead sandflies from under the spray dodger and in various nooks in the cockpit. Norm repaired the short in the wiring from the battery to the lights in the cabin. Then he unscrewed the round inspection seal in the flotation compartment under the double bunk at the bow and found a lot of water there. He sponged out ten buckets full, handing them up to me to tip overboard. This was not a good sign. I inspected the storage bins and found only one with a little bit of water in it. The slow seepage in the floor was something we had been putting up with for a while, sponging up the mess even at 3am. But this?

"We ought to keep a close eye on these leaks," I said. "We will need to do some repairs soon." But Norm was calm about it.

"It'll be all right. We could get home like this and then do the repairs."

Not likely, I thought, but said nothing. I hoped we could get to Bluff quickly.

We made a list of supplies to buy when we got there. We had not touched our reserve supplies of tinned or dry-freeze food, but after Norm had topped up the tanks we were down to 47 litres of petrol in reserve. We were the only boat moored in the calm, isolated Kaipipi Inlet and we had a good sleep that night. In the morning we found we had collected 4.5 litres of fresh water from the overnight rain that dripped from the boom tent.

Friday's weather report was good for a crossing, with a moderate sea, 20-knot southwest wind, coastal showers and some cloud but a three-metre southwest swell. The sun rose at 7:30am and soon we were away, motoring out of the cove and into Paterson Inlet. The high tide at Bluff was at 2:39pm and we estimated that it would take us seven hours to get there. We had breakfast on the way and after we had navigated our way between the Muttonbird or Titi Islands a light westerly wind came in to fill the mainsail and steady the yacht for an hour. There were numerous islands, rocks and reefs to avoid. We could see Ruapuke Island to the east, and the peaked Bluff hill in the north, but what was the tall mast ahead, and what was that beacon? When we got closer we established that the 'tall mast' was the chimney of the Tiwai Point smelter and the beacon was the lighthouse on Dog Island. How different things can look from out at sea.

Meri called us at 9:30am with an inquiry from Sam. "Tell him we hope to be at Bluff by 2pm," I replied.

"Go closer to the headland as you approach, and call Bluff Harbour Radio an hour before you arrive," were her instructions. We radioed at 12:30pm and were told to go to the fishermen's wharf.

As we approached the entrance, a shoal to the east of the channel had small swells on it and we caught one of the waves. We could see we needed to be closer to the headland to get into the deeper trough, and we moved over. As we motored into the harbour and passed the beacons we saw the tide racing in fast at about five knots. We were glad it was with us and not against us.

The tidal current slackened a little as we approached the wharf. Meri Leask had organised a berth for us and her husband, Ian, was at the end of the third jetty to show us where to go. Well timed. Soon we were alongside the berth and Ian helped us to secure *Starlight* to the wharf with mooring ropes, two springs and fenders. It was almost high tide.

*Starligh*t had safely taken us from Stewart Island across Foveaux Strait in six hours and we were now at Bluff.

14

Bluff – Dunedin

Day is dying in the west,
Angels watching over me, my Lord,
Time for me to take my rest,
Angels watching over me.
All day, all night, Angels watching over me.
Negro spiritual

Sam Medland was looking forward to joining us at Bluff and we were equally looking forward to his help and company. On 9 March I phoned him to say we had arrived and gave him a shopping list. That afternoon he arrived with Heather and Graham McKenzie who were retired farmers, and they stayed for a cuppa and a chat. Sam wanted to stay on board even though we would be in Bluff for a week or two, and he put his gear on the starboard quarter berth – his spot in *Starlight*. This suited him well.

After his hosts had gone, we told Sam about the leaks. We explained how *Starlight* had withstood the storm on the spit in Bruce Bay, and the 'unplanned beaching' in Isthmus Inlet. He agreed with me that Bluff, with its boat repair facilities, was a good place to inspect the hull and fix the leaks, and between us we soon won Norm over. We made inquiries about lifting the yacht out for repairs, but Bluff did not have a travel-lift for launches and yachts. The Harbour Board crane services and the charges per day on the hard were very expensive and more suited to fishing boats or ships.

We were not sure what to do. We told Sam that we were still trying to read the Bible from cover to cover and pray for the people at each place we visited, and he suggested we also pray for God's guidance about the repairs. We did this together.

The answer to our prayer came the next morning when Keith Aitken, a friend from the Goldwing motorcycle club, called to see us.

"Don't worry about getting a crane," Keith told us. "My son-in-law Earl Hoffman repairs boats all the time, I'll ask him to arrange a trailer and pull *Starlight* out for you." This was good news and I was reminded of a Bible verse, Daniel 9 verse 23, which says that as soon as you begin to pray, God is working on the answer.

I walked to the motor camp to do the laundry and have a 'proper' shower. There was an automatic washing machine but no dryer, so I had to carry the load back to the jetty where I pegged it to a makeshift clothesline and the brisk southerly wind soon dried the clothes. It was very different from the marina in Auckland where boaties were forbidden to have their laundry on show. I was surprised to hear that the forecast was for frosts inland. We had been wearing long-sleeved shirts for the last few weeks, mainly as protection against the sandflies, but now the temperature was dropping. It was down to 9 degrees Celsius that morning and it was still early March.

Sam rang his friend Alf Beckham, who offered to pick us up for the Sunday morning Salvation Army service and give us lunch afterwards. However Alf had difficulty finding our berth because of the dense fog around the wharves at Bluff that morning. He drove us to Invercargill where we joined in the service led by Captains Dean and Glenys Fairhurst. Norm took his cornet and played in the small band, and we found the hymns and choruses uplifting and cheerful. The message was from Deuteronomy, chapter 5 verse 29, after God had delivered the Ten Commandments, when he said, "Oh, that they would always have a heart for me, wanting to obey my commandments. Then all would go well with them in the future." It gave us much to think about.

Alf was a widower who lived with his adult son John. He cooked us a delicious hot meal which we shared with his friend Margaret, and after lunch they all came back to look over our yacht. Then Alf took us to the lookout on the top of Bluff Hill. The fog had lifted and we had a panoramic view of Foveaux Strait. We could see where we had come from, such a wide expanse of ocean with islands dotted here and there. Next we went to the Land's End Restaurant at Stirling Point for Devonshire scones and coffee, and watched the boats coming into Bluff Harbour. When he dropped us back at the jetty, Alf said he had really enjoyed our visit. We had enjoyed our day too.

Very soon the yacht *Wild South*, owned by Earl and Lynn Hoffman, berthed on the other side of our jetty. They had been fishing beside one of the offshore islands, and gave us some cod fillets. Earl told us how valuable his radar had been that morning as they had narrowly avoided hitting another boat coming towards them in the early morning fog. Keith Aitken had already spoken to Earl about our need to repair *Starlight* and he was ready to help.

"I'll arrange a trailer and pull you out at high tide on Monday," he offered. "There's a concrete ramp near the clubrooms not far away." We all agreed that was really good news. It gladdened my heart.

The next morning Keith called again and he and Norm talked for hours. I walked to the post office to post our census forms and was pleasantly surprised at the friendliness of the local people. Total strangers treated me like an old friend and chatted about local matters.

True to his word, Earl turned up just after five with his truck and a big boat trailer. We motored to the ramp, lifted up the centre-plate, rudder and outboard motor, then floated the yacht onto the trailer. We had to use all our fenders and bits of wood to support the hull on the trailer, but there were no problems pulling it out of the water and we were soon parked high and dry on some flat land near the engineer's workshop.

Earl was quick to inspect the GRP hull and his well-trained eye soon found the bruises. One, the size of a fist, was in the middle behind the centre-plate. There were also several deep grooves in the side of the bow where water had been seeping into the storage compartments under the double bunk. A tiny hole was drilled in the main bruise, and water trickled out all night.

Next morning the men drilled a larger 2.5cm hole. Then the water poured out fast. They made an inspection hole in the floor of the cabin just above the damaged area, to find out how much water was still in the hull. Because of the heavy crossbeams there was quite a bit. Norm said it needed pumping and drying out.

The bright yellow yacht was conspicuous on the hard and word soon got around that we were doing repairs. One firm let us use their power and an extra long lead was coupled up to our 240-volt system. This meant we could use the lights, the electric jug for boiling water, the battery charger and some of our power tools. The owners of Bluff Engineering and Welding Co Ltd allowed us to use their toilets even when they were closed. People popped in to lend us various items like a heat lamp, a jack to level the trailer and a piece of wood. "Might come in handy," Norm said. We also asked Stephen of Southern Ocean Safety Ltd to repair our dinghy.

The Maritime Museum near the Island Wharf Bridge was open from 1 pm to 5 pm each day, and we were intrigued enough to spend some time there. Southland's maritime history included oystering, whaling and the development of Island Harbour, which was reclaimed from shallow sandbanks on the western side of the harbour to become Bluff's main shipping port in 1960. I really enjoyed climbing aboard the old oyster boat *Monica 11*, which is on the hard as the museum's largest exhibit.

We visited Keith and Helen Aitken who cooked us roast pork for tea on Tuesday. The view from their lounge window of the entrance to Bluff Harbour was spectacular.

Goldwing rider Mel Shaw and his wife Alice came the next day and we went to their 315-acre sheep and cattle farm at Waianiwa in Southland. He also took us to Riverton. The southwest swells coming in the entrance to the river showed up the shallows as surf and brown sandy patches. We could see it would be tricky coming in at half tide unless we had a local boat to guide us, but it might have been possible on our own at full tide if we read the waves correctly. We saw the wharves and shelter inside the Aparima estuary, where a number of fishing boats were berthed or moored, but we were glad we had not tried to get in there during the storm.

Mel helped us buy some large shiny paua shells for our granddaughter Talitha, and we stayed at the Shaws for tea.

On Thursday we were invited for afternoon tea at Ian and Meri Leask's home. Meri's VHF and SSB radios were placed conveniently in her kitchen, and I wondered how she managed when she went out to social events. She told me she had a portable radio, but most calls came at scheduled times. Her father and husband had both been fishermen and she knew all the local boats. Her dedication as a volunteer over many years was much to be admired. We were very grateful for her timely advice and conveyed our heartfelt thanks. Another invitation came from Jon Beask, who was repairing his 16ft Hartley trailer-sailer. Jon had recently retired to Bluff because of the cheap housing. He was enthusiastic about boating which was a new experience for him, a previously landlocked forestry worker, and was very interested in our trip. Then the owner of a green Gazelle stored in the Bluff Yacht Club's enclosure sought us out to say he had heard about our trip around the South Island.

We met Keith Yates, the owner of *Ulla* which was a 36ft keeler on the hard near us. He told us he had been motoring at night from Puysegur Point towards Bluff in rough seas and strong winds when his yacht was knocked down and lay on its side. Most of the gear inside her shifted to the downside, but fortunately she stayed afloat and did not fill with water.

"What happened, how did you manage?" I queried.

"A large wave spun the yacht around 180 degrees the next morning and it became upright," he replied. "I eventually came into Bluff and put the yacht on this cradle. I plan to add extra lead weight to the keel," he added.

Another vessel on the hard was a catamaran, *Cat Knapp*, owned by 69-year-old Jack. He had sailed around the world in a mono-hull yacht at four knots, but was now planning another trip in this much-faster catamaran, expecting speeds of fifteen knots or more. As we looked over his catamaran, he told me how rare it was to meet a woman who liked sailing. He said he'd surveyed about 150 sailing couples and only five women had said they enjoyed it – the rest just went along for the sake of their husbands. I was interested, but not surprised.

Several years ago I was asked to give a lecture to a boating club on sailing from a woman's viewpoint. I talked about men not 'hogging' the sailing tasks;

their partners needed practice at steering, hoisting the sails, starting the outboard and handling the anchor. "You never know when you might fall overboard, at anchor or at sea, when your wife is the only person on board. She needs to know how to handle the boat, and not just do the cooking," I told them. "If the outboard pull-cord is too strong for her, get an electric start. If the anchor is too heavy, get a winch." At the end of my talk, however, the questions were mainly about recipes because most of my audience did not have wives willing to go with them and they had to do their own cooking. "You're very lucky," they told Norm.

On Friday, Norm inspected the hull and considered it dry enough to start the repairs. The weather was fine and I took off on a bus to Invercargill to buy warmer clothes and some groceries. I left it to the men to do the smelly fibre-glassing, using the repair kit we carried on board. They scraped off the GRP gel coat and smoothed the surface, then using the two-pot polyester resin mix and some fibreglass cloth they filled the hole from below. To make extra sure that the entire bruise was covered, they put more resin and cloth on from the top through the inspection plate. When I arrived back the task was done and Norm told me that it would need all night to harden. The next morning I polished the hull. It took several hours and a lot of polish but at last it was clean and shiny again. While I was working I noticed a number of trucks carrying big loads of logs, crossing the bridge to the Island Harbour wharves where the logs were being shipped out. On the other side of the channel was a very long wharf spanning the shallows from the deep water to the Tiwai Point Aluminium Smelter on the eastern side. Bauxite from Queensland in Australia was chemically treated to form alumina, then shipped to Bluff for smelting at Tiwai Point where it was electrolytically reduced to aluminium ingots. The Tiwai Point plant, opened in 1971, was huge by world standards.

Daylight saving time ended on Saturday night, 17 March 2001, giving us an extra hour of sleep. We could now expect shorter daylight hours and cooler temperatures.

Sam and I went to the 10:30 am service that Sunday at the Bluff Christian Fellowship, a small happy congregation that made us welcome. But Norm stayed with the yacht because he had found a small leak in the hull, near the repair he had already carried out. He spent the morning drying the spot and filling the crack with resin and cloth. I was relieved that *Starlight* was still on the hard.

In the afternoon, Sam went for a three-hour walk around Bluff Hill, taking the scenic Foveaux Walk and then the Glory Track. Norm and I walked to the motor camp to have a shower and do the laundry. Before we left, we locked the cabin hatch and lifted up the stern ladder for security reasons but when we came back we found a police officer waiting for us. Some children had dropped the ladder, climbed up into *Starlight*'s cockpit, taken our petrol can and poured petrol into the fuel tank of a diesel tractor parked nearby. They had also lifted the cover on our 10-hp outboard. Luckily Sam spotted the oil dipstick in the nearby grass where it had been thrown. The parents, who had been busy cleaning their boat while their children got into mischief, were very apologetic and gave us four fresh paua in their shells as a peace offering. Not much harm had been done.

We walked to the Paua House on Marine Parade and met 98-year-old Fred. He and his late wife Myrtle had collected thousands of paua and other shells, some from overseas, and displayed them in several rooms inside the house. They had won numerous awards from the tourist industry for their unique collection. It was a visit not to be missed.

On the way back, Sam noticed an old two-storey hotel for sale. It was called Sea View, the same as his old homestead on Great Barrier Island, and this brought back happy memories. Ian and Meri visited us that evening. It was good to see them and we appreciated getting to know them personally, not just as voices on the radio. Every day it seemed that someone stopped by to ask about our trip around the South Island. Most of them were amazed and gave us plenty of encouragement along the lines of, "Good on you" and "Go for it". Keith also called most days and was a great help and encouragement.

We arranged for Earl to put *Starlight* back in the sea at high tide on Tuesday 20 March, and we were ready at 11:30am when he arrived with his truck. In no time at all *Starlight* was floating again. We couldn't thank Earl enough for his timely and willing help. We motored back to the jetty and our previous berth. After a late lunch I read a book for a while and went to sleep. Norm followed my example and soon we were both snoring loudly. We had not had any daytime rest for weeks, and our systems seemed to be saying the hull's repaired, it's time to relax.

That evening Norm rang Raewyn, to let her know that we were back in the water. I started watching the sea again, noting the smaller tides and slower currents under the jetty which were a big contrast to the full moon conditions of the previous week. The forecast was for easterly winds and rough seas in Foveaux Strait, so there was no question of leaving the next day. That night we all slept soundly in calm water.

From studying the charts and the *Stewart Island Cruising Guide*, I found that there were only a few places along the south coast to anchor safely. To follow the coastline round to Dunedin would take at least 30 hours and include sailing or motoring overnight. We needed an offshore or light southwest wind, slight to moderate sea, small swells and fair weather. Not asking much, were we?

Rain set in early on Wednesday morning. Norm's list of repairs was all ticked off. Water, petrol, food were stocked up. The gear was stowed and the dinghy firmly fastened down flat on the foredeck. We were just waiting for the right weather, and we waited all that day. For tea I cooked fresh lamb cutlets, cabbage, pumpkin and potatoes followed by a cuppa, a piece of luncheon cake and an apple.

People ask me what do yachties do in wet weather when we're holed up in a harbour or at anchor. I usually answer sleep, chores, read, cook, eat and sleep again. Sam liked to do crosswords and play chess. He got me interested in crosswords, but not Norm, and challenged me to a game of chess. Our first game lasted an hour and a half, and he won. The second time our game lasted two hours and I won. He would have to challenge Norm next time.

A weak front was passing over the area and the marine forecast, at 5am on Thursday 22 March, was for a calm sea, no wind and some light cloud. We were off. We had an early breakfast, filled the Thermos flasks and left Bluff at 6:45 am, putting in a TR call to Meri at 7am. We motored out at slack water and turned east after clearing the shallows. Sunrise was at 7:15 am and we were north of Dog Island soon afterwards. We followed the coast using chart NZ 681, which covered most of Foveaux Strait. At 10:15am we were off Waipapa Point, which had a light on it, and I marked a GPS waypoint. It was necessary to steer slightly south of east to keep two to three miles off this rugged coast till we came to Slope Point, also with a lighthouse on it. I unrolled chart NZ 68, which covered the area from Centre Island to Nugget Point. I had marked the possible anchorages with my pink blob, but all were exposed to the southern swells.

Sam was keen to sail so as soon as a light northeast wind came we hoisted both sails to assist the motor. We followed the coast in an easterly direction, passing Chasland Mistake and Tautuku Peninsular. After we passed Long Point the yacht was heading into the northeasterly wind so we dropped the sails. The low-lying hills and farmland along this coast were a complete contrast to the high mountains in Fiordland.

Meri called us on channel 61. "A yacht called *The Shag* is coming over from Paterson Inlet on Stewart Island, heading for Dunedin," she told us, "Contact them on channel 8 or 10." That was great. We could see their white sails in the distance to the southeast – they had some wind out there, but there was none for us closer to the coast. We radioed John and Robyn Armstrong on *The Shag* and arranged to keep in contact. It was good to know we had company for this leg. We lost sight of them for a time but then saw their slim mast several miles behind us. They too had lost the wind and dropped their sails.

The sea was slight and became very calm at 5pm as we slowed down in the lee of Nugget Point. The tide was low and the kelp hung down from the rocks. We saw seals swimming close by, and we were close enough to the lighthouse to see tourists behind the netting fence. Norm and Sam took photographs, and we had a hot meal of eggs, baked beans and toast. It had been a very pleasant day's journey. *The Shag* caught up with us shortly after we left Nugget Point and passed us at 7pm. We all called out and waved. The third chart, NZ 66 from Nugget Point to Katiki Point, was unrolled. The sea became moderate with a northeast wind on the nose and a one-metre northeast swell. We motored north for a time keeping near *The Shag*. In the distance we could see the Otago Peninsula. Norm took a compass bearing and set Fred, our Autohelm, at 30 degrees to head for the point. With *The Shag* close by we had no qualms or fears about an overnight trip. How wrong could we be?

Darkness came at 8pm while Norm was on watch. At 10pm I put on warm, waterproof clothing, as a bit of spray was coming over the cockpit, and joined him on deck. We could easily see *The Shag's* masthead and navigation lights ahead. The sea became rough with a two-metre northeast swell and *Starlight* pitched into a stiff 20-knot northeasterly wind, but she rode splendidly over each wave. At midnight the clear night sky was ablaze with bright stars and we could see the lights of Dunedin South along the shore. Sam woke from a good four-hour sleep and came on deck, and Norm went below to rest although the movement of the yacht made sleep difficult.

Half an hour later a dense sea fog suddenly enveloped us. The shore lights disappeared and it was difficult to see *The Shag*. The speed and course of each yacht varied so much that we gradually lost sight of each other, and Sam and I strained our eyes as the fog thickened. *The Shag* could be very close or far away from us, we did not know. At 1:30 am I turned the VHF radio to channel 10 and very soon John called us.

"I am following my waypoints on the GPS along the coast and you are leaving us. Our radar shows you a mile away from us to the east, almost off the screen," he said.

"Radar?" we all exclaimed. Sam and I realised that if they had radar our GPS would not be needed. Their radar would pick up rocks and reefs, boats and any other objects in our path. Norm picked up the mike and said, "Great news but we can't see you."

John and Robyn guided us towards their yacht, slowing down until we could see their masthead light. We steered minus 10 degrees and then another minus 10 on the Autohelm until we could see their yacht and we fell in behind and stayed there, steering carefully and adjusting our speed as needed. They had radar, and they were local Otago yachties who knew the way. At times the sea was rough and the strong northeast wind blew right on the nose as we motored at four knots along the obscured coastline.

Norm came on deck at 3am and I went below to monitor the VHF radio, now on channel 8. It was very comforting to know that *The Shag* was close by and in contact. I heard nothing on the radio until 5am, when news came that a large ship was due at the Taiaroa Heads and that the pilot was coming to take it into the Otago Harbour. It was still dark and very foggy, so both yachts hove to for some time. We kept a close watch out, hoping not to lose sight of *The Shag* in the fog. I took a GPS reading to find that we were to the east of the Heads.

The grey fog was very thick. "Nil visibility," Robyn called it. The lighthouse on top of the cliffs at the Taiaroa Heads was still flashing at 7:30am but could not penetrate the fog. However we could see the sharp rocks at the bottom of the cliffs. We caught sight of the ship we had been warned about, but then lost it in the fog. The grey-green sea was slight to moderate and the wind a fresh northeasterly. The dawn came slowly that morning. Eventually we saw the ship entering the heads and both yachts followed it in. The entrance was narrow with a breakwater to the north.

We followed *The Shag* up the channel, past many markers and beacons. Each post was numbered with even numbers to port and odd to starboard, in ascending order from the entrance. The fog started to lift and we had more visibility, but it was low tide and John and Robyn wisely decided to wait in Hamilton Bay. They guided us in and we tried to follow their course but missed the deeper channel and got stuck on a sandbar. We had to lift the centre-plate to halfway and free *Starlight* so we could motor towards *The Shag*, now at anchor, and tie up alongside them. It was 10am and we had been at sea for over 27 hours.

We all had breakfast aboard *The Shag* that morning. We talked about our night's adventure and we called John and Robyn our 'Guiding Angels', much to their embarrassment. We had greatly appreciated their local knowledge, sailing experience, GPS and radar skills as this area was new to us. Even though I had the charts, to have a local boat to guide us in was a bonus.

They told us of their experiences over the years as well as their just-completed circumnavigation of Stewart Island, which had taken three weeks. We also shared our dream of circumnavigating New Zealand in our trailer-yacht and spoke about some of our trips, particularly the adventures along the west coast and in the fiords.

It wasn't long before the tide was on the make and we motored out, heading into a stiff southwest wind. *The Shag* led us past Port Chalmers, negotiated around Goat Island and took us in towards the Otago Yacht Club. The channel wound around lots of mud-banks, now being slowly covered by the rising water.

"Go in after beacon number 63 and line up the two white markers; these will guide you into the enclosure," were John's instructions. We soon found a place to berth near a pontoon, while *The Shag* rafted up to another yacht. We went ashore and were warmly welcomed by Kevin Martin, the marina manager. We enjoyed a shower and then joined members of the Otago Yacht Club for a well-cooked hot meal.

There was much to talk about. Keith Maydon was on duty at the bar and recognised us. "Yes, we're still getting around the South Island in *Starlight*," Norm told him with a grin. Keith had moored beside us in his Noelex 25 trailer yacht, *Blue Inn*, back at Tarakohe on 4 January, almost three months before. He was intrigued to find us down there and curious about our trip. I found out that Robyn Armstrong was a Past Commodore of the Otago Yacht Club and held the Ocean Yachtmaster Certificate. She was the first woman I had met who had these qualifications. John was also very skilled and experienced, and between them they were well qualified to sail anywhere. Three weary seafarers slept well on board *Starlight* that night, but not before we had read our two chapters from the Bible and thanked God for guidance, for bringing us safely into the harbour and for our two 'Guiding Angels'.

Next morning we decided to shift to our allocated berth on the floating jetty while the early morning sea was still calm. We were able to hook up to power and water and the fees were $4.50 per night plus $3.40 per person – good value. We rang Raewyn to give her an update, and since the Otago Yacht Club was within walking distance of the central city we took the opportunity to stretch our legs.

Norm telephoned his cousin Christine Fitzpatrick and her husband Colin. They came to see the yacht, invited us for tea at their home in George Street, and offered to lend us Christine's Subaru station wagon. We shared our experiences of overseas travel (we had each visited the Anderson families in Wisconsin during 1998). We exchanged family news and talked about yachting and motorcycling. Colin still had the 16ft Pelin trailer-yacht he had built more than twenty years earlier.

The use of a car was a real bonus. We found the Dunedin North Salvation Army Hall in time for the 10:30am service the next day. Among the many students in the congregation was Fui Washburn, an 18-year-old Samoan from Porirua, who welcomed us with much excitement. She had recently started studying health science at the university and was missing her family and familiar faces. Captain Joanne Baynon led a lively service with some of the students taking part.

Freda Almond, Sam Medland, Norm, Mavis and Reg Almond at the Otago Marina

We were invited by David Ojala and his wife Dawn, to join the students in a barbecue lunch, and had a relaxing time sharing food and talking with them under the shady trees. Later we took Fui to look over *Starlight,* and in return she showed us around Cumberland Hall which housed and fed 315 students. About a quarter of the Dunedin population were students and there were many halls of residence in the city. Dunedin folk also took pride in offering board and home hospitality to the students. On Monday we shopped – at the supermarket, The Warehouse, Macdonald's (for lunch), and the second-hand shops. We filled a container with good spring water from the tap at Speights, topped up the petrol cans and ended up at Reg and Freda Almond's home at Abbottsford for tea.

Keith Maydon contacted us with an invitation to talk to the Otago Trailer Yacht Squadron meeting that Wednesday night. Ever since we had arrived we had a stream of interested visitors to *Starlight*, wanting to hear about our experiences and giving us their valuable local knowledge in return. Those visitors included Keith's friend Murray Watson, who had been with him at Tarakohe in his Farr 6000 trailer-yacht *Ceol Mara.* They had towed their yachts non-stop from Dunedin to Nelson, a 12-hour trip, then launched them and toured the Abel Tasman National Park coastline to Tarakohe and back. It was hard to believe that we were here in Dunedin after travelling those many miles around the coast. Keith and Murray were keen for other trailer-yacht club members to hear our story – how we did it and what happened on the way.

I found some notes of our North Island trip in 1997 and gathered up a few useful books, charts, photographs and postcards to illustrate our talk. Norm collected together various pieces of equipment including a car tube, the one-litre shower, the GPS and the Autohelm.

Later on that day, Norm checked for leaks in the yacht but found none – praise be. Sam and Norm were fascinated by the ingenious 100-year-old system for hauling out boats using a cradle on rails and a pit that had a trolley running at right angles to the stands. Norm was also intrigued by a small 16ft teak clinker boat called *Plucky* that had come from Scotland as a lifeboat many years earlier and was now on a hard stand. The owner told him that it had belonged to Roger Carey, a well-known boat builder.

While walking around the trailer-yacht yard, Norm noticed a yacht full of water because the cover had blown off in heavy rain. He contacted the owner who was only too happy to accept his offer to clean it out. Sam pitched in and gave him a hand.

After we had been to the city in the car to get supplies, we found that the subway underneath the railway line was flooded to a depth of half a metre because of a particularly high tide. It was the only road to the yacht club so we had to leave the car on the city side and walk back along the railway line to where *Starlight* was berthed. When Captain Annette Garrett, formerly of Porirua, called to visit us she had to do the same. On Wednesday Christine needed her car so we returned it with our grateful thanks.

Keith picked us up at 7pm and took us to the Leviathan Hotel lounge where he had organised the Otago Trailer Yacht Squadron meeting. About 25 people turned up. I used the North Island and South Island map transparencies to show the places we had visited – highlighted by my 'pink blob' marker pen. Norm explained the special construction of our Gazelle yacht, and Sam talked about some of his experiences growing up on Great Barrier Island and then some details of the Gisborne to Whakatane section of the North Island trip. We took turns to highlight different aspects of the trip. I gave some details of going into the bar harbours on the west coast, up rivers and the unplanned beaching. We talked for over an hour and a half, but still only covered our experiences briefly. The questions flowed on and on as the audience showed their intense interest and attention to detail. At 9:45 pm Keith thanked us and tried to wrap it up, but still the questions came. Even after we had finished, people kept coming up to us and talking. We were warmly thanked for sharing our experiences, and felt it had been an encouraging night.

The weather report for the next few days was for a southwest front coming over the South Island bringing cold showers, strong winds and rough seas. While we waited for the weather, I did research for Freda's Cooper family history at the public and the Hocken libraries. Later Freda and Reg called and took us driving around Dunedin, their home town.

By Friday we were all ready to move on. A $7 meal at the Otago Yacht Club was a treat and we enjoyed talking to John and Robyn and the other members. They gave us hints on sailing north, especially on the approaches to Oamaru Harbour and how to miss the sandbar at the entrance. They gave us computer printouts of the weather patterns and the latest forecast for the next day – fine weather, a 25-knot westerly, three-metre southerly swells and rough seas easing. We paid Kevin $117.60 for the eight days we had been there, and kept the receipt as a memento.

Most days the marine weather forecast began with, "A gale warning is in force at …" But on Saturday 31 March the 5am marine forecast had no such warnings and was favourable for our leg north to Oamaru, so we cast off and motored out of the club's enclosure into the channel in the clear morning air. What a change from the day of our arrival.

The tide was coming in and we had to combat the rip at the narrow channel near Goat Island. It took over two hours to get to the heads, and as we rounded the last bend a big Sealord fishing boat came in so we pulled well over to port. We could see the cliffs, the lighthouse and the Royal Albatross colony, all sights we had missed on the way in. Before we left the shelter of the Otago Harbour we had our devotions and thanked God for all the people we met. Their hospitality, kindness, local knowledge, intense interest and encouragement had meant a lot to us and we were grateful.

What lay ahead along the east coast we were yet to discover.

above: Graheme and Pat Sowman welcome us at Resolution Bay, the start of our circumnavigation of the South Island, on 16th December 2000

right: At Nelson, Diane and Harley Watts from Waitara, Taranaki

below: *Starlight* on the sand at low tide, Awaroa Inlet, Abel Tasman National Park

Starlight moored in Tarakohe Harbour, Golden Bay

Starlight berthed at Westport

Low tide at Greymouth Wharf – note the long vertical ladder

Starlight floating in an eddy off the Mahitahi River, Bruce Bay

above: Julie Lougesen, who with her husband Bruce runs the Bay Takeaways caravan at Bruce Bay

left: Jim Fern, president of the Westport Yacht Club, came on board *Starlight* to meet us

A brilliant sunset seen from the Nelson Marina

Starlight follows the fishing boat *Kutere* into Greymouth Harbour

Norm replaces a damaged outboard bracket on *Starlight* at the launching ramp, Deep Water Basin, Milford Sound

top left: Starlight leans down a hole in the Mahitahi River, Bruce Bay, at low tide during the night.
top right: Mavis returns a spade to Brian and Eleanor Titheridge after Norm had used it to dig out the admiralty anchor embedded in the sand after the storm.
above left: Carol Brown maintains the Fiordland Radio service from Te Anau. *above right:* Norm, Mavis and Morgan Slykerman on *Starlight* during a fishing trip in Milford Sound

Starlight on a flat sand spit at Bruce Bay at low tide, with five anchors spread out

top and middle left: sleeping bunk and two-burner cook stove aboard *Starlight*. *top right:* Helena Falls, Deep Cove, Doubtful Sound. *above:* keeler *Time Lord* in the mist at Crooked Arm, Doubtful Sound

High mountains and reflections in Crooked Arm, Doubtful Sound

Norm rowing to find a water pipe, marked by stripes on a tree, to collect brackish water in North Port, Chalky Inlet

Starlight anchored in Kisbee Bay, Preservation Inlet, Fiordland

The "unplanned beaching" on the rocks behind Little Island, Isthmus Sound

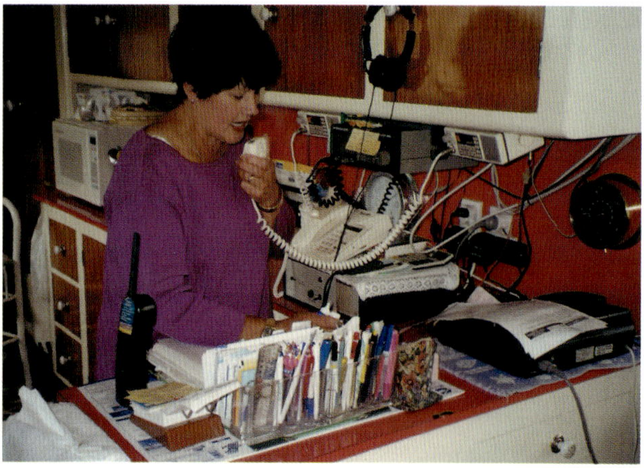

above left: Lyn and Bill Ayto and their ten passengers on mv *Takaroa* visit us while we are moored behind Stick Island in Wet Jacket Arm

above: Mavis with Mark Sowman, manager of the Big Glory Bay Salmon Farm, Stewart Island

left: Meri Leask in action on Bluff Fishermen's Radio

below: *The Shag* passing us at Nugget Point on the southeast corner of the South Island

above: Mavis, Robin and John Armstrong and Sam Medland rejoice aboard *The Shag* in Otago Harbour after safely negotiating a fog at night.

above right: Ted Boraman on his fishing boat *Angitu* at Oamaru.

right: Earl Hoffman supplied trailer and truck to haul *Starlight* out of the water at Bluff

below: *Southern Bear* at anchor in Kaipipi Cove, Paterson Inlet, Stewart Island.

Fishermen Gordon Mitchell and colleagues gave us good advice at Timaru

above: Dinner for three aboard *Starlight*

left: Sam Medland and Geof Fathers at Oamaru

The Collett and Hutson families visit us on board *Starlight* at Lyttelton

Ron Bingham took Norm to buy petrol while we were at Akaroa

Sam Medland looking at the entrance to the Oamaru Harbour at low tide

Starlight looks so small compared with the bigger fishing boat and the high wharf at Timaru. Margaret Bailey and her daughter, Treena, took Norm in their car to buy petrol

Kaikoura fisherman Victor Foster on *Takapu*

An early morning farewell from Joan and Ray Martin and their dog Deefa at the South Bay Marina, Kaikoura

Kay and Mark Backhouse (back left) with Rex and Irene Greenwood and Mavis, and Greenwood grandchildren Angus and Rebecca (front left) at Lyttelton

The launching ramp at South Bay, Kaikoura, with an early dusting of snow on the Kaikoura Range

Looking back at the entrance as we motor up the Wairau River at full tide

Doris Holdaway takes the rope as we tie up in the Opawa River

Starlight motors out towards the sea, 4 June 2001. Photo Doris Holdaway

Mavis aboard *Starlight* at Ted Perano's jetty on the Opawa River, near Blenheim

Norm and Mavis on their 1986 Honda GL1200A Goldwing motorcycle, ready for another adventure

Starlight's 'lady skipper' hauls up the pink anchor for the last time on their South Island journey - Oyster Bay, Port Underwood

Home at last - Mavis and Norm pose in their lifejackets at the Onepoto jetty, Porirua Harbour on 7th June 2001

Starlight moored at the Mana Cruising Club's wharf after crossing Cook Strait at the end of the South Island circumnavigation

15

Oamaru – Lyttelton

When night has fallen on the stormy deep
And the sailor's home is far,
He lifts up his eyes to the heavenly lights,
And steers by the faithful star.
Grace Gleam and F A Jackson

It wasn't long before we passed the entrance breakwater and left the shelter of Otago Harbour on that fine Saturday morning. Outside the breakers the blue Pacific Ocean welcomed us with a low one-metre southeasterly swell that pushed *Starlight* along.

"Enough wind to sail," Norm called out eagerly. Sam and I soon had the two sails unfurled. But we sailed at two knots for only a short time before the breeze died and we were motoring again. We dropped the jib but kept the mainsail unfurled to steady *Starlight.* Norm steered a northerly course and we passed several bays and low headlands, keeping about three miles off the coast. We cleared Danger Reef and, just before we reached Shag Point, we spotted the 13-metre cairn erected in memory of Otago settler and politician Sir John McKenzie on Puketapu Hill 343 metres above the town of Palmerston. It was certainly a conspicuous tower.

I changed from chart 66 to chart 64, Otago Peninsula to Banks Peninsula, long before we reached Katiki Point since the two charts overlapped. As we approached Moeraki, a big clump of seaweed got wrapped around the hull, centre-plate and motor so Norm put the motor into reverse and went around in a circle while Sam pushed the bulk of it off with a boat hook. In a few minutes we were on our way north again. We noticed many patches of discoloured, brownish seawater about two miles from the shore. Was it krill? No. Had the sea currents stirred up brown sand? Hardly. Maybe it was plankton. We didn't know, and resolved to ask the next lot of fishermen we met. (Later we did, and they told us it was a harmless algal bloom.) Sam tried to catch a fish on a lure trolling behind, but caught only large and inedible barracouta so he gave up.

A little bit of easterly wind developed in the afternoon, so it was up with the jib and we sailed for a while again, but there was not really enough puff and as we wanted to get to Oamaru before sundown we motor-sailed. The gentle swell created a good surf which helped us identify the reefs. At 4pm, when I took a GPS reading, we were two miles off Orore Point and could see the Oamaru headland to the north. I tried to call the Moeraki Radio on the VHF channel 62 but there was no reply. However Keith and Martin spoke with me from the Otago marina, where they had just finished their Saturday regatta.

"Where are you?" they asked.

"Near Oamaru headland," I replied.

"You've done well to get so far," Martin said, and told us how to negotiate the shallows and avoid the sandbar at the entrance to the Oamaru Harbour.

We had a call from Ted on his fishing boat *Angitu*. He had been listening in and offered us a berth alongside his boat at the wharf. "Follow me in," he suggested. But we established that he could see a larger yacht approaching from the north near the harbour entrance, and didn't realise we were still about two miles south. He took his boat in alone and by the time we got to the entrance there was another fishing boat there for us to follow. We watched carefully as it avoided the shallows and surf near the entrance.

Norm lined up the yacht club's two white markers then skilfully steered *Starlight* through the entrance, turning closely around the western end of the Holmes wharf, then gliding us towards the berth. By 5pm *Starlight* was rafted up beside *Angitu*. Ted Boraman welcomed us and offered water, power and toilet facilities aboard his 44ft motor-cruiser which was set up for fishing parties. Very soon Alasdair Sime, a member of the North Otago Yacht and Power Boat Club, turned up to offer us the use of the club's facilities on the other side of the harbour and lend us a key for the showers. John Armstrong had telephoned him about us. What a lot of thoughtful people, caring for a visiting yacht crew coming up the coast. On Sunday 1 April we woke up to the sound of our alarm clock at 6.45am. Ted was due to leave at 7am for a fishing trip and we had to cast off from beside his boat. His ten passengers arrived, all warmly dressed on this cool morning and equipped with waterproof coats, rods and reels. Ted takes his guests twelve miles off the coast to a reef where blue cod is plentiful, and they were expecting a good catch.

We motored across the little harbour and tied up to a small jetty near the club's facilities. We had showers and then watched powerboats being launched at the nearby ramp, their owners taking advantage of the fine Sunday morning. There were hundreds of shags sitting along the mole. I couldn't even attempt to count them. The small swell coming into the harbour rippled towards the jetty, making the yacht lurch against it, and we had to put all our fenders, mooring ropes and springs out to combat the surge. It was definitely not a comfortable place to be so we motored back to the Holmes wharf and berthed near the small landing platform.

We walked into town past historic buildings of creamy-white Oamaru limestone. The large and impressively-decorated Victorian buildings were part of the old town area, constructed between 1870 and 1890. We found the Salvation Army Citadel, recently rebuilt in this same splendid Oamaru stone. The service started at 10:30am and the large congregation included people of all ages and many family groups. A brass band accompanied the hymns and a praise group, consisting of guitar, flute and keyboard players with three singers, led the singing for the more modern choruses. A visiting pastor gave the Bible message. Captains Mark and Brenda Ennever, who had been in charge of the Porirua Corps in 1997, made us welcome.

That afternoon, several interested yachties came aboard *Starlight.* Among them were Eleanor and Eric Weir who had a 25ft Noelex trailer-yacht. Later an Aquarius trailer-yacht, just in from sailing, stopped alongside us. There was a lot to share. At 3pm Lucian and Dot Middleton arrived with Sam who had been to their house for lunch. *Angitu* came back from a successful fishing trip at 4pm and we rafted up against her so we could have a comfortable night without worrying about the rise and fall of the tide.

That night we read from chapters 45 and 46 of the Book of Jeremiah, the prophet who told God's message to the Israelites. Chapter 46, verse 28 says, "Fear not, says the Lord, for I am with you." So our prayer for the people of Oamaru and all of New Zealand was that they would honour God and fear not. I too should learn to trust God more, as at times I had been afraid.

It was difficult to climb down the vertical ladders from the wharf onto *Angitu* so we could get across to *Starlight,* particularly at low tide when the wharf was four metres above the sea level. We found it easier to invite our visitors aboard from the steps by the loading platform. But this area was very wet, slimy and slippery, and also very difficult to manage at low tide. We took the rudder out of its frame and used it as a gangplank to get some people across. However when Ian Hamilton, a Salvationist and keen motorcyclist, called on us he slipped and badly bruised his elbow. This incident made Norm resolve to do something about the slippery platform. Later on he bought some chicken netting and fastened it to the landing with staples. "That should give it more grip," he explained.

Ian took us home to his house where his wife Dawn gave us lunch. Then we went to admire their son's collection of ten motorcycles. On the way home we stopped at the lookout for a view of the bay – big swells and rough seas off shore – and we were glad we were safe on dry land. The light showers in the morning had passed over and the sky was now clear with no wind in the sheltered town and valleys.

The next day we had tea with the Ennever family and came back to the yacht at dusk to find a strong southwesterly wind blowing across the harbour and whipping up a nasty chop. Ted suggested we move our sleeping bags over to *Angitu*, since he went home each night. We appreciated the offer and had a comfortable sleep aboard his big, roomy boat, while *Starlight* jiggled and bounced in the choppy harbour waves all night.

Rebecca Anderson, a reporter from the *Oamaru Mail*, came on Wednesday to interview us. She was very competent and put us all at ease. She took notes in shorthand and took a photograph on a new digital camera. The article and photograph made the front page under the headline, "Age no limit for trio".

The night sky was clear. I looked at the stars at 10pm and woke at 2am, hoping to catch sight of the *Aurora Australis*. The Southern Cross was shining brightly in the south, Orion was setting in the west and Scorpion was rising in the east – but no Aurora. A Christchurch newspaper had printed a photograph of a blazing red Aurora captured the previous night and I was hoping the sight would be repeated. But there was nothing there when I looked. Perhaps I needed to be more of a night owl.

After the newspaper story was published, we had six more yachtie visitors. One was Geoff Fathers from Great Barrier Island, who was soon talking with Sam about life on that island. We noticed that it was a very low tide, so we walked to the end of the wharf and took a photograph of the shallows. There was very little deep water left.

On Friday, Bev and Malcolm McCaw took us to their home built on a hill overlooking the town. They had a magnificent view of the ocean, and I was invited to use their powerful binoculars to watch a fishing boat negotiate the shallows and come into the harbour. We also used their washing machine and our clothes were soon fluttering in the strong breeze. Their daughter Lynley Campbell joined us and we looked at Malcolm's motorbikes. He had a 1986 Suzuki Cavalcade motorcycle with a 1400cc V4 motor and matching sidecar. We had been on a few rallies with him and he had taken me for a ride on it but I preferred our Honda Goldwing for its comfortable, smoother ride. He also had a beautifully restored vintage Harley Davidson motorcycle.

After lunch their friend Jim Caldwell popped in. He had looked after a small colony of yellow-eyed penguins at Bushy Beach as a volunteer for more than twenty years. We told him about the young penguin we had seen that morning by the launching ramp. It was one of that year's young chicks, not yet fully grown, but plump with a lot of fluffy feathers.

"I'll keep an eye on it," Jim told us. "If it's distressed, hungry or exhausted, it will need care until it is strong enough to feed itself." Jim checked the colony every week and cared for birds that needed a helping hand. We thought he did an admirable job protecting this endangered species.

Bev and Malcolm took us to the Oamaru Motor Museum, the Oamaru Stone Quarry, which was a very productive quarry but very dusty, and to the Whitestone cheese factory which made a large variety of organic cheeses from cow and sheep milk. While we had transport we filled the LPG gas bottle, bought 27 litres of petrol and stocked up on groceries. We were getting ready to move on.

Strong gusty southwest winds prevailed on Saturday, causing very rough seas with 4.5 metre swells. It was no weather for sailing so we did some chores and had a rest day. Ted did not go out that day but spent some of the time cleaning *Angitu*, helped by his lovely young Romanian daughter. Ted and his wife had adopted her and her brother at great expense after his own family had grown up. We took the opportunity to thank Ted for his friendly welcome and the use of his facilities, and that night Norm and I slept on *Angitu* again. It suited everyone. We had an early night while Sam slept comfortably on *Starlight* and was able to read a book till late.

I woke at 5:33am in time to hear the VHF marine weather report – a very good forecast. I was soon roused by a group of keen fishermen calling out, "Ahoy! Anyone there?" I ran up to the deck and saw them there high up on the wharf in the darkness.

"Ted's not here yet," I answered, "What's the time?"

"Quarter to six," they replied.

I suggested they ring Ted on his cell-phone, then Norm and I quickly shifted back to *Starlight*. By this time Sam was awake and we reviewed our plans. The weather had calmed down inside the harbour and the forecast was for slight seas, light or variable winds and a two-metre southerly swell. We decided to leave and go north to Timaru. By the time Ted arrived to embark his passengers, we had untied all our mooring ropes and fenders and were ready to cast off. We said goodbye to Ted and thanked him again, then we motored across the harbour to the jetty by the yacht club. Here we returned their key, together with a thank you card and – you've guessed it – another two packets of chocolate biscuits.

It was almost low tide as we left the harbour at 6:55am on Sunday 8 April. The surf was breaking over the shallows between the narrow channel and the breakwater but we negotiated the deeper water at the end of the wharf. We skirted around the shallows outside and then headed north in a slight, deep-blue sea. I telephoned the McCaws and Hamiltons to say thank you and let them know we were leaving. Malcolm had said that he wanted to watch us through his binoculars as we headed out. We were so grateful to all the people here who gave us hospitality and took an interest in our journey. Our prayer for these folk and the people of Oamaru included an extra request; "Dear Lord, can you do something about clearing the entrance for the locals using the harbour?"

The northwest wind freshened a little and we hoisted two sails. The speedo showed six knots as the wind and motor pushed *Starlight* along. Norm put the outboard motor on half throttle and would not hear of turning it off as the ribbons in the shrouds only fluttered slightly, showing a very gentle wind. We were only getting about one or two knots of sail-power. Then at 9:30am the breeze failed completely so we dropped the sails. The sea was as calm as a mill-pond except for the one metre southeasterly swell. We kept almost three miles off the coast, well beyond the surf that broke a long way off the shore. We took turns at steering but Fred did most of the work. While Sam was on watch, he saw two dolphins and an albatross nearby.

The coastline was low and flat with no headlands, so it was difficult to detect our progress visually. At 1pm I took a GPS reading and marked the chart which showed that we were on track for Timaru. Later that morning the sea became moderate and confused as a light ten-knot northeasterly breeze sprang up – it was on the nose so we did not hoist the sails. Shortly after this the motor stopped. We had run out of petrol. We poured another 16 litres in, replacing what we had used in six and a half hours of running. Our average usage over all our trips was 2.4 litres per hour.

We could see the traffic on Highway One close to the shore, and the meat works chimney ahead. We soon altered our course to a little east of north. Three yachts were sailing south, using all their sails in the slight northerly breeze. The ketch *Kokoamo* was a glorious sight under full sail. However they had great difficulty tacking back, and ended up coming into port several hours after we had berthed.

At last a headland came closer and we identified the white structure of the lighthouse on Tuhawaiki (Jacks Point). The two-metre swell crashed on the rocks below and the shallows created higher swells, making tiller steering more difficult. We looked out for the large leading beacon and it soon appeared in the distance, looking like a small stake. Then, motoring closer, we saw the port and starboard beacons that marked the channel and guided us into the large harbour. After we passed the breakwater the swells eased, and the sea inside was calm.

I had earlier called the Port of Timaru on VHF channel 9 and they told me that a berth on the north side of the number two wharf was available.

However when we arrived we could not identify wharf number two, so I radioed again and the security guard came down in his ute to show us where to berth. We saw his flashing lights and gave him a wave as we glided in to the allotted space at 2:25pm. We had taken seven and a half hours to do this leg.

We chatted to the security guard as we tied up to the wharf, using long mooring ropes and springs to allow for the two-metre drop in the tide. There were big truck tyres slung outside the tall piles of the wharf, and we put all our fenders out to combat the surge as we were berthed close to the shore. The security guard asked me to fill in an identity form naming *Starlight*'s owner, skipper, home port and cell phone number. This was the first time we had been asked for these details, but we supposed it was a necessary precaution in such a large port with so many vessels coming and going.

There were fishing boats each side of our wharf and a big cargo boat was being loaded at the next one. One yacht came in later, gliding past on the other side of the number two wharf. The crew picked up two stern lines on a floating buoy and took a rope ashore from the bow. Norm walked round the foreshore to see this 28ft keeler called *Knickers,* and was soon chatting to the owners, Chris and Barbara Sowerby. They had seen our yacht at Oamaru and were planning to sail there at Easter to join in a regatta. Chris asked lots of questions, and we told him that getting there and back over the long weekend would totally depend on the weather.

The Sowerbys took us to the Salvation Army Hall where we hoped to find a Sunday evening service but it was closed – there had been a senior citizen's meeting that afternoon – so we went to the home of Majors David and Myrtle Clark. David was my cousin, and had taken up the appointment as Timaru Corps Officer in February 2001.

When David took us back to the yacht at 9:30pm, we were weary but well satisfied with the day's events. The area where *Starlight* was berthed was very dark and the tide was low. I found it almost impossible to climb down the vertical iron ladder as the rails leaned in slightly under the wharf and the top of the ladder had no handholds. My short legs could not touch the next rung as I leaned backwards, almost toppling over. Norm had to hold me firmly from the top of the ladder as I made the third attempt. At last I was able to climb down. There was also a gap between the last rung and the deck of our yacht. "Jump," they called. I looked at the short distance, jumped and landed on the deck safely. Whew!

The next morning Norm was up early and I didn't hear him go. He had a bright idea – to fix the top of the ladder so that I could climb down easily. He located an engineering firm that helped him make up two pipes, two feet in length, with two-and-a-quarter inch rings welded onto the end of each. The rings fitted snugly over the top of the ladder's short uprights to make an extension to allow me, and others, to have something to hold onto while we climbed down this awkward, bent and rusty ladder.

I climbed up and down the ladder twice to test it. His ingenuity had solved the problem, and his invention worked wonderfully well. Thank you, Norm.

While we were at Timaru we had lots of visitors. Three fishermen leaned over the wharf and talked about their experiences. They were two brothers and their brother-in-law. Another fisherman was Dale Coker, the husband of Valmay whom we had met at Milford. She had told him to look out for us. In the afternoon David and Myrtle Clark came aboard with Margaret Bailey and her daughter Treena, from Porirua. Margaret was living in Timaru to care for her 89-year-old mother Ruby Wood, and after they had looked over *Starlight* we went to visit her mother.

That night we joined Chris and Barbara Sowerby for a lovely home-cooked tea. We had a long chat about life's experiences, shared many jokes and of course talked yachting. They had bought their yacht at Taupo, had it hauled overland to Tauranga, then Chris, with a crew of three young women, sailed it to Napier and then non-stop to Timaru. "Quite an adventure," we told them. They were equally impressed with our circumnavigation in *Starlight.*

The northwest winds blew strongly. Inside the harbour the sea was calm but outside it was turbulent with lots of 'white horses' and surf pounding on the breakwater rocks. We walked around to the yacht club and looked at the launching ramp exposed to the surf on Caroline Bay. We noticed that most of the keeler yachts were moored by the mole inside the harbour, but there was no walkway there and little room for visitors. We watched in awe as a large cargo ship slowly turned around inside the harbour and berthed at the container wharf assisted by two tugs.

Robyn and Owen Brown, friends from the Goldwing motorcycle club, called to see us on *Starlight.* They were amazed at how small she was. "Fancy going all the way around New Zealand in this little boat," they exclaimed.

"Not for me," Robyn added. They told us that the report of our visit in the Greymouth newspaper had been used in the March copy of the *New Zealand Goldwing Riders* magazine. News does travel. "I'll pick you up on Wednesday afternoon and take you to our new house for tea," Owen said as they left.

Gordon Mitchell and two of his relatives came aboard. Their whole family was involved in the fishing business. "It's not like it used to be," they told us. Gordon advised us to move to number three wharf near his fishing boat to avoid the surge. We moved *Starlight* and found that the surge was much less at the new position, and that the wharf had a good, easy-to-climb ladder.

Myrtle and David Clark visited *Starlight* at Timaru

I made enquiries at the Port of Timaru Office about paying the wharf fees but the clerk could not tell me what to do. "Come back later," she advised.

The next time I called she said, "The Harbour Pilot wants to see you." I went into his office and he questioned me about our berthing arrangements.

"Who told you where to go?" he asked.

"The security guard told us on Sunday when we came in to berth at number two wharf," I replied. "Then the fishermen told us to go to their number three wharf."

He told us that yachts usually moored near the clubhouse. He had a computer screen that monitored the activities in the harbour, but our tiny yacht was too low at the wharf to be picked up by the cameras. No wonder he was puzzled. By this time the clerk had looked up the fee schedule but could not find a category for our small boat.

"How long are you staying?" she asked.

"About five or six days," I replied.

"Make it ten dollars then." She had given up working out the calculations, so I quickly paid the money.

Later we walked to the town centre and visited the historic St Mary's Anglican Church, which had a spectacular ceiling shaped like a ship's hull upside down. On the way back we stopped at a service station selling used car tubes for a dollar. Our fenders and car tubes were getting worn and dirty from chaffing against the many wharves and jetties we had tied up to. These tubes were already inflated so we bought three.

It was Easter weekend. On Good Friday, Major David Clark called at 9:30am and took us to the service at the Timaru Salvation Army Citadel. Norm and Sam played in the brass band and several people took turns to read the portions of scripture depicting the Easter story. David asked the three of us to talk about our yacht journey and what Easter meant to us. Fellowship over a cup of tea and an Easter hot-cross bun followed, and several people took the opportunity to ask us more about our travels. They included Majors Merv and Bev Layt, Mrs Ferguson, Margaret Bailey, Vaughan and Jenny Nicholson. We felt at ease with these folk.

David and Myrtle invited us to their home for lunch and that afternoon Myrtle, their son Brent and daughter-in-law Tania and their two-year-old grandson Timothy went for a short ride in *Starlight*. We motored out of the harbour so they could experience the swells, the view of the land from the sea, and the navigation system of red and green beacons that marked the channel for the big ships that came into Timaru. When we came back at 4pm we tied up at to the pilot boat jetty, for ease of disembarking.

We shared our Bible reading and prayed for the many people of Timaru, thanking God for their friendliness and immense help. After tea we listened to the 5:33pm marine weather forecast for the Rangitata area. It was for a moderate sea easing and the southwest wind becoming a variable ten knots. A northeasterly swell of one metre was developing, and the outlook was for ten knots of northeasterly with no rain. There would be clear visibility, and we thought it was a good forecast for the next leg, Timaru to Akaroa. We expected it would take between fourteen and eighteen hours, almost an overnight trip, so at 6pm we cast off and headed out of the harbour.

The southeast swell was strong but the sea was only moderate. A fresh southeast wind allowed us to hoist the mainsail and then the jib. The wind strength varied a lot. Sometimes it was too strong as *Starlight* bounced and flew over the swell at four or five knots, at other times it was too light to keep us heading northeast. The swells were taking us towards the shore. Then, as the wind eased the yacht sailed at only two knots, so we started the 15hp outboard and Sam dropped the jib.

"I enjoyed the feel of the deck under my feet even though the bow was heaving in the two-metre plus swells," he recorded in his diary. With our speed increased to five knots we could finally make progress in a northeasterly direction. We had been warned that a heavy southerly swell could push a yacht into the Ellesmere Bight, where some vessels had been known to founder. Chart 64 recorded a caution.

After dark we kept steering a northeasterly course. I checked with a GPS reading every two hours and at 10pm we were twelve miles off the coast. The waves were splashing over the starboard side at times, so Sam and I put on wet-weather gear for our watch. Norm was seasick and went below to change his wet clothes. The Autohelm was given a rest that night as it could not cope with the turbulent sea and the strong southerly swell. Sometimes the swell would push us north or northwest before Sam could correct the steering. The sky was clear and the stars were shining brightly. Sam recorded that night's experience in his diary.

"Because I am a night-owl, I did not find it hard to watch the sun set and still be on watch to see the sun rise the next day. Usually most of the sailing was in daytime near the shore, so we could appreciate the shore and countryside beyond. This night as we sailed, the sky was clear with twinkling stars and no clouds. To see the glow of the lights of Timaru slowly fade astern – then, while we were in the total darkness, I had a great feeling of being on a new journey," Sam wrote.

"The course was 60 degrees but I steered by the stars, only occasionally leaning over to check the compass," Same told me. "I felt very close to God and found myself singing the Sunday school song:

If I were a beautiful twinkling star, I'd shine on the darkest night,
I'd seek where the dreariest pathways lie and shine then with all my might."

The tune is called 'Starlight' and was number 801 in the Salvation Army tune book. I was reminded that when we named our yacht *Starlight* we asked for the sail number 801, but it had already been allocated and we were given the number T1017.

While I was on watch, I saw some lights on the horizon that looked like a huge cruise ship all lit up at night, but when I looked again I realised the light was the three-quarter moon rising behind a patchy cloud. The moon soon climbed over the cloud and shone a bright ray of light all the way towards *Starlight,* lighting up the sea all around us. The next two hours passed quickly and the next GPS reading showed us twenty miles off the coast. A change of course to 20 degrees made sailing more comfortable and we gradually drew back towards the land.

When dawn came we were only five miles off the coast and could see Banks Peninsula under a blanket of cloud in the half-light. "Steer east," I told Sam. "We are too close to the Ellesmere Bight. I can see the streetlights of Birdlings Flat in the distance."

Morning came and the hills and valleys became clearer as we motor-sailed along the south coast of Banks Peninsula. The sun rose at 7am and the cloud dispersed. We passed cliffs, rocks and seaweed, and some dolphins came to swim beside us. We saw a couple of farmhouses, and some cattle grazing on the hills. At 8:50am I took a GPS reading and marked our position on chart 6324, a detailed one of Akaroa Harbour. I opened up an old booklet, *Cruising Banks Peninsula*, that was given to us many years ago by Doug and Carol Rattray. It had a detailed map and much relevant information.

It took more than two hours to progress along the coast before we identified the magnificent entrance to Akaroa Harbour. We passed several more Hector dolphins swimming and frolicking in the slight sea. The lighthouse poised on a point to the north was hard to see in the haze and because of the sun which was directly ahead of us. As we entered the heads, there were clumps of big, long, floating seaweed ahead – it became hard to avoid. Then we saw a number of powerboats coming towards us, obviously intent on using this fine Easter Saturday morning for fishing.

Once we were inside the harbour we dropped the mainsail and, since we were in calm waters, started to tidy up the yacht. The trip had taken sixteen hours.

At French Bay the large and small yachts were lining up for their races. As we rounded Green Point, noting its warning light on the end of the reef and the power line taking electricity to it, Norm heard the sound of the race horn.

"That's the same noise as my fog horn," he said. He got out his homemade horn, made out of a shortened 'peashooter' trombone and a heavy mouthpiece, and blew it loudly. All the little yachts took off and started racing.

"I started that race before the timekeepers were ready," Norm declared. The race was definitely on, but we never knew if he had really started it.

As we approached the Akaroa town wharf, we could see that there was just enough room for us to berth between a keeler and the tourist cruiser. The place was full of holidaymakers who were fishing from the wharf, boating, playing on the beaches or walking around the shore. The whole area was in holiday mood, enjoying the sunshine and shelter of this idyllic harbour. Sam was still alert after being awake all night, and he cleared the seaweed from under the hull with the boathook, then went for a walk. Norm and I slept, exhausted, for three hours.

That afternoon I walked to the yacht club for a hot shower. The last races were finishing and the clubhouse began to fill up. When I arrived back at the yacht, Norm was chatting to Ron Bingham who operated Canterbury Cat Tours. Ron offered him a lift in his van and took him to a service station two kilometres away to buy 18 litres of petrol.

Akaroa was an early French settlement and this was reflected in the names of the streets and in the style of architecture. Even a modern motel had French-style balconies with creeper growing up the walls. I was intrigued by the Eyris Pearl Centre built on the wharf, and found that paua was cultured to produce artificial pearls, just as oysters are cultured in other places. The prices of the blue pearl pendants and strings were 'out of this world' as far as I was concerned, but they were very beautiful and smooth, with intermingled hues of blue, green and red.

While I was away from the yacht, the most unusual episode occurred. Norm took pity on a young man who had fallen into the sea from a slippery ladder as he was attempting to board a large yacht. I arrived back just in time to find the young man, size SM, getting dressed in Norm's size XXL shirt, underpants and shorts. Norm was organising safety pins and a piece of string to hold up the clothes. He had chosen a vivid green pair of shorts that I thought too gaudy, and I couldn't help but be amused at the scene. After drying the lad's shoes a bit and supplying a dry pair of socks, Norm sent him and his friend on their way with the sodden clothes in a plastic bag. "No need to return my clothes," Norm told them, "I'll get some more from the thrift shop."

He told me afterwards that the young men had been drinking beer from cans and were a bit tipsy, hence the fall into the sea. They had decided they wanted to buy a boat – they thought in terms of $100 or so – but the one they had their eye on was worth more than half a million dollars. The dip in the sea sure woke them up and stopped their daydreaming.

The light wind died down overnight and all three of us slept well while *Starlight* was tied to the wharf with mooring ropes and several fenders in place.

Easter Sunday services were advertised in the local newspaper. The Anglican service was at 9am, a bit too early for us, but the Presbyterian service starting at 10:30am seemed a more appropriate time. We made our way there by walking along Beach Road, passing the shops until we came to the corner of rue Lavaud and rue Brittan to find Trinity Church set among some big trees. This church was established in the 1860s and the present building erected in 1886. The few faithful locals welcomed us and, as we were early, showed us through the church. One of the features was the mouse choir puppets, which could be seen through peepholes. The church was packed for the Easter service, mostly with visitors including teenagers, young children and babies. The service was well-organised and reverent, the acoustics were good, and the organist played very well. We found the atmosphere in the old wooden church very peaceful. I enjoyed the older hymns, some of which I had not sung for a long time. A guitarist accompanied the chorus 'This is the day', an appropriate one for Easter Sunday. The *Good News* Bibles in the pews had all the readings book-marked – someone had been busy – and the short sermon was followed by the sharing of bread and fish in remembrance of Christ's breakfast on the shore with his fishermen disciples. The reading was from John chapter 21, where Jesus asks Peter, "Do you love me?" A quiet time of prayer renewed my spirit in abundance.

Visitors were invited to the adjacent church hall for a cup of tea and a biscuit, and this gave us the opportunity to talk with the few regular local members who told us that they looked forward to the influx of visitors on holiday weekends "to keep the church going". We met a farmer who had seen us sailing along the coast the previous day. "You were fast," he said. He told us that he had his binoculars on us for some time from his farm high up on the hill overlooking the sea. It was a timely reminder that when we were at sea, anyone could be watching us.

As we walked back to the wharf we watched numerous powerboats and jet-skis being launched at a ramp, which was wide enough for three trailers to be using it at the same time. It was a busy place. Many visitors were picnicking, flying kites, or just strolling along in family groups. Watching all this activity made the afternoon fly past.

We found that a fresh northwest wind made *Starlight* bump against the wharf. We discussed moving to the other side of the wharf or anchoring in the shelter of the bay opposite, and decided on the latter. The calm of this bay relaxed and charmed us. This quaint Akaroa harbour was made long, long ago by three volcanoes which erupted and sent lava flows to form valleys and ridges radiating out towards the sea. Two deep harbours and numerous inlets were created around Banks Peninsula. Our devotions that night reflected on God's creation and goodness.

After a pleasant, still night, we hauled in the anchor and headed out of Akaroa Harbour in a calm sea towards the ocean. Several powerboats passed us heading for their favourite fishing spots. The charter boats cruised to the entrance of the harbour and, because they feed the little Hector dolphins regularly, were treated to a lively display.

The lighthouse on the point was clearly visible as we motored along in slight seas close to the shore. There was little wind, although a light northeasterly was predicted, and the sky was clear. We were amazed at the way the cliffs cut off abruptly from the sloping hillsides as if a giant had bitten them out. We passed the numerous bays and inlets of Banks Peninsula and *Starlight*, propelled by the 15hp outboard, made good time. Soon we were heading in to Lyttelton Harbour where there were a number of yachts sailing in a stiff northeasterly breeze. We saw a huge container ship leaving the wharf, so we kept to the eastern side and headed towards Diamond Harbour. The wind dropped and the sea became calm in this harbour, which was sheltered from the northeasterly winds.

People here were enjoying the fine weather. Some were on the wharf waiting for the ferry to take them back to Lyttelton, others were just mucking about along the shore. There were yachts and launches tied to poles and other boats were anchored nearby. We called out to one yacht owner, "Is the water deep enough to anchor here?"

"Plenty," he replied. "It's half tide." So we dropped the anchor quite close to the shore. It was 3pm on Easter Monday, 16 April, and *Starlight* had completed a good seven-hour run.

A Noelex 25 trailer yacht came alongside. Eric and Eleanor Weir, on *Alyeska,* recognised *Starlight* and greeted us warmly. They had met us and had come aboard when we were at Oamaru. They lived in Ashburton but kept their yacht at Diamond Harbour. Before we settled for the night I rang Raewyn to let her know we were at Lyttelton, and she passed on the sad news that our niece Elizabeth had given birth to a full-term but still-born baby girl. The funeral was in Christchurch the next day and I felt that we should go to support the family.

The next morning we spoke with Mark and Tracey McGill and their son George, who were moored nearby in their 25ft Trojan trailer-yacht *Southern Belle*. They had decided to go home early and offered to show us the way into the marina at Lyttelton. This was much appreciated as a strong southwesterly storm had recently destroyed many of the boats and several of the floating jetties in the marina, and we were uncertain how to negotiate the debris still strewn about the harbour. They skilfully guided us, in misty low cloud, past the buoys, flotsam and posts into the now-much-smaller marina where we tied up to a small floating jetty near the club's launching ramp. We were blessed yet again by meeting yachties with local knowledge.

Mark offered to take us to the funeral in Christchurch. We were able to have a shower at the Canterbury Yacht and Motor Boat Club's facilities and change into our good clothes while he retrieved his yacht and took his family home. He went the second mile by helping us find the church in good time for the funeral service. Thank you, Mark.

The church was packed. Elizabeth and her husband, David, spoke of their traumatic experience. The tiny white coffin, with a posy of pink and blue flowers on top of it, was a poignant reminder of the baby that died without drawing even one breath. I could relate especially to the grandparents, as we had lost a twelve-week-old granddaughter some years earlier.

Norm's brother Jim Millar gave us the keys to his spare car. "Use it while you're here," was his generous offer. Sam had left us to stay with his family in Christchurch, but as we were staying on board *Starlight* in Lyttelton and planned to be there for a week or two, the car would be very useful. We caught up with Norm's cousins Novene Jacobs and Moira Wear and went to tea at Novene's home where we met her husband Jake and another cousin, Laurie Millar.

We visited Merle and Trevor Hamilton at Leeston where we talked about Norwegian family history, viewing old photographs and heirlooms, then had tea with Fred and Doris Collett who lived near New Brighton. We admired Fred's 1988 1000cc Kawasaki motorcycle and sidecar, immaculately painted in glossy black.

During the week we watched the secondary schools' Sunburst sailing regatta. The very excited, well-equipped and competent young sailors went off each day to sail their heats, with the semi-finals on Friday and the final races on Saturday. Their unfurled sails were a kaleidoscope of colour as they waited to launch their little two-person yachts.

Our mobile phone was busy that week. All day Thursday, visitors came to *Starlight* which was conveniently tied up to the floating jetty. Our nephew Jonathan Millar and his children Samuel (7) and Frances (6) brought our elderly friend Joyce Pilgrim to see the yacht and have morning tea with us, then Lorna and Stan Harris came for lunch. Stan had grown up with Norm at Blenheim and they enjoyed a catch-up. That afternoon another nephew, Andrew Millar, came with his three small sons and we shared our lolly boxes with them. Then granddaughter Adrianna Slykerman and her friend Lance came out for a short trip around the harbour, motoring in a choppy sea and fresh northeasterly winds. They stayed for tea, and Adrianna treated us with lots of chocolate Easter eggs.

That Friday a southwest wind was predicted so we arranged to shift *Starlight* to berth A7 on part of the remaining marina. The fee of $6 per night was good value. A key for the security gate cost us $20 for the deposit, and water and power were available. We soon had all our mooring ropes and fenders in place, and another nephew, David Millar, arrived with his wife Sharon and two-year-old son Josiah. The yacht was a bit bumpy for them, although we felt only a slight rock. The lolly boxes were popular nevertheless, and when they left they took our laundry home to do.

One night we went to Moira and Robin Wear's home at Kaiapoi for a dinner party with family and friends. Conversation was lively and it was very late by the time we arrived back at the marina. The strong southwest wind made the yacht bounce violently around, so much that it was too risky to try to board so we slept fitfully in the car until the wind eased in the early morning. We were finally able to get on board *Starlight,* now resting in calmer water, and catch up on lost sleep, and I made a resolution to put some pillows and blankets in the car in case it happened again.

While Norm was walking along the jetty next day, he met Ken Ryler whom we had last seen at Oban on Stewart Island. Then, he had been on his way to Picton to buy a boat.

"Hello. Did you get a boat in Picton and sail all the way back here?" Norm asked him.

"Oh, no," he replied. "I only got this far." He had found and bought a 34ft steel ketch called *Jasmine* at Lyttelton. Finding him there surprised us, and when he invited us to come aboard we readily accepted. He had used all his savings to buy *Jasmine,* but he was living permanently on board and it was cheap rent.

Yachts being rigged for the Secondary Schools Regatta at Lyttelton, Easter 2001

We left early on Sunday morning for the Linwood Salvation Army service, where we met many friends – Corps Officers Captains Dean and Edwina Herring and family, Chris and Maurie Allan from Ashburton, June Matheson (previously from Porirua), Pearce and Winifred McNabb, Dr Ngaire Ellis (whose parents we had met at Tauranga), the Hutsons, Colletts and their families. We invited them to visit us on *Starlight* and the week soon filled up with return invitations, including one to Simon Hutson's ninth birthday party.

I was busy on Monday checking the charts for the next leg when a voice called out to us. It was Bruce Anderson from the Canterbury Trailer Yacht Squadron. We invited him aboard and he asked us to give a lecture to the club about our travels around New Zealand.

"When?" we asked him. "We don't know how long we will be staying. It all depends on the weather, we could be here for weeks or we might be gone soon."

"What about Wednesday night?" Bruce suggested "It's Anzac Day and our members can easily be contacted."

We agreed, and were told to be at the club rooms at 7pm. Little did we know what we were letting ourselves in for, but we would prepare as well as possible.

Kevin and Christine Glanville, who had been in charge of the Porirua Salvation Army the previous year, came and gave us a tour of Lyttelton and the shops. We watched the black ball drop from the top of the 15-metre mast on the Lyttelton Timeball Station to mark 1pm. It was a timepiece from yesteryear that intrigued us.

On Anzac Day, the radio news told of record attendances at New Zealand and Australian remembrance services – this was heart-warming as there are fewer veteran soldiers each year. We tided up the yacht in preparation for visitors, and I selected a number of photographs and put them into a folder with the overhead transparency maps for the evening lecture. Norm found some gadgets including the foghorn, the Autohelm and two car tubes and ropes. We contacted Sam to come and help us.

The Collett and Hutson families came at 2pm – all eleven of them – and that made thirteen people on board *Starlight*. Somehow we all fitted into the cabin and cockpit. It was impossible to serve afternoon tea but the two lolly boxes were passed around and enjoyed, especially by Simon.

They left at 4pm just as Dr Dee Ongley arrived with his fiancé Michelle. Dee is a house doctor at Christchurch Public Hospital and was on night duty. We talked of our past boating experiences with his mother, Dr Jane Avery, and as soon as they left we had a quick tea and prepared for our lecture.

The clubroom was soon filled with people. Bruce introduced us, and I started off by saying, "This talk could be titled 'waiting for the weather' or 'living out a dream'. We could be called courageous or crazy." I used the map to show our travels around the North Island, then Norm talked about the preparation and construction of the Gazelle trailer-yacht with its special strengthening. I went on to talk about the places we had been to around the South Island, especially Fiordland. Sam spoke of his involvement and crewing experiences, and mentioned our day in the fog when the Armstrongs in *The Shag* had become our guiding angels.

We told our attentive audience of more than 40 people about our devotions. We said we prayed for the people at each place and we were trying to read the Bible from cover to cover, but confessed we hadn't made it yet. They all laughed.

When Norm explained how he filled the compass with half vodka and water by blowing through a tiny tube, Sam interjected with, "I have to watch that he doesn't suck instead of blowing – he might be kicked out of the band." More laughter.

The questions came readily, and there were more explanations of our gear and the petrol, water and spares we carried. Many wondered how it all fitted in, so we gave them an open invitation to call on Saturday and see for themselves. Even after Bruce had thanked us, the questions still flowed and it was 10:30pm before we were able to pack up our gear. It had been a good evening, with a lot of interest and much hilarity.

On Saturday the first visitors arrived before we even had time for breakfast. Peter and Ina Knappen brought a big bag of muffins, which we enjoyed with a cup of tea. They owned a 1990 Gazelle trailer yacht that had been built at Levin. Their yacht was the same size as ours, but they had altered the cabin layout, and they were surprised at how we stacked all our equipment and stores into the available space. Then Bruce Anderson and two friends came on board. Bruce asked more questions and made notes.

"How did so many yachties hear about the talk?" we asked.

"We all keep in contact, mostly by email," he told us.

We expressed our gratitude for the petrol vouchers we had been given, and he explained that the audience had made gold coin donations. As they left, Moira and Robin Wear arrived, and we were called on to demonstrate *Starlight's* equipment; the stove and table that folded away, the square bucket for our dishes, the Autohelm, foghorn, GPS, charts and first aid kit. What, no fridge? We used powdered milk and margarine, and keep only a couple of days' supply of fresh meat aboard. The lolly boxes were passed around yet again.

Rex and Irene Greenwood and their two grandchildren Angus and Rebecca called, then Stan and Lorna Harris. Lastly Mark and Kay Backhouse came. They all asked questions. "Where do you do the laundry?" "Where do you shower?" "Do you ever get seasick?"

"Ask Norm," was my reply to that one.

"Have you caught any fish?" We told them we had been given tuna, crayfish, cod and salmon at various times during our voyage, sometimes more than we could eat.

We were pleased to answer their questions and allay any fears for our safety. It was if someone was at the gate to the jetty letting our visitors in one group at a time, almost every hour, and letting the others out. As Mark was leaving he invited us for tea on Monday and offered to call for us after work.

The sun set early behind Magazine Bay that evening, and it was dark at 6:15 pm with no wind and a calm sea. We were glad we had hosted so many visitors, fifteen in all. Most were over-awed by the gear we carried. "Like a caravan on the water, or a home away from home," were their comments. We whole-heartedly agreed with them. I served an omelette on toast for tea, and Norm remarked, "What a wonderful place for a picnic." It had been a busy day.

Stan invited us to play in the band at the Sydenham Salvation Army service. Norm took his cornet and Stan found a trombone for me to play. We joined five other musicians in a song arrangement, 'Because He lives I can face tomorrow'. Captain David McKenzie led the service and the message was 'Listening to God'.

We met Majors Glenis and Rex Cross, who came later to see our yacht, and Bill Luxton, who remembered seeing us at Takaka. That afternoon we went to the Christchurch Cathedral for a special concert that included organ and trumpet music, several choirs, a string duet and the Salvation Army Citadel Band. The cathedral was packed, the acoustics were good and we enjoyed excellent music. Afterwards we met Brian and Liz Edwards (formerly of Tawa), Rex Arbuckle (Norm had been to school with him at Leeston) and Brian and Heather Kench (Heather, née Brown, had lived with us in 1973 when she was teaching at Porirua).

The next day Mark Backhouse called for us and took us to his house at Redwood, and Kay's parents Colin and Elaine Nuttall joined us for a scrumptious dinner. Colin had built and sailed a large ketch, *Kokoamo*, but had recently sold it. His ears pricked up when we told him that we had seen it sailing at Timaru. Mark was interested in buying a trailer-yacht or a small keeler, so we had a good talk about boats, which their boys Heath and Blake eagerly joined in. Mark was a builder by trade, and we admired their large painting of Christ as a carpenter.

Later that week, Kay told us that Mark was a changed man.

"He can't stop talking about you. I've been praying for him for years and you've done it. Now he's going to church with me and interested in the Bible. You've changed him," she explained.

"Not us," we replied. "It could only be the Holy Spirit that has changed him." We were too overcome to speak further. How could God, through his Holy Spirit, speak to this businessman in a lecture on yachting, we wondered. Even though we knew that all things are possible to God, it still puzzled us.

"We will pray for you and your family," was our response. And we have kept in touch.

While we still had Jim's car we visited Bruce and Marilyn Tremain (they were living at New Plymouth in 1997), Ken and Kara Sellars (Ken had been on the scows with Norm in the 1950s), and Brian and Ann Garguilo who grew tomatoes in large hothouses. Our association with Brian's family from Nelson went back a long way. We attended a Sunday service at the Grace Vineyard Church where the pastor spoke about 'Trusting God in the Storm'.

During the next few days we had a meal with Rex and Irene Greenwood (Norwegian family history) at Templeton, visited Judith Earl (Millar family history) and husband Peter Williams at Sheffield and our niece Pam (née Clark) and Roger Blakemore and their family at Darfield. We ended up having a roast dinner at Richard and Jean Crawley's Hororata deer farm. Thank you to one and all.

Norm spent some time chatting to Peter who looked after the Lyttelton boat yard. He told us more about the recent storm and the boats that were lost. The rubble from the broken jetties was still piled high. Peter came to our yacht and noticed that our rigging was loose, so Norm adjusted the shrouds – a timely tip from Peter.

On Tuesday 8 May, our mobile telephone rang. It was Jane Anderson, from *The Press*. "Can we come and interview you about your trip?" she asked. All was a flurry of activity to put our stores away and to tidy up the cabin and cockpit. Norm quickly finished changing the oil in the 15hp outboard motor before Jane and the photographer arrived. The caption, 'What a swell trip it's been' and the report, with a coloured photograph of us standing on the bow of *Starlight* (it made the yacht look very small), was on the front page of *The Press* the next morning.

All thoughts of moving on were on hold, as the weather continued to be either foggy or windy with strong northerlies. We had been at Lyttelton for three weeks. The light rain was gently soaking into the parched land, and fresh shoots of young grass were evident in many places. However I looked up the *Nautical Almanac* and found that the full moon was due soon, so we would have moonlight if we did an overnight trip. I wondered where we could shelter on the way north.

John Hecker, who kept a 40ft keeler at Waikawa Bay, called and gave us a contact at Kaikoura.

"Ring Ray Martin", he advised. He told us how to approach the entrance to the marina at South Bay where the tourist boats were kept.

"Look out for the sharks-tooth rock on the headland," he told us. "There are lots of rocks and reefs near the entrance. Touch the green float with your starboard side and line up the coloured post on the house with the black and white post by the launching ramp. Then turn in to the jetty." He also told us that there was shelter behind Motunau Island and that he had motor-sailed from Lyttelton to Waikawa Bay in 29 hours at seven knots. We would only be able to do half that speed and would take almost twice as long, but the conversation made me look forward to moving on.

Adrianna came with her friends Jude and Josh for a trip around the harbour, but as it was foggy we only took them for a short ride at high tide around the boats on swing moorings in Corsair Bay. The faithful 15hp outboard conked out on the way, and we had to use the 10hp to complete the half-hour journey. I was very aware of the shallows, rocks, drizzle and thick fog, so was relieved to get back to the berth. Norm later fixed a small blockage in the outboard's carburettor.

On Thursday 10 May, Sam rang to say he had decided to leave Christchurch and go back to Wellington by train and ferry. He wanted to join his wife Eva, to baby-sit their grandchildren for a few days, so we went to visit him at his son's home and stayed for tea. We looked at each other's photographs and talked about the trip we had shared from Bluff to Dunedin, Oamaru, Timaru, Akaroa and Lyttelton.

Sam's seamanship skills and willingness to steer were great assets to us, and he told us he was well satisfied with his trips along the East Coast especially the overnight journeys, and the experience of meeting so many helpful people.

We kept listening to the marine forecasts, taking special note of the Rangitata and Conway areas. Thursday was raining and Friday night was stormy, with heavy rain and strong northeast winds that rocked the yacht. A complex low-pressure weather system was making its way from the northwest of the North Island and passing south. The five-day forecast was for southwest winds and more showery weather. We were anxious to move on. I wondered if we would ever get the right weather pattern to take us north.

We made our preparations for the next leg, filling the LPG gas bottle – only the third time in nearly six months – and checking the fresh water and petrol supplies as well as stocking up on groceries.

Much to our surprise the forecast on Saturday was for 25-knot southwest winds and moderate seas easing. Our eagerness was apparent as we made final plans. We left a cheque for the jetty fees and returned the car to Jim and Ann Millar with some petrol vouchers and two tow ropes as a token of our grateful thanks. We said goodbye late on Saturday night.

How could we pray for all the people who had given us hospitality and for those who had willingly passed on information? Our Bible reading and prayer encompassed them all, as well as those who lived in the area we had not yet met. "God bless them all," summed it up.

16

Kaikoura – Port Underwood – Porirua

Through many dangers, toils and snares
I have already come;
'Tis grace has brought me safe thus far,
And grace will lead me home.

John Newton

On Sunday 13 May we left Lyttelton at 8am and motored out of the harbour in a slight sea with very little wind. I rang Raewyn to let her know we were on the way and heading for Kaikoura. It was Mothers' Day, and Telecom had given me a special rate. The minutes on my mobile phone Goldcard had expanded from 69 minutes to 189 – I couldn't believe it. I rang most of our family, and left messages with the Colletts to let them know we were off. I rang Doris Holdaway at Blenheim to say we were on our way, and Adrianna to say thanks. I used the phone until we were out of range.

A north-northeast course took us well into Pegasus Bay. I marked our GPS readings on Chart 63, Kaikoura to Banks Peninsula. The sea was still slight with little wind so we kept on motoring and the southeast swell gave *Starlight* a push from the stern. The sky was clear as we approached Motunau Island at 4pm, but a westerly wind had sprung up making the sea around the island very choppy, so we anchored off shore in the lee of some cliffs, south of the river entrance. This leg had taken us eight hours.

The sea was joggly but it was comfortable in the cabin and I was able to cook a hot meal. I reported our position to Barry, who manned the Waikuku VHF radio on channel 63, telling him we were stopping for the night. It was good to know that someone knew where we were anchored. I slept intermittently on the central bunk.

The 5am forecast was for a slight sea, a northeasterly one-metre swell and a five-knot westerly wind. We lifted the anchor at dawn and were motoring northeast at 7am when the sun rose over the unbroken horizon. We noted some high cliffs along the coast and at 10am we passed Point Gibson with a lighthouse on it. The sea became moderate with a slight southwesterly wind that seemed to change direction often. We made sure we missed the Busnett Rocks. The Haumuri Bluffs were about five miles ahead and the Kaikoura Peninsula could be seen faintly in the distance, when we had a very unpleasant surprise. There was very tragic news on the midday report on National Radio.

"The body of a young woman, killed in Wellington three weeks ago, has been found in a gully near the Rimutaka Hill road. She was Helen Frances Wickliffe, aged 22."

"That's our granddaughter," we both said at the same time. We were shocked. Within ten minutes of the news release, Barry was on the VHF radio with a message from the police to ring our daughter, Carolyn Wickliffe. We had been found, and the mobile phone now had coverage so I spoke to Carolyn and heard that Helen had not been in contact since Easter Monday. Family and workmates were suspicious and called the police, who arrested Helen's boyfriend. He told them what he knew about Helen's death, but her body was only found on Sunday afternoon, the day our mobile phone was out of range. The family had been trying to contact us.

"I'll come home as soon as I can," I told Carolyn.

The 15hp outboard motor churned on in a calm sea and a southerly swell pushed the yacht along nicely. The tide was with us and the GPS recorded an excellent speed of 6.9 knots. *Starlight* made good time heading towards Kaikoura and at 2pm we were getting close. I contacted the Kaikoura Coastguard on the VHF and spoke with Caroline Giles to arrange a berth at the marina. As we neared South Bay we could see reefs and rocks everywhere. It was half tide with a calm sea and only a little swell breaking on the rocks. Even though John Hecker had given us specific instructions on how to enter the marina, we were not sure.

"I'm going to go around in a circle," Norm called out. Then I caught sight of a fishing boat approaching the entrance from the east and realised it was going in, so we followed. The fisherman pointed to a large green floating buoy as they passed close, his boat almost touching it, indicating for us to do the same. In no time at all we were inside the marina and there was Peter Giles waiting to show us where to berth. We threw him some ropes and the yacht was soon firmly tied up to a jetty high above the sea level but there was no means of climbing up. We used our rope ladder that had proved useful on many other occasions, and were soon on dry land.

The marina had recently been built to accommodate the flourishing whale watching and dolphin diving tourist operations. A large breakwater had been built and inside the deep excavated marina were big concrete posts and jetties. The dolphin tour boats were pulled out each day at the ramp by huge tractors and the guests disembarked from the bow, via steps, straight onto the land.

The large 40-passenger catamarans used for whale watching were berthed at specially designed jetties, and buses ferried the tourists to and from Kaikoura.

Ray Martin, who maintained the fleet of tractors and trailers, invited us to his nearby home for tea and showers. I arranged to catch a courier bus to Koromiko and a flight from there to Wellington, and I rang Carolyn and told her I would be home the next day. I should have had a good sleep on board *Starlight* in this sheltered haven, but my mind was racing with thoughts of Helen's death under such bizarre and tragic circumstances.

I was up early and ready for the trip home when Peter Giles arrived in his truck to take me to Kaikoura. Several people I met expressed concern and sympathy for us, as they had heard the VHF messages and knew of our involvement in the tragedy. The shuttle bus passed through Ward, Seddon and Blenheim and I was soon at Koromiko, where I boarded a small aeroplane. The flight over Port Underwood and Cloudy Bay gave me a clear birds-eye view of the coast and the entrance to the Wairau River system and I wondered when I would be back.

My sister Joan Hutson, and Barbara Millar were waiting for me at Wellington airport and they filled me in on some of the details. We went straight to Carolyn's home where she was overjoyed to see me and asked me to stay.

Grief came in bursts especially at night and first thing in the morning. The hardest thing to bear was knowing that Helen had been dumped in a gully and had lain there for nearly a month. Her boyfriend later pleaded guilty to manslaughter. Why hadn't he called an ambulance? Why had he hidden her? It puzzled us. But at least we could now arrange the funeral.

Norm had stayed at Kaikoura to keep an eye on *Starlight* and was wonderfully hosted by Ray and Joan Martin, who fed and cared for him as if they had always known him. I was able to telephone him each night with progress reports. One evening while we were talking to him on the mobile phone, Carolyn asked him to bring home a crayfish. "Not likely," he replied doubtfully. But just as he put the phone down a boat came alongside and a fisherman threw him two crayfish which he cooked and put in the Martins' freezer to bring home. Ray promised to keep an eye on the yacht, so Norm was finally able to come home on Sunday 20 May.

The funeral was arranged for Monday 21 May at the Porirua Salvation Army Hall and conducted by Norm's cousin, Graham Millar. Many of Helen's friends and relatives came, and the church overflowed with more than 350 people. Many tributes, in word and song, expressed shock, grief and sympathy at this unnecessary tragedy. The news media had been following the story and TV cameras filmed Helen's casket being carried out. A large number of mourners followed us to the Whenua Tapu Cemetery at Pukerua Bay.

I slept at Carolyn's home until Tuesday 22 May. "I'll be all right now," Carolyn assured me. We both supported her for the rest of the week replying to messages, cards and emails.

"Are you going to finish the circumnavigation of the South Island?" we were asked.

"Its nearly winter but we haven't got far to go now to complete it," we replied, "It may take a week or two, that's all."

"Get back to *Starlight,*" Carolyn told us. "You have to finish the trip and bring her safely home." So on the following Saturday Raewyn and our granddaughter Talitha took us to the Interislander terminal and we caught the 9:30am *Arahura* sailing to Picton.

We were back in Kaikoura, via the shuttle bus, at 3pm and rang Joan Martin who willingly picked us up and took us to the marina at South Bay. There she was, our *Starlight,* moored safely where we had left her.

Murray Davidson called early on Sunday morning. He had seen *Starlight* berthed at the marina. He was a keen yachtsman and owned a keeler that he kept at Waikawa Bay. He recognised Norm but couldn't remember where they had met, until Norm told him that he had owned Kapiti Motors at Paraparaumu.

"That's it. I once took my parents' Bellett car to you for servicing," Murray recalled. The parents and their red Bellett car had been well known to us. Murray invited us to attend the Presbyterian service at 10am, and came back in time to take us in his car to St Paul's Church, perched up on a hill. It was a very cold frosty morning and I wondered why the church was so cold. The switches to the electrically heated oil-filled bars under the pews were turned on at the wall but no heat was radiating out. About 25 worshippers, mostly elderly, nearly froze (or so I thought). Nevertheless the congregation sang heartily, accompanied by a competent violinist and an enthusiastic pianist. We enjoyed singing modern songs and old hymns, and listened intently to a good sermon from a dedicated minister recently arrived from Hawera.

After the service, a hot cup of tea and a small electric bar heater (that worked) warmed us up. When they investigated the heating system, they found that the time switch had malfunctioned. Then Murray showed us the inner workings of the organ that had recently been overhauled and repaired at great cost. We met Murray's wife Marie, who was the church secretary. "Come for lunch tomorrow," they invited us.

After we returned to South Bay, we were invited to have tea with Ray and Joan. A hot roast of rolled hogget with seven vegetables and a delicious desert of apricot crumble soon warmed us. We wondered why anyone would choose to live in Kaikoura after Christchurch city. "It came gradually," they told us. They had owned a small bach, had come up at weekends and then found work close by. They loved the peaceful, seaside atmosphere, so the bach was replaced with a two-storeyed brick house that had a magnificent view of the bay.

Back at the yacht, the gas stove soon heated up the cabin but I filled a hot water bottle and used an extra blanket to keep me warm. It was a very cold night with snow falling on the Kaikoura ranges. Ray lent us his ute to get petrol and stores, and we visited Murray who showed us over his farm of 250 dairy cows, run by sharemilkers. He told us about some of his sailing trips and gave us encouragement.

"You're doing what I only dream of," he said.

Over lunch, Marie Davidson told us she did not go yachting with her husband but was a keen tramper. She talked of her trips to Stewart Island and in Nepal, where she had been up 14,000 feet or more. The thought sent shivers down my spine.

Clear skies, cold air and fresh snow greeted us on Tuesday but the forecast was for showers along the coast. The Whale Watch boats had a lay-day, as the sea was very rough with three metre southerly swells. The forecast was for 25-knot southwest winds at Conway and over 35 knots in the Cook area, but the southerly was expected to ease. The five-day forecast for the Marlborough district was for fine weather, and the fishermen said that the southerly wind would give us a two-to-three knot push if we went north. What a bonus.

I looked up the charts and books to prepare for the next leg. It would take eight to ten hours to motor-sail at five knots to Cape Campbell and a bit longer to find shelter in the lee of the cape, perhaps at Marfells Beach. We were keen to move on but the weather was a big factor in our decision. Sunrise was about 7:45am and sunset at 5pm, so we had less than ten hours of daylight. The moon was in the first quarter, rising in the afternoon and setting just after midnight, so there was no use depending on moonlight at night.

I walked to the Coastguard quarters and thanked Peter and Caroline Giles for their support. They said they loved their time-consuming voluntary work and had been encouraged by the number of younger members training for rescue work in the two Kaikoura Coastguard vessels. They did 25-30 rescues a year. "Keep up the good work," I encouraged them.

At 7am on Wednesday, the southwest wind was roaring and rain had set in with low cloud and poor visibility. It was not a good time to start, so we decided to stay another day. The rain was on and off all that day and more snow fell on the tops of the Kaikoura Range. In between the showers we went for a walk, but put on warm clothes and took an umbrella.

Our devotions that day were a mixture of thankfulness for all the kindness and hospitality given to us from the folk at South Bay and Kaikoura, and concern for our family back home still recovering from the shock of Helen's death. Grief and sorrow would be with us for a long time but we believed that a loving God would supply our needs.

On Thursday morning, the marine weather forecast for the Conway area was for a 15-knot southerly easing to variable 10-knot winds, with a slight sea and a two-metre southerly swell easing. There would be clear visibility and the outlook was good. It was a cool, crisp morning and by daybreak we were ready to leave. Ray and Joan were out walking their dog Deefa, and came over to say goodbye. They helped us retrieve the rope ladder and cast off the fore and aft mooring ropes, and we were on our way. We could see the rocks and reefs easily and we motored past the green floating starboard buoy without a hitch. Chart NZ 6212 had a detailed 1:25,000 section of Kaikoura Peninsula on which I had marked, with my pink blob, the many reefs and rocks.

Starlight cleared the Kaikoura Peninsula by keeping well offshore, passing the long reef and dodging several crayfish floats and lots of seaweed. We set a northeasterly course. I unrolled chart 62, Kaikoura to Cape Palliser (on the south of the North Island), and had the feeling we were getting nearer to home. The variable light wind was mostly westerly, off the land, and for a time we thought sailing might be possible but the wind was light and later changed to a 15-knot northeasterly which was right on the nose. The southerly swell gave the yacht a lift while we had a slight sea, but later we punched into a moderate sea, and there was no chance of sailing at all. The sight of the mountaintops of the Seaward and Inland Kaikoura ranges, resplendent in fresh bright white snow, was so spectacular that I had to reach for my camera and take some photographs even though we were some distance away.

At 11am we were about two miles off the Clarence River mouth. The 15-hp outboard motor churned on at five and a half knots. Norm thought that if two motors were going the yacht would go faster, but when he started the 10hp outboard, the bow rose up and the stern was sucked down despite some heavy water containers placed forward of the centre-plate. The displacement hull was pushing water and even with the power of the two motors we only gained an extra half a knot, while the yacht bounced a lot more and gave us a rough ride. Before long we were back to using just the faithful 15hp motor to churn up the miles. After a light lunch, Norm refilled the petrol tanks and I kept up the routine of taking a GPS reading every two hours.

The afternoon passed quickly as we noted the headlands and peaks. At 3pm we were off Needles Point, conspicuous with its stark white rocks protruding like points into the sea. The sun was getting lower, almost behind the western hills, as we approached Cape Campbell. Chart 6212 also had a detailed sketch of this rocky and reef-strewn area, and we kept more than three miles off to make certain we would clear them all. The swell and waves were splashing high on the rocks and we had to steer *Starlight* out in a wide circle until we were well north of the danger zone.

At 5:05pm the GPS showed that we had just passed Bowler Reef. We then turned northwest into Clifford Bay, and saw a confused sea and a southeast swell crashing onto the shores of Marfells Beach. We would get no shelter there, and it would be a most uncomfortable mooring for the night so we decided to head for Port Underwood. We had the charts for this secluded haven and knew that there was a light at the entrance. We had been there twice before but only in daylight.

In an earlier TR, I had given our ETA at Cape Campbell as 4pm but our progress had been slow due to the northeast head wind and the moderate seas. I called Wellington Marine Radio on channel 71 to let them know we were just past Cape Campbell and were heading for Port Underwood. A revised ETA of 9pm was recorded.

The sun had set behind the hills and the half moon began to shine brighter as the twilight faded. Several stars appeared as we motored towards White Bluffs. The light from the Fighting Bay Lighthouse high up on the hill, two flashes every 20 seconds, was easily identified as it had a long range, but it took us a long time to see and recognise the light at the entrance to Port Underwood. It was on a lower hill and had a shorter range, with one flash every five seconds. Once we had identified them these two lights guided us and gave us confidence as we motored in the darkness. Gradually the moonlight began to illuminate the sea area around *Starlight,* and the lights from the houses at Rarangi shone onto the turbulent surf that crashed on the shore.

I telephoned Doris Holdaway (née Perano) of Longbend Farm, Blenheim, to let her know we were nearby and heading for Port Underwood. She owned a bach there and had a wealth of local knowledge.

"Look out for the mussel-farm floats on your starboard side. They will have lights on them," she advised us.

"We will let you know if we can visit, but the southeast swell on the Wairau River bar is a bit heavy tonight," I told her. "It's not a good sea for crossing the bar."

We used another section of chart 6212, Port Underwood, to help us navigate in the entrance and past the various inlets. The mussel farm lights twinkled along the shore and I was glad that Doris had mentioned them. At 9:20pm I called Wellington Marine Radio and signed off our TR. "We are inside Port Underwood," I reported. The radio operator was very helpful and offered further assistance if needed.

Just as we entered Oyster Bay, I went to the bow to have a closer look at the sea. "Two rows of mussel floats ahead – turn around!" I yelled to Norm who was steering. He took *Starlight* around in a circle while we both had a closer look. There were two parallel rows of ripples in the sea, but when we looked harder we realized it was an apparition. My fear of running over ropes and floats in the dim light was unfounded.

We could now see the very strong lights on the shore by a jetty and some fishing boats that were moored nearby. A few more minutes and we were in the middle of the bay. I dropped the anchor in the not-too-deep water at 10:20pm. We had been at sea for 17 hours. We enjoyed a late hot meal and flopped into the bunk, grateful to be in this very calm bay.

In the morning the view was magnificent. We were surrounded by hills. The road wound between the pine trees, beside the frosty farms and around the shore. The tranquillity of this peaceful bay was a complete contrast to the bouncy seas we had encountered the day before in the open waters. It was a cool, clear morning and after a late breakfast we made the yacht ship-shape and listened to the weather forecast. It was all good. Little wind, low swell, slight sea and clear skies. I knew that Norm had been many times up the river to Blenheim when he was an engineer on the Eckford and Company's boats in the 1950s. These shallow-drafted boats took approximately one hundred tons of cargo each between Blenheim and Wellington, doing two return trips a week.

"Do you want to go over the Wairau bar?" I asked him anxiously. "The weather's good here. How can we decide?"

"I'll know once we are out of the shelter of Port Underwood," Norm replied. So I hauled in the anchor and we motored out, passing the lighthouse that had guided us the previous night, and into Cloudy Bay. The sea became very calm and there was no wind as we motored towards the river mouth. It looked perfect for a bar crossing. I looked up the *Nautical Almanac* and found that high tide for Cloudy Bay was at 3pm. The scene was set for an attempt to go up the river. At 12:45 pm I telephoned Doris and said, "We're on our way."

Even though Norm had been familiar with the bar crossing in the days when he was on the boats, he had difficulty in recognising which group of trees marked the entrance. At 1:40 pm he asked me to take a GPS reading, which placed us outside the overflow canal, an artificial safety outlet for huge floods.

"Another half-hour or so and we'll be there," I reported. The centre plate was winched up half a metre and Norm steered *Starlight* in a trough just outside the breakers. We were soon in a position to see the entrance. We motored past to make sure we could see exactly where the waves were breaking and where the channel was. The bar, built up with rubble, mud and sand deposited from the outflow of the river against the southeast swells, makes a barrier across the entrance that can shift from time to time. That day we could see the river outlet channel running north, parallel to the beach. We could see the deeper water where the waves were not breaking.

Norm turned back and skilfully steered *Starlight* through this deeper water and into the narrow outlet of the river at 2:40 pm. There were several people fishing from the stony embankment on the north side, and we were so close that we nearly collected a fishing line as we passed. Norm kept the yacht at a steady speed to maintain steerage. We had been across this bar before, in a powerboat in 1977, but it seemed different in the yacht. Once we were motoring across the flats I could relax – but not for long.

We recognised the former pilot station and the fishermen's jetty on our starboard side. Norm remembered Percy Miles on the pilot boat coming out of the river and leading the *Echo* or the *Wairau* across the bar, particularly after an easterly storm had changed the channel. The homestead nestled amongst some trees on the Boulder Bank, where the Charlie Perano family used to live, was on our port side. Then we passed the entrance to the large 2000-acre Vernon lagoon. Ahead of us was the wide Wairau River estuary, strewn with large logs and big tree branches. Norm steered a little too close to a grassy bank and the rudder touched the mud. We were in about one metre of water so we lifted the rudder half-way up. We carried on with the motor running at quarter speed, keeping the stumps and logs on our starboard side.

As we approached the entrance to the Opawa River, which flows into the Wairau, we disturbed hundreds of birds resting on the calm river-water. Swans, ducks, shags, hawks, kingfish and swallows flew up as we passed them. I was told later that there were many Royal Spoonbills nesting in the lagoon, but we did not see any. We carefully entered the Opawa River, winding through grassland and then through tree-lined banks. We followed the sweep of the river for about five miles – about halfway to the town of Blenheim.

Doris had told us to tie up at her brother Ted Perano's little jetty near her farm on Dillon's Point Road, but we missed it. At 3:30 pm, we turned around in the thick weed of the narrow river and then motored back until we saw her car parked on the embankment. She was all smiles as she greeted us.

"Fancy crossing the bar and getting up the river," she laughed. We threw her a rope and *Starlight* was soon securely tied to the jetty. To our surprise, a reporter and a photographer from the *Marlborough Express* came to interview us about our travels in a trailer yacht. They asked us lots of questions and were interested the equipment we carried on the yacht. They took several photographs of Norm blowing the foghorn but they used one of us both standing by the cabin hatch, framed by the spray-dodger.

The interview and photograph was published on the front page of the next *Saturday Express* with the title, "Retired couple complete sea circuit – South Island circumnavigation brings 20-year dream to reality." Underneath the photograph was the caption, "Sailing Sallies: Mavis and Norm Millar on board their yacht Starlight after sailing up the Opawa River."

"*Starlight* will be safe as a bank tied up here. There is very little river flow and minimum tide rise. Come and stay at my home," Doris insisted. We gratefully accepted her offer, collected some personal gear and the laundry, tied down the dinghy, threw all the cushions and gear into the cabin and locked it. She whisked us off in her car. Her spacious farmhouse was only half a mile away.

Oh, the comfort of a warm house, a roast dinner of beef and wild duck, the luxury of a big bed with an electric blanket and two duvets, and the plate of hot oatmeal porridge for breakfast. It was so different from our lifestyle on the yacht. In the morning, we saw a heavy hoarfrost that turned all the large farm fields white. Doris lent us her car on Saturday to visit friends June Knight and her sister, Shirley Bridle (née Brooks), to call on Norm's aunt Florence Blick at the Bethsaida Rest Home, and again on Sunday to attend the Blenheim Salvation Army service. Norm had grown up here and knew many of the congregation. We were impressed with the tuneful contributions of the brass band and the songster brigade. Captain Dusky Miller (no relation) made us welcome and we caught up with old friends at the 'over 60s' lunch held at Dean and Daphne Brook's home. Norm even tried to fix Don and Margaret Hoare's car but ended up towing it to their house, where we had a chat over a cup of tea. We made a quick visit to see Paul Blick at his flat and to the service station to buy some petrol and LPG gas before returning the car.

Monday 4 June was Queen's Birthday and a public holiday. The weather was still calm but not so frosty, so we decided to try getting out over the bar near the high tide at 5pm. In the afternoon, Doris took us to *Starlight*, safely resting against the jetty. Barry Holdaway came alongside in his boat just as we were putting away our petrol, LPG, stores and the clean dry laundry. Barry asked us questions about our trip and was especially interested in how we had managed to get over the bar. Soon it was time to thank Doris for her wonderful hospitality and say goodbye.

We cast off and *Starlight* glided along the calm river. Norm steered the yacht into the deeper sweeps of the river and tried to avoid the overhanging leafless trees. We had to keep looking up. The calm river reflected the bush and trees, the grassy bank where a horse was grazing, the bulrushes and the eroded mud banks exposed at half tide. We passed two canoeists paddling along the edge. When we came to the estuary, *Starlight* got stuck on a mud-bank. We were too early for the full tide, so we dropped the anchor to hold the yacht in place.

Barry came over to see us after he had set a fishing net. He was unsure about crossing the entrance bar, so was going to watch us go out into the open sea. Norm told him how Ivan Guard used to go over the bar regularly in his launch to take the mail and stores to Port Underwood in the 1940s, before the road went through. Norm also remembered going into Port Underwood in the *Echo* to collect the wool bales from the farms. We talked until 4pm, when the tide had risen enough for us to motor on towards the entrance. We wanted to get out of the river and across the bar in daylight and the sun set at 5pm.

There were little waves rippling at the entrance and small breakers rolling in, but there were gaps that showed up the deeper water. We motored out using the 15hp outboard and with the rudder in the half-way position. Norm steered *Starlight* over the swells and between the gentle breakers, without a bump, until we were out into the calm bay. Barry had anchored his boat by the shore inside the bar and walked along the entrance spit to watch us negotiate the bar. We knew that he would give it a go one day. We dropped the centre-plate and the rudder down to full positions as we were now in open waters and heading for Port Underwood. After sunset, the sky turned a brilliant red, orange and pink colour. Then the fluffy clouds above the hills of Port Underwood turned purple. As darkness fell the light at the point flashed, showing up the entrance, and we were soon anchored again in the calm waters of Oyster Bay.

In the morning it was 'up anchor and away.' The slight swells were breaking on the rugged rocks at the point and along the coast as we motored north, in slight seas and with no wind, towards Tory Channel. As we approached the entrance, the Interislander ferry *Aratere* was coming out so we moved to the starboard side while it passed by. Soon we were inside, combating the many tide rips and cross-currents. The cargo boat *Kent* thundered past, and shortly afterwards the *Arahura* came into the channel, so we steered closer to the shore. Next, the fast ferry *The Lynx* passed us. Numerous fishing boats, launches and powerboats were also using the narrow channel. In all our travels around New Zealand we had hardly ever seen another boat, but Tory Channel was certainly a busy waterway that day.

We turned Dieffenbach Point and motored into Queen Charlotte Sound. Our well-used chart 615, Marlborough Sounds, was consulted but we hardly needed it as we had been boating there for many years and all the many coves and headlands were familiar to us. However we kept a sharp lookout for navigational changes and sea traffic on this sheltered waterway. Later on, we noted a new post marking the end of the reef off Snake Point at the entrance to Bay of Many Coves.

The entrance to the Waikawa Bay marina had a sign saying. "5 knots only – No Wake Zone". It was a busy marina with a lot of activity.

Norm wanted to find Bill Pettigrew so we tied up at the set-down jetty and found that the shed previously used by Trojan Boats was empty. "The workshop has been moved to Picton," we were told, so we were off motoring again. Before long we were at the Picton wharf. We found Bill at his new premises and, much to his surprise, Norm gave him our spare crankshaft that we knew he needed for his Honda 10hp outboard.

On Wednesday 6 June we were up early after a good sleep in the surprisingly calm water at the Picton wharf. The forecast for Cook Strait was for slight seas, a one-metre northerly swell and a light 15-knot northwesterly wind, so we set off for Resolution Bay. We had started our circumnavigation of the South Island here on 18 December 2000, nearly six months earlier. We called in to see Graheme and Pat Sowman and had lunch with them on their sunny front lawn. We said a big thank you to them and at 1pm we were off again, ready to leave the South Island behind us. In our prayers that day we included our gratitude for the people of Marlborough and all the folk we had met on *Starlight's* circumnavigation of the South Island.

We motored towards the Northern Entrance and then set the jib but, because the wind was very light, we kept the motor going as well. The sea was slight as we passed White Rocks and the out-going tide gave *Starlight* a lift – 6.9 knots on the GPS. The current at Cape Koamaru was swirling a little but it was relatively calm compared with our previous crossing on 6 January 2000, the last time we had crossed south to north, when the turbulent current had tossed the yacht around like a cork. We consulted chart NZ 46, the one we had used right at the beginning of the trip, and it made me realise that *Starlight*'s circumnavigation of the South Island had been accomplished.

The final leg of our journey, crossing Cook Strait, went without a hitch. The sea was slight, the swell was small, the sky was clear and the wind a light northwesterly. We were able to steer for Mana Island which was clearly visible; not hidden by the usual thick cloud hanging over the North Island. I put in a TR to Wellington Marine Radio at 1:30pm and cleared it at 5:30pm when we had passed Mana Island. The sun had set and a beautiful full moon was rising over the hills behind Plimmerton. When I tried to take a photograph of this scene, the flash of the camera lit up the sail. Our friends had been in touch with us and were looking out for us but night had fallen and they could not see the yacht's navigation lights.

"There they are," Yvonne called out excitedly when she saw the flash light up the sail. "They're nearly here."

The navigational tunnel lights guided our approach and at 6pm we were in the Mana Cruising Club's marina, tied up at the wharf jetty at low tide. The crossing from Resolution Bay in five hours was a record for us as we usually took six or seven hours. It was great to be back near our home.

I went to the club to arrange the use of the jetty and met Powell and Rae Lewis, who recognised me.

"When did you get back?" they asked.

"Five minutes ago," I replied.

Some of our family and friends gathered near *Starlight* to greet us – Raewyn and Ken Te Tau and our grandchildren Talitha, Ezra and Ezekiel, Glen Wood, Clive and Yvonne Stephens and their grandson Jesse. They had seen us off nearly six months ago. It was a grand welcome home.

Many folk on the email, telephone or word-of-mouth grapevines had followed our travels with great interest.

"Where are they now?" was an often-spoken question.

Now that answer was, "They're home at last."

The next morning we motored across the Porirua harbour and tied up to the Onepoto jetty at high tide. Ken, Carolyn, Ivy Paul and Clive Stephens were there. Ken took me home to collect our van and the yacht trailer, and our neighbours Roy Meyler and Brian Williams came to the ramp and used their strength to wind up the heavy yacht onto the trailer. We really appreciated their help. Willing hands also helped us drop the mast and soon we were home with *Starlight* back on the lawn.

We were safe at home and exhilarated. It was 7 June 2001, over five and a half months since we left to go around the South Island and nearly four and a half years since we had started on this adventure. Our dream of circumnavigating New Zealand in our trailer yacht, *Starlight*, motoring or sailing, had become a reality. We were grateful to all the people we met for the local knowledge and hospitality they willingly gave us, and for the answers God gave to our prayers. We never did manage to read the Bible from cover to cover, but our prayer for New Zealanders is still the same –that God will wonderfully bless them.

We realised that we had been privileged to see God's creation from a different perspective. To see the rocks, reefs, headlands, farms and forests, to ride the storms and calms of the sea, and to watch the stars, clouds, sun and moon above us, was an experience that filled our souls.

This is my Father's world, and to my listening ears
All nature sings and round me rings the music of the spheres.
This is my Father's world, I rest me in the thought
Of rocks and trees, of skies and seas; His hand the wonders wrought.

Maltbie Davenport Babcock

Starlight – a Gazelle 25 TS trailer yacht

The Gazelle 25 has the accommodation and performance of a small keeler, but the absence of a skeg enables it to be launched and retrieved in less than half a metre of water and to be easily transported by road.

Designed by Trevor Adams in 1974, the Gazelle 25 was modified by Daryl McGee of Wellington who took over the manufacturing in 1978. Since then around 160 have been produced. In 1980 the moulds (plugs) for the hull and deck were sent to Paraparaumu where boat builder Val Chubb manufactured Gazelles in Te Roto Drive. *Starlight* was the second boat off his production line.

The wide beam and gunwales allow the crew easy access over the entire deck. Stanchions and headsail sheet blocks are attached to the full-length slotted toe-rail. The ballasted centre-plate, containing 410kg of lead, provides a very high self-righting component. In the cabin there is room to walk right around the centre-plate casing, which is braced to the cabin top with two stainless steel struts. The centre-plate is raised and lowered by an electric motor, using three pulleys and a strong wire.

The gas stove folds away to form a backrest and a table slides away under the cockpit floor. The seats in the cockpit hold six people. There are two stern quarter berths with sealed flotation, two berths in the cabin and a double forepeak berth with a flotation compartment under it. The backrests under the shelves in the cabin have flotation and the space between the cabin floor and the hull is another flotation area, making the Gazelle almost unsinkable. Storage is provided under the cabin bunks and along the deep shelves, and in two self-draining cockpit lockers for fuel, spare ropes etc.

There is a deep, self-draining anchor well in the forepeak with a tightly-drawn cover over it. *Starlight* also has an electric anchor winch, a spray-dodger and lee-cloths. *Starlight* does not have the 300mm transom step of subsequent Mark 2 models, but has a stainless steel divers' ladder mounted on the transom. The outboard motor sits in a well inside the cockpit where a vertical rise and fall mechanism can raise or lower it, and a bracket was fitted to the starboard side of the transom to support a second outboard

Starlight now has a 12-gauge aluminium mast, a stronger spreader and collar and heavier shrouds than were originally fitted. The 13/16th rigging has a stabilising backstay but no topping lift. A larger teak-based sliding double hatch has replaced the fibreglass main hatch. The foredeck now has a screw-down Perspex hatch of the type used by ocean-going yachts. The Gazelle Mark 2 has fewer bulkheads than the Mark 1 and is both stronger and lighter. The Gazelle is a popular cruising yacht and it also has a proven racing record in both New Zealand and Australia.

Starlight - layout

Inside layout

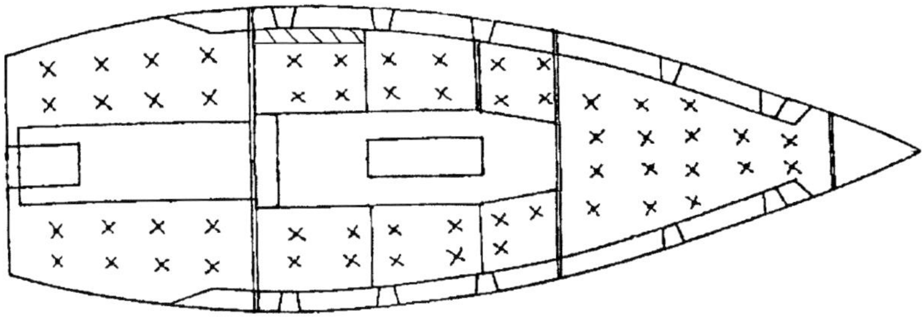

Deck plan

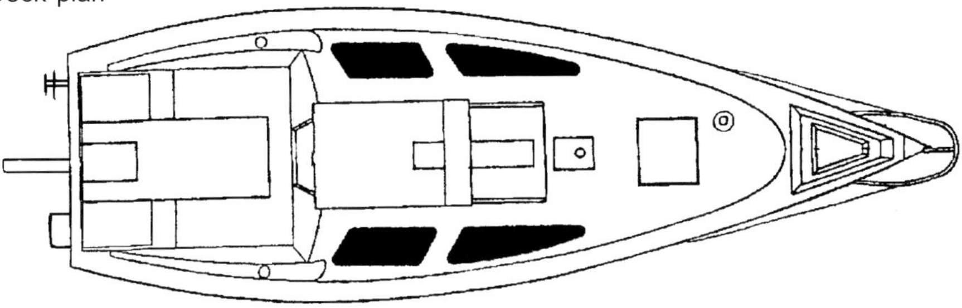

Side plan

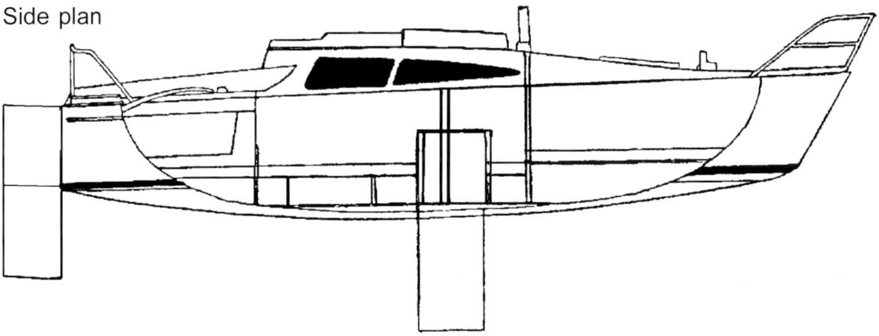

Specifications – Mark 2 Gazelle

LOA	7.42m
LWL	6.76m
Beam	2.49m
Draft min	0.38m
Draft max	1.37m
Ballast	410kg
Towing weight (including trailer)	1600kg
Height of mast (from the deck)	8.53m

RECIPES

Bottled Fish

Prepare fish by filleting and skinning it, taking out most of the bones. Cut fish into medium pieces and place in clean, warmed small Agee jars. Add a small teaspoon of salt (nothing else) and press down the fish pieces. Place seal and ring on the jar (I do 2 jars at a time).

Place a trivet or spare rings on the bottom of the pressure cooker and fill with water up to about half way up the jars. Put on the lid of cooker. Cook over a hot flame until the air vent has a steady stream of steam hissing out. Put on the medium pressure weight and turn down the flame to a slow or medium heat – just enough to keep the pressure up – and cook for 45 minutes. Let the cooker cool down slowly and only then remove weight and lid. (If using a large saucepan or preserving pan instead of a pressure cooker, boil jars for 3-4 hours.) Remove the jars from the cold liquid in the cooker, wash the outsides and check that the seals are in the down position. The bottled fish will keep for a long time.

Seawater Bread made in a Pressure Cooker

1.5 cups lukewarm seawater
1 tablespoon sugar
1 tablespoon dry yeast
4 cups flour

Mix well and stand for 5 minutes. Dough is sticky.

Grease the inside of the warmed pressure cooker, put the dough directly into it, put the lid on the cooker and leave to stand in a warm place for 2 hours (can use some warm water in a bowl). Stand the cooker on a toasting rack over the lowest possible flame and cook for about 45 minutes or until the dough is firm (do not use the pressure weight).

Shake out of the cooker (the crust of the bread comes away from the sides), turn over and replace in the cooker with the topside now on the bottom. Cook for a further 15 minutes to brown the topside of the loaf, using the toasting rack and the lowest flame.

Billy Bread

2 cups flour
2 teaspoons baking powder
half a teaspoon salt
1 cup sultanas or raisins
half a cup golden syrup
half a cup milk

Add the melted syrup and milk to the dry ingredients. Mix well. Grease the bottom and sides of a large tin (a catering 3kg tin fits in well, and I usually double the mixture for this size) and put a piece of tinfoil on the bottom (for ease of tipping out). Fill the tin with the mixture and place a rack or trivet in the pressure cooker with warm water to cover about half way up the tin. Cook on low heat using the medium weight on for 45 minutes. Let the cooker cool down slowly.

Remove tin from cooker and turn out the Billy Bread.

Stores and equipment carried for the circumnavigation

Sails: Main, small main, storm jib, working jib #2, genoa jib #3, sheets and fittings, runner and ropes, lightweight yellow-green spinnaker and ropes. Most of the time the small main and the #2 jib foresail were attached to the boom and the forestay. The other sails were folded up and stored in their bags in the portside quarter berth (the squab had been removed).

Outboard motors: 10hp Honda four-stroke in the well of the cockpit, subsidiary outboard on the stern bracket. (8hp Yamaha two-stroke Porirua to Auckland, 15hp Yamaha two-stroke Auckland to Porirua, 15hp Honda four-stroke for the South Island trip)

Petrol: Two petrol tanks of 22.5 litres each in the rear compartments of the cockpit, with flexible petrol pipes, squeeze pumps in the lines and connections to either outboard. A spare 22.5-litre petrol tank with fittings was stored in the well of the cockpit. Remaining petrol (up to 67.5 litres) was stored in 4.5 and 10-litre plastic containers under the transom. The extra 127 litres of petrol bought at Milford was stored on the forehatch or on a seat in the cockpit in five 20-litre and one 27-litre containers. Maximum petrol carried was 262 litres (approximately 58 gallons). The 15hp Honda outboard used approximately 2.3 litres (half a gallon) per hour. A big funnel for pouring petrol and kerosene was stored, with the 30/40 oil and the chemical for the Porta-loo, beside a petrol tank in a rear compartment.

Water containers: 67.5 litres (15 gallons) was stored in 1, 2, 3 and 4-gallon containers, plus drink bottles and buckets to catch rainwater. Our minimum consumption of water was 4.5 litres (1 gallon) a day. The kettle held 2.2 litres, and hot water not used for breakfast was put into Thermos flasks or cooled down to fill our drink bottles. Our 18-litre water container had a pump and a small basin for washing. We used half a cup of fresh water for cleaning our teeth and a cupful for a sponge wash.

Batteries and power supplies: Four 12-volt car batteries, assorted sizes of spares for torches, cameras, GPS. Battery charger and extension power lead, high-rate discharge meter for testing car batteries, torch-battery tester, two hydrometers, 240v electric jug (for use with shore power)

Lifejackets: Two lifejacket coats, four adult lifejackets, two children's lifejackets, two survival suits (in a small pouch)

Anchors: 17kg Danforth with 6 metres of 10mm chain and 100 metres of 14mm rope, 4kg Danforth with 4 metres of 6mm chain and 200 metres of 10mm rope, stored in front well. A collapsible brass rock anchor, an Admiralty anchor and another small Danforth stored under the double berth behind the Portaloo with a lot of extra ropes. An electric anchor winch was fitted to the foredeck but we rarely used it.

Ropes, fenders, tools etc: Long ropes for anchoring, shorter ones for mooring lines, small thin ropes for reefing, a roll of thick string. Four fenders and four flotable cushions, three car tubes, spinnaker pole, boat hook, diving flag, two long oars, two short oars, two fishing rods, fishing lines, spare hooks and sinkers, bait board, homemade danbuoy, Portaloo, pottie, bucket with lid containing laundry powder, thin clothesline ropes and pegs, square bucket for dishes, detergent, mop, Steelo pads and scraper, extra baking soda and detergent for cleaning up spills, car polish for deck and hull, outboard motor spare parts, electric drill, large screwdriver, bolt cutters, 12-volt soldering iron and solder, gumboots and waders, shoe-cleaning gear, scrubbing brush with a broom handle attached.

Tool kit for repairs included miscellaneous bolts and nuts, duck tape, insulation tapes, rubber gloves, fibreglass repair kit, stainless steel arc welding rods, sewing repair kit for clothes and sails, rubbish bags, cleaning rags, sponges and old newspapers.

Navigation, safety and communication equipment: 32 charts for the North Island, 40 charts for the South Island. These were rolled up in four draftsmen's tubes and hung by stretchy cords from shelves in the cabin. Other books and sailing aids were kept in a small bag. Flares (6 red parachute and 10 smoke), two EPIRBs, Garmin hand-held GPS (global positioning system), two VHF radios, Venturer multi-band radio with direction finder, transistor radio, car cassette radio, three big square torches, four smaller torches, two kerosene overnight lamps, small Silva hand-held compass, tide clock, two wrist watches, two clocks and one alarm clock fitted above the foreward double bunk, two barometers, five fire-extinguishers and a fog horn. The main compass and the speedo were fixed to the cockpit walls either side of the main hatch. Invincible dinghy, bailer, rope and oars, two battery-operated bilge-pumps and hoses

Diving and snorkeling gear: Two sets of wetsuits, flippers, belts and weights, masks, snorkels, diving knives and pouches, compensator vests, two air-tanks holding 3000lbs compressed air

Cooking and utensils: Two 3kg and one 2kg LPG gas bottles, cigarette lighters, flint-striker, matches (including some waterproof ones), fold-away two-burner gas stove with fiddle rails, griller and toast rack. Cooking oil, salt. cutlery, plates, mugs and cups, glasses, three saucepans and two frypans, pressure cooker (and spare seal and valve), large preserving pan holding eight jars of bottled fruit and eight jars of homemade jam

Food storage: Two chilly-bins, one for margarine, cheese, eggs, bacon, ham and meat, one for potatoes, vegetables, fruit and tomatoes. Air-tight Tupperware containers for bread, biscuits, fruitcake, freeze-dried food, rice, pasta, flour, yeast, sugar, cereals, cornflour, milk powder, instant soups. Tins of meat and vegetables, baked beans etc were placed in gaps between, but 30 tins were kept as a reserve supply, stored in a box covered with two layers of plastic in the bin under the stove. Small jars of jam, honey, peanut butter, Vegemite, tea, sugar, instant coffee and Milo were kept in a small cupboard above the steps near the foldaway table. Under the second step there was room for two Thermos flasks and several 1.5-litre bottles of cordial or fizz. Fresh milk was sometimes hung over the stern to keep cool in the salt-water, as we had no refrigeration.

Clothes, linen and bedding: Summer clothes in small carry bags, warmer clothes in a small backpack. We also took swimsuits, two sets each of Line 7 and PVC waterproof clothes, waterproof hats, sunhats, gloves, scarves, woollen hats, toiletries, toilet paper and spares. 4 sleeping bags, 2 rugs, sheets, 4 pillows and pillowcases, tea towels, towels, small 4-man tent, double Lilo airbed

Personal equipment: First-aid kit and medications, sun-screen and insect repellents, Aloe Vera soothing cream, hot-water bottle and cover, fly-spray, sunglasses and spare bifocal spectacles, antibiotics

Books, papers and entertainment: Log book, stamps, envelopes, telephone calling card, telephone numbers, visa and bank cards, cheque book, pens and pencils, two cameras, films. *The Living Bible* (pocket edition published 1989), *The New Testament and Psalms* (New American Standard, published 1979), *The Salvation Army Song Book,* Norm's Besson cornet, two *Salvation Army Band Solo Cornet Tune* books, band learner's manual, cornet case. Also several novels, Reader's Digest books, chess set, diary and notebooks

Bibliography

Chart Catalogue and Index, NZ 200. Hydrographic Office of the Royal New Zealand Navy, Auckland, 1980

Coastal Cruising Handbook: a guide to the north-east coast of New Zealand and anchorages from the North Cape to the East Cape. Royal Akarana Yacht Club, Auckland, 1982

Bell, Noel, *A Boaties' Guide to Fiordland,* Mana Cruising Club, Mana, 1994

Drayton, Keith & Treleaven Ian, eds, *Cruising Banks Peninsula, A Pilot for Small Craft.* 2nd edition, Lyttleton Maritime VHF Assoc, Lyttelton, 1992

Eckford, HS (Bert), *History of the Eckford Shipping Company and Blenheim River Traders 1881-1965,* Blenheim Print, 1995

Foster, Peter, *Stewart Island Cruising Guide,* Mana Cruising Club, Mana, 1996

The Holy Bible, Oxford University Press, London (King James ed)

The Living Bible, Kingsway Publication, Eastbourne, UK, 1989

McNeill, Robin G, ed. *Moir's Guide South: guide book to the tracks and routes of the great southern lakes and fiords of New Zealand,* Great Southern Lakes Press, Christchurch, 1995

Murray, Keith WJ & Von Kohorn, Ralph, *Sounds Cruising Guide including Cape Palliser to Farewell Spit,* Steven William, Wgtn, 1986

Owen, William, *The Northland Coast: a boatman's guide.* David Bateman, Auckland, 1993

Scanlan, Mike, *The New Zealand Boating Handbook,* Reed, Wgtn, 1980

Scanlan, Mike, ed, *Safety in Small Craft,* NZ Coastguard Federation, Auckland, 1994

New Zealand Nautical Almanac, Marine Division, Ministry of Transport, Wellington, 1997

New Zealand Nautical Almanac, Marine Division, Ministry of Transport, Wellington, 2001

Small ships radiotelephone service: general instructions. Ministry of Commerce, Wgtn, 1991

Von Kohorn, Ralph S, *Columbia Cruises South.* Cape Catley, Queen Charlotte Sound, 1977

Von Kohorn, Ralph S, *Columbia Cruises North.* Cape Catley, Queen Charlotte Sound, 1979

Index